LOOK BEHIND YOU!

Sketches and Follies from the Commons

Matthew Parris

*Best wishes to Jonathan

Matthew Parris*

Robson Books

To my father, Leslie

First published in Great Britain in 1993 by Robson
Books Ltd, Bolsover House, 5-6 Clipstone Street,
London W1P 7EB

Copyright © 1993 Matthew Parris
The right of Matthew Parris to be identified as author
of this work has been asserted by him in accordance
with the Copyright, Designs and Patents Act 1988

British Library Cataloguing in Publication Data
A catalogue record for this title is available from the
British Library

ISBN 0 86051 874 4

Typeset by EMS Photosetters, Thorpe Bay, Essex
Printed in Great Britain by
Butler & Tanner Ltd, Frome and London

From: Matthew Parris

The Times' Room,
House of Commons,
London SW1A 0AA

17th May 2001

Dear Mr. Congreve,

Mr. Parris was in London briefly last night and saw your letter of the 14th May.

He has one spare copy of *Look Behind You* and plenty of *Read My Lips* and so he has asked me to send you a copy of that as well.

He wonders if you are related to Congreve, the playright?

Yours sincerely,

Eileen Wright *(MRS)*

Private Secretary.

Mr. Jonathan Congreve,
2, Highgrove,
Long Sutton,
Lincolnshire,
PE12 9ER

From: Matthew Parris

The Times' Room,
House of Commons,
London SW1A 0AA

17th May 2001

Dear Mr. Congreve,

Mr. Parris was in London briefly last night and saw your letter of the 14th May

He has one spare copy of Look Behind You and plenty of Read My Lips and so he has asked me to send you a copy of that as well

He wonders if you are related to Congreve, the playright?

Yours sincerely,

[signature]

Private Secretary.

Mr. Jonathan Congreve,
2, Highgrove,
Long Sutton,
Lincolnshire,
PB12 9BR

Acknowledgements

Articles included in this collection appeared first in *The Times*, except where the *Investors Chronicle* is acknowledged.

For all her help in keeping and filing my work, her occasional praise, occasional criticism and constant common sense, I am indebted to my secretary and friend, Eileen Wright. She, Mark Mason and Guy Roberts helped me choose and edit these sketches.

In *The Times* room at the Commons, Peter Riddell, Phil Webster, Nick Wood, Bob Morgan, Sheila Gunn, Jill Sherman, Arthur Leathley, Jonathan Prynn and Andrew Pierce helped me write them. Three successive editors of *The Times*, Charles Wilson, Simon Jenkins and Peter Stothart have been my quiet patrons, while *The Times* sub-editors at Wapping have silently corrected hundreds of stupid errors, and otherwise left me alone. Thanks to all.

And to my mother! Phoning me the other day to say how she enjoyed reading my sketches, she was overcome with enthusiasm and burst into tears. Encouragement like this matters as much when you are forty-four as when you are four. She should know that all those thousands of hours reading me Dickens, and her own stories, when I was a boy, were not wasted.

Introduction

These sketches are perhaps less than a fiftieth of those I have written in the last half decade but include what I hope are the best. 'Best' only because, so often, the parliamentary pantomime itself has been such a hoot.

Lord knows the plot has been exciting enough! The book covers the fall of Margaret Thatcher and the rise of John Major, the fall of Neil Kinnock and the rise of John Smith, and the incredible general election in between. We start in a time when a minister was intercepted on the telephone, calling Mrs Thatcher an old cow, we move through a time when one backbencher called another an inflated pig's bladder on a stick, and we end at a time when Mr Major was caught off-mike (as he thought) calling his Cabinet colleagues bastards.

To the bastards, the pigs' bladders on sticks, and to the old cow, I raise my glass. Parliament is a show or it is nothing. It may be wise, it may be good (it may be stupid, it may be bad) but unless it catches and holds our attention then how will we notice? And if we do not notice, how is democracy to work? Tangled with all the important and worthy work that parliament does, and quite inseparable from it, is a strand of good old fashioned showbiz: vulgar, silly, shallow, cheap – no doubt – but *watchable*, thank heavens.

No MP, however grand, and no commentator, expert and informed though they may be, should ever feel ashamed of playing to the gallery. The gallery is perfectly capable of deciding for itself what matters but the gallery does need to be entertained.

The gallery is the people. If I am doing my job, I write for the gallery. I dedicate this anthology to those MPs who, once in a while, remember whom this pantomime is supposed to be for.

Look *Behind* You . . . .

Guy Fawkes Day 1992 took me to a radio studio for an interview about the Commons. The topic was the whipping system, not gunpowder; but for his last question the interviewer asked me to suppose that Fawkes's plot had not been foiled. Imagine, he said, that the whole Palace of Westminster had gone up in smoke. How would I replace it? What sort of parliament would I build from the rubble? Could we improve on the old place?

Though the question caught me unawares, an idea sprang straight to mind. As our legislature is really a pantomime, shouldn't we build it and bill it as theatre? All the Commons is a stage and all the MPs merely players. We should reconstruct both the building and its procedures to reflect that.

Why fight the farce? Let's stop pretending parliament's anything but showbiz, cease to resist the shock-horror, boo-hiss and tee-hee, and celebrate it instead. We could have curtains, an interval, final bows and encores. We could even have music. Actors in 'A Palace of Varieties' was how Julian Critchley described his fellow MPs. Then we should build for them a palace where they can do in style what they do best, and we best love to watch.

For a start, the audience seating should be vastly expanded. The present arrangements are a disgrace: a tiny 'strangers' gallery with inadequate loos, no popcorn and a prohibition on 'making a disturbance'. Why shouldn't the public cheer and boo, too, like the MPs?

Second, though the present Punch and Judy, Left vs Right theme works well dramatically, and the layout needs to reflect it, MPs ought to face each other across a floor raked not only (as now) up to each side (so they can see each other) but also tilted down from the Chair (at the far end) towards the 'bar of the House' (at the audience end) – so we can see them.

At present the audience and the press are suspended up near the ceiling. This offers an excellent view of Bryan Gould's bald patch, as seen through the wrong end of a telescope, but makes it as hard for an MP to address the public as to address the swallows on an overhead pylon. Anyway it's forbidden. My third proposal, then, is that the bar of the House should be renamed the 'stage apron', and MPs permitted to march on to it, with Madam Speaker's permission, and address the audience direct, in a loud stage whisper.

> The Foreign Secretary's lying!
> Oh no he isn't!
> Oh yes he is!

Which brings me to the pantomime itself. Of all the dramatic forms, pantomime is the one which suits our legislature best. Just consider why . . .

To define 'pantomime' I cannot do better than my dictionary: 'a kind of play characterized by farce, lavish sets, stock roles and topical jokes'. The dictionary adds that the performance is directed especially at children.

Well, politicians, too, have to direct their performances at the most infantile in the audience, because these make up the majority and MPs need votes. Their stage set is indeed lavish, designed and constructed (and now maintained) at a cost which would have made Cecil B. De Mille blush. And anyone who doubts that the MPs' kind of play is characterized by farce must have been asleep for the past six months.

But it is the 'stock roles and topical jokes' which really define panto, and parliament.

Take panto first: why, in pantomime, do we fall back on stock situations leavened with modern instances? Because it's easy: easy for the playwright, whose plot, dialogue and dramatis personae are ready and waiting, half-made and parboiled for him with no need laboriously to construct or explain unfamiliar plots and subtle new characters.

Easy for the actors, too, who walk straight into characters they know and can act in their sleep. And easy for the audience, who only need half a brain to follow stories whose outlines they learnt in childhood, acted out by stereotyped clowns, heroes or villains, as familiar to them as the stars in *EastEnders*.

Now, isn't precisely the same true of parliament? As a writer of 650-word sketches, I have no time to familiarize my readers with any but a handful of the 651 MPs. Just the party leaders, plus Dennis Skinner, Norman Tebbit, Edwina Currie . . . the famous demons, fairies, goblins and dragons of the political world. A small, caricatured, comic-strip, obvious cast. You know where you are with household names.

And the plots? Well, take as an example a plot which wouldn't work. Have you ever tried to explain the common agricultural policy? It may be the object of most of the EC's expenditure, but as a panto (or Commons) story, forget it. 'Tarzan' Heseltine's marathon quest for power (he's *behind* you!), Neil Kinnock's alleged tendency to exaggerate ('Kinnockio'), the Belgrano Bee in Tam Dalyell's bonnet, Eurosceptics vs Europhiles (much clashing of imitation swords, fake blood on the carpet), 'savage cuts' (*oh* yes they are!), 'profligate' Labour councils (*oh* no they aren't!), 'heartless' Tories (boo! hiss!), 'economic miracles' (abracadabra!) . . . oh yes! – as John Major would say, wouldn't he? – there's nothing like the old tunes. You need something you can whistle, at Westminster.

In some strange, unspoken way, the actors (MPs), the audience (you), and the playwrights (politicians and the media are joint playwrights) all sense each other's need for something *simple*. It must contain familiar characters and a familiar plot. Frankly, if they make it too complex or subtle, we don't report it. If we did, you wouldn't read it. 'Stock roles and topical jokes' – it's just as true of parliament as it is of pantomime.

Should we, then, now that we are rebuilding our legislature post-Guy Fawkes in time for Christmas, take the process one step further to its logical conclusion, and restrict the show to a single pantomime?

During Baroness Thatcher's long reign I often wondered. So adept was she at playing, in turn, the wicked stepmother, both the ugly sisters, the fairy godmother, Prince Charming and Widow Twankey, while imagining herself Cinderella all along, that it sometimes seemed she could do the whole show virtually alone as a one-woman *tour de force* – with short walk-on guest appearances by Nigel Lawson as Baron Hardup and John Major as Buttons; assorted Labour and Tory backbenchers as the rats, mice and lizards; and Neil Kinnock as the pumpkin.

But those days are gone. Mrs Thatcher is on the panto shelf – a sort of Sleeping Beauty waiting in the Lords, perhaps a little optimistically, to be kissed to life. Lord Tebbit has been hacking through the briars towards her, but it may not do the trick. More recently the panto seems to have moved to *Jack and the Maastricht Beanstalk*.

In this, John Major plays young Jack, whose mum, the Nation, sends him to the Common Market to exchange the cow for something useful. Poor Jack Major comes home with a handful of funny Dutch Treaty beans, which his European pals have told him are magic and considerably valuable. Everyone had warned him about being duped, including the cow. After a cool reception at home, he sets off up the beanstalk to the fairy-tale world of a Federal Europe, where the ogre Delors waits. 'Fe, fi, fo, fum, I smell ze blood of ze Eengleeshmun.'

This panto has many possibilities, including an engaging role for Kenny (Clarke) as young Jack's goofy pal and fellow Euro-adventurer. The ogre's castle can be stocked with thugs like Helmut and his Bundesbank hounds.

John Smith presents problems for the casting director of our panto. In one version of *Little Red Riding Hood* (libretto by Conservative Central Office), Mr Smith plays Grandma in her bonnet and nightie ('My! what big spending plans you have, Grandma!' – 'All the better to tax you with, my dear'). In Walworth Road's production, all togged up with sword, garter and protesting tights, Mr Smith is what happens when you kiss Gerald Kaufman, sitting on a lily leaf. By way of riposte, Tory Central Office offers us Robin Cook playing all seven of the dwarfs against Virginia Bottomley as Snow White. Paddy Ashdown makes a more plausible Prince Charming, or perhaps Puss in Boots, but also invites a possible casting (alongside Ken Livingstone's King Rat) as the panto cad: Prince Paddy Not-So-Charming-After-All . . .

And throughout all these libretti, 500 government and Opposition backbenchers leap to surface as elves, blue and red wood sprites, wolf packs, soldiers, sailors, and bands of thieves for *Aladdin* (starring Ted Heath as Ali Baba).

Or what about a camp version of *Babes in the Wood*, in drag, with Dennis Skinner and Geoffrey Dickens as the two innocent Babes, and Denis Healey, eyebrows bristling, as their evil abductor.

No, stop me. I'm getting carried away. These ideas work far, far too well. Besides, there's one big advantage to traditional pantomimes of the extra-parliamentary sort. They stop after Christmas.

One Day I'll Show Them

7.12.88

Why are all those MPs – those, that is, who are not called Norman – called Reggie, Ronnie or Stan; Cyril, Cecil or Archie? Why are people with ludicrous names driven by some unseen force to stand for election?

As with so many great discoveries the answer came to me by chance, while pondering another great question of our time. Why can so few politicians pronounce their rs?

In a flash it was all clear. Both questions have the same answer: MPs were desperately unpopular at school.

They were the boys and girls who got teased in the playground. Some had funny names. Some had speech defects. Some had squidgy little faces, awful freckles, or problems with girls. And the whole of their lives since have been a desperate attempt to compensate. Plump little Kenneth hid in the loo from the other boys, sobbing silently: '*I'll* show them. One day, I'll be Secretary of State for Education. I'll wear flashy ties and be popular with all my mates.' Correct Miss Margaret-Hilda flinched at classmates' taunts: 'Snobby-Roberts!' Inwardly she vowed to work even harder, to be even *more* superior, and – one day – to be the first woman prime minister in the Western world, *and* end up a duchess.

Thin, shy, studious young Michael Meacher ('Meacher, Meacher, suck-up to the teacher') knew he'd grow up to be a working-class hero. Oh yes! They'd be sorry they'd bullied the bloke they now needed to protect *them*! He'd stand at the Opposition dispatch box championing the unemployed.

So he did yesterday, at Employment Questions. Opposite him was the Secretary of State. Who is called Norman. And cannot pronounce his rs. When he was Minister of Transport his Labour opposite number was called Albert (really!) and couldn't pronounce rs either. The repartee on 'redundant British Rail rolling-stock' was richly rewarding.

Someone called Conal from York wanted to know why some tourist information centres were closed in winter. Then Cyril from Rochdale spoke. But soon Cecil from Barrow-in-Furness was on his feet, worried lest Norman's relaxing of the rules about employing teenagers might usher back chimney-sweeps.

Norman from Chingford looked in. Dale, Derek and Kenneth (Workington, Leeds and Blackley) intervened.

Then on to a Mr Rooker's question ('Rooker! Rooker! You're a silly . . .') where Bernard from Castle Point came to Norman's aid. Alistair's exchange proved interesting to Dafyd, so there was hardly time to hear Irvine. And none for Dudley, Archy or Spencer. As for Hugo and Trevor, there was no chance at all of questions 79 and 80 being reached.

For it was time for Prime Minister's Questions with Hilda. The first was from Keith of Manchester; the second from a Ms Walley. Hugh from Hornsey was away, but a freckled person called Neil seemed especially agitated, while a chap called Robin Maxwell-Hyslop was furious about a girl called Edwina.

With Hilda sat Tristan (a whip, or class monitor). In garish tie was Kenneth who (since our story started) has become Education Secretary. Still waiting at the back was Sydney from Barnet. Standing at the Bar of the House, yet another Kenneth, next to a Miss Fookes and a Mr Brandon-Bravo.

We never reached Humphrey's question.

Priscilla the Peril
5.5.89

To make space for her, Cabinet colleagues shuffled bottoms sideways in a series of furtive little bounces to ensure that none got too close. Upon every face was a smile but nobody wanted a cuddle. The PM sat down with a seemly gap to left and right.

Denis Healey once compared her to the deadly Upas tree. A vigorous and broad-branched tree, the Upas spreads wide; but nothing grows beneath its shade, and seedlings wither all around.

It was her tenth anniversary as Prime Minister and she was there to face PM's Questions.

The whips had put it about that the PM wished nothing to be made of the occasion, but Malcolm Bruce, for the Democrats, rather soured his own congratulations by asking her whether she would in future keep her mouth shut. Mrs Thatcher's reply – that to give him the answer he sought would be a logical impossibility – is probably the only thing she will ever say that would have pleased Bertrand Russell.

Neil Kinnock offered a dreary whine about St Francis of Assisi and his prayer. She replied – more in the spirit of Joan than Francis – that people were better off these days and knickers to anyone who said otherwise. Islington's Chris Smith (Lab) asked about the trade deficit and was told that we should be proud of Britain's overseas investments, so suck. Alf Morris (Lab, Wythenshawe) asked about the National Health Service proposals and she replied that there were more funds, more nurses, and more doctors than ever, so yah boo sucks. Jim Sillars (SNP, Glasgow Govan) said Britain was betraying the people of Hong Kong. Mrs Thatcher replied that we weren't and anyway Sillars had asked that last time and hadn't he anything new to say, and yah boo sucks with knobs on.

Knickers, knickers, knickers. What are we to make of it? When we were young, there were two different kinds of girl who were entirely maddening in the playground. One type was horrid and contrary. She spoilt the boys' games, used rude words, carved obscenities on desks, and never, never owned up. She is immortalized in the *Dandy* as Beryl the Peril.

The other sort was the goody-goody. I remember a boyhood nightmare called Priscilla. Priscilla always got full marks for her homework and never let you copy. Priscilla used only polite language and was the only girl ever to get 50 out of 50 for presentation.

Listening to the Prime Minister yesterday, the secret of her maddening effectiveness dawned on me. Margaret Thatcher is both little girls, Beryl and Priscilla, in one.

For these last ten years she has been shouting the polite equivalent of knickers to all and sundry, without ever offending good manners, using bad words, or engaging with any serious thought anyone has ever put to her. And why not? She knows what she wants and knickers to anyone who disagrees.

Sometimes, yesterday, when they barracked her, Mr Speaker fidgeted nervily, concerned that a lady's courtesy should be so abused. For is she not the very model of civilized behaviour? Mrs Thatcher is the politest, most genteel nose-thumber in history. These ten years past have been the longest continuous nose-thumb ever recorded.

The Liftman

After seven years of being punished for impertinence, it is an exhilarating experience to find myself paid for it. But the Press Gallery presents special problems for an ex-Member, gamekeeper turned poacher. When debate gets heated, the temptation to join in is almost unbearable.

'Faced by this dilemma,' I heard a frontbencher declaim, the other day, 'what should I do?'

'Resign!' I swear the cry was only a micro-second from my lips before, in the nick of time, it struck me that I was no longer a Member. Think of the ignominy. Hauled out of the Gallery by policemen, to the growls of my old colleagues and the titters of my new.

Still, it's nice to be recognized by erstwhile fellow MPs, a couple of whom (I suspect) have not registered the change either. Alistair Goodlad has only recently stopped sending me those 'Have you any spare PM's Questions Gallery tickets?' notelets.

Keith Joseph used to make the opposite mistake, as became clear during a strange ride in the lift from the Special Gallery (East) during my first year as a Member. Keith, who was in the same lift, mistook me for a lift-attendant.

'Take me to the Members' Lobby,' he said, courteous but brusque. Then a worried look crossed his face. Perhaps, I thought, he has realized his error. Better for me to say nothing.

'East–West trade,' he muttered, half to himself and then, turning to me, the only other occupant of the lift, 'By cutting the link, would we gain strength, or simply lose a potential lever?' I stammered out some half-baked reply.

Sir Keith looked at me intently, listening. 'Yes. Quite possibly . . . Ah, we're here. You can let me off. Thank you. Goodbye. I shall think about what you said, and perhaps discuss it further, next time I am in your lift.'

I suppose the story could be cited as unintended discourtesy, a testimony to Keith's absent-mindedness. To me it serves better as testimony to his intellectual openness – an unintended courtesy. Keith addressed his colleague as a lift-attendant, but was as interested in a lift-attendant's views as he would have been in a colleague's. Other ministers would address you as a colleague, and be as interested in your views as in a lift-attendant's.

They Shoot Horses

18.7.89

The question has to be asked: Is the Prime Minister on crack? This drug is said to produce a feeling of mildly aggressive well-being. Nothing better described Mrs Thatcher yesterday, reporting on the Paris summit.

'The vast majority of people in the streets of Paris were cheering,' she told an astonished Chamber, 'and saying "Madame *T'atcher*, Madame *T'atcher*!"'

But who should wonder – for she projected a kaleidoscope of global certainties.

'Every free country in the world is a *capitalist* country!'

'And then we discussed the Uruguay Round . . .'

'And we have some *excellent* meteorologists.'

For had she not just returned from the biggest acid-house party of them all?

These gatherings are now very common. Guests party the night away. Some think they can fly. Others that they can reduce inflation to 4 per cent by next year. Some think they can stare at the sun. Others that they can conquer the Third World debt crisis. At its wildest extreme, guests even come to believe that they can reduce agricultural subsidies.

These people need help. Yesterday, Labour's Brian Wilson (Cunningham N) tried a douche of scepticism.

'Isn't that just *typical* of the pathetic small-mindedness of the Opposition?' she retorted. 'That's *just* what they are like!'

Mrs Thatcher gave us a taste, yesterday, of her new style: a punchy but often jokey grande dame. 'Wait a moment, wait a *moment*,' she scolded Eric Heffer (Lab, Liverpool, Walton).

As for Mrs Thatcher's career, there is much partying in Paris still to come. 'Why limit your timescale?' she replied, when Dennis Skinner suggested the next election might blow the whistle.

We have a word of advice. The 'high' she was enjoying yesterday needs ever larger doses of stimulant – experts warn – simply to maintain the same level of elation. Soon she will need a mega-party in a major European capital at least once a week. How much longer can she keep up the waltz?

They Shoot Horses, Don't They?

Hit and Run

14.10.89

The 1989 Tory Conference . . . .

Walking in Blackpool, I glanced into an amusement arcade. A young girl was playing at one of those car-chase games, where (hunched behind an imaginary wheel) trees, pedestrians and crash barriers flash at you from all directions on a screen.

She was wholly absorbed. As she opened the throttle, teeth clenched, her eyes had a manic expression. I walked on. At the newsagents the headline asked: 'Can Maggie save the day?' Later, at the Empress Ballroom, the Empress herself was to help us answer that question.

To the strains of 'Oh I Do Like To Be Beside the Seaside', Mrs Thatcher appeared in royal blue, pearls, and what seemed to be a diamond replica of a military medal pinned to the shoulder of a jacket cut in the 'power-dressing' style.

And she was away. With more poise than I have ever observed in her before, she began to extol the virtues of liberty, charity and Kenneth Baker.

Much followed. There was the fond glance at Denis as she announced the end of the 'earnings rule', which taxed elderly pensions. There was the journey of Challenger II to Jupiter and Mars, which proved the need for Mr Patten's new litter Bill. But it was when she spoke of Freedom that a strange insight dawned. Where had I seen that manic look before? Yes! The girl in the amusement arcade, on the car-chase machine!

For is our Prime Minister not the ultimate hit-and-run driver? It was Ted who gallantly opened the car door to her. She grabbed the wheel, floored the accelerator and threw him out. Passengers counselled caution – Jim Prior, Francis Pym – and she threw them out too. Willie Whitelaw clung grimly to the bonnet as she swerved onwards.

Sometimes there was the sound of sirens. Sometimes she bounced off crash barriers, leaving pedestrians bleeding in the road. Sometimes there were flashing blue lights in her rear-view mirror. Always she hit the gas pedal and accelerated out of it.

Once, on a bend called *Belgrano* she almost overturned. Then she lost her way and crashed straight through a helicopter factory. Did she stop? Did she heck!

Just at present the sirens grow louder, the Law closer. Chewing Polo mints and praying hard, she obeys every road sign and drops temporarily within the speed-limit – 'what, me, officer?' 'We will never privatize the NHS,' she declared yesterday. 'We were never going to!' How she longs for the open road . . .

But that look in her eyes as she barked the word 'freedom'! As thousands cheered and Whitelaw, tears streaming down, bellowed like a beached hippo, I fancied her – even then – to reach in her handbag for another 50p piece, and fumble for the throttle-lever.

Sixty-four today, and the oldest girl in the amusement arcade. Just one more game, O Lord, just one more game!

31.10.89

In Combative Form

On London's South Bank, the political event of the week was about to occur. Mr Brian Walden was about to withdraw his support from Mrs Thatcher's leadership.

How would she react? I watched the occasion on television, forming so clear a view of the Prime Minister's performance that there seemed no need to check my recollection against that of others.

Or so I thought. Then came yesterday's newspapers. 'Resolute,' said the *Financial Times*.

'Hm,' one thought, 'well, the *FT* does need to maintain a certain dignity. But perhaps the *Guardian* will sock it to 'em . . .'

'Sticks to tough line,' read its front page.

'True as far as it goes,' one thought, 'but what about the really interesting thing? Perhaps it will be in *The Times*?'

'. . . Showed commendable good sense' – no, not there. The *Telegraph* perhaps?

'In combative form' – not there. I waited for the London *Evening Standard*: 'Confident and characteristically assertive'.

I sat down in bewilderment. Was Sunday a dream? Was I plagued by delusions from which the rest of the world was free?

Had I just *imagined* that I saw a woman going completely crackers?

It took me back to an unhappy encounter I once had in a number 77 bus with an elderly lady who thought I wished to make an indecent approach. She was in combative form (*Telegraph*) as she swung at me with a plastic bag, screaming accusations.

I denied them. Sticking to her tough line (*Guardian*) she repeated herself half a dozen times and told me to get off. I said it was she who should move but she was resolute (*FT*). I challenged her to substantiate her accusations but, showing commendably good sense (*The Times*), she refused to be drawn. Finally, as we reached Vauxhall Bridge, she moved off to berate one of the other passengers. She was confident and characteristically assertive (*Standard*) to the end, when they took her away.

Those in Peril on the Sea

1.11.89

An eager young new boy once enthused to Churchill that it was a thrill to sit on the government benches, surveying the enemy opposite. 'No sir,' Churchill is said to have retorted. 'Across the floor are the Opposition. The enemy is all around you.'

Mrs Thatcher sat, yesterday – tense, composed – facing an Opposition attack from Shadow Chancellor John Smith.

He welcomed the new Chancellor. Mr Major, he said, had been Kuala-Lumpured as Foreign Secretary in October, only to face being Strasbourged as Chancellor next month. We glanced at Geoffrey Howe, badly Bruged in a continental road accident last year.

Mr Smith's greatest good-fortune yesterday was Mr Robin Maxwell-Hyslop (C, Tiverton).

All but skewered by a demand (from Northampton's Tony

Marlow) that he list Labour's conditions for entry into the ERM, Mr Smith couldn't think of any, on the instant.

He didn't have to. Maxwell-Hyslop started a series of disruptive 'points of order' and, while the House bayed, Mr Smith wrote out some policies on an envelope, then read them – despite, he said, 'organized wrecking tactics from the benches opposite'.

I must advise Mr Smith that Robin Maxwell-Hyslop is a *dis*organized wrecking tactic.

Major got better as he went on. But he did go on – and on. He was best when sparring with substantive interventions, answering figures with figures, for which, happily, Mr Major seems to have some kind of a facility.

'Why,' shouted a Labour heckler, 'did Lawson resign?'

And in due course, Mr Lawson rose to speak.

Grim, pale and strained, he stared around the Chamber. 'That article,' he said – he meant the offending article in which Mrs Thatcher's adviser, Sir Alan Walters, had called the European Monetary System 'half-baked' – 'that article was significant' (and he paused) 'only in that it represented the tip of a singularly ill-concealed iceberg . . .' Mrs Thatcher turned her face, expressionless, towards him . . . 'with all the destructive potential that icebergs possess.'

You could have heard a pin drop.

I scanned the government benches. The tips of a dozen singularly ill-concealed icebergs heaved gently in the swell. The rounded surface of Ted Heath rose and fell on the forward bench. Near him a jagged pinnacle they call Ian Gilmour spiked through the waves. John Biffen, innocent above water, lethal beneath, lay behind. And – right over to one corner – Michael Heseltine, the ultimate hazard to shipping, glinted in the television lights – razor-sharp with all the destructive potential that *he* possesses.

How is she to navigate a passage through all this? Can she trust her first mate, Sir Geoffrey Howe? Can she rely on her new pilot, John Major? Was that a smooth rock, just under water on the other side, or was it Kenneth Baker? And where was Douglas Hurd? Sitting on the steps, some distance away – plenty beneath the surface there . . .

Some of these could sink her, now. And, all around lesser perils bobbed up and down in the waves: backbenchers she had disappointed, and the flotsam and jetsam of discarded junior ministers.

A sea of troubles. Ah for that trusty old ice-breaker, HMS *Whitelaw*! Why ever did they decommission him?

After the Event

28.11.89

It was not Michael Heseltine who first challenged Mrs Thatcher for the leadership but the 'stalking horse', Sir Anthony Meyer. . . .

There now follows a review of this morning's Press:

Following his shock victory in the Tory leadership election over the weekend, Sir Anthony Meyer has gone to ground. Senior Conservatives, however, have been talking freely to journalists and their comments dominate the front pages of today's papers.

It appears that Sir Anthony was far more widely admired than had been suspected.

The *Daily Telegraph* leads with an exclusive interview with party chairman, Kenneth Baker. 'I always said,' comments Baker, 'that this election was a distraction. And what a marvellous and helpful distraction it has been. It is no secret that many had doubts about the previous leadership. What I think Anthony did was to focus those doubts and courageously to resolve them.

'In this great purpose, Ant will have guessed, I know, that he has had my quiet support throughout. I should be honoured to serve him.'

A number of junior ministers, previously thought to be hostile to Sir Anthony's ambitions, have emerged through this morning's papers as supporters. The *Independent* quotes Michael Howard, the 'dry' water minister, as backing Meyer's opposition to the poll tax. 'I always said,' says Howard, 'that only loyalty kept me from mentioning my doubts about this farce.' Every minister interviewed praises Meyer, most referring to secret doubts about the previous leadership.

The Times quotes a speech pre-released by Michael Heseltine, hailing Meyer as 'English visionary and European prophet'.

'Anthony dreams dreams,' Mr Heseltine will say to the Henley Dyno-Rod operatives' annual dinner tonight. '*We* must awake and make them reality.'

In *Today*, Norman Tebbit puts it more bluntly, under the slogan 'TURN TO TONY!' 'Tone and I,' he says, 'are very different blokes. He's a philosopher. I'm a kicker of backsides. I always said we need both. Tone knows that.'

From elsewhere on the back benches the unanimous chorus of approval is maintained. Beneath the *Daily Mail*'s banner headline THE IRON DONKEY, influential Tory backbencher Anthony Beaumont-Dark (who had earlier described Meyer as 'not so much a stalking horse: more a stalking donkey') clarifies his thoughts: 'This magnificent beast,' he says (referring to the donkey), 'is rightly celebrated for its iron will and endurance. Yet it is also famous for the gentleness we respect in Tony, too. Naturally I voted for him.

'His first task will be to bring new blood into the ministerial ranks. I always said . . .'

The scoop of the day, however, goes to the *Guardian*, which carries an anonymous eyewitness account of the vote in the Tory 1922 Committee. Apparently the vote revealed a small majority for Sir Anthony.

The announcement, says the *Guardian*, was accompanied by a vigorous and unanimous thumping of desks. Committee chairman Cranley Onslow explained this seeming about-turn: 'It is not always easy – even for the MP himself thumping the desk – to know at the time whether it is a hostile or friendly thump. Subsequent events have helped us to clarify. I have always said . . .'

Sir Anthony himself, apparently, was carried out – too shocked to speak.

Taking No Part

The staircase outside our Westminster room has a dustbin-alley air. Overshadowed by the black metal caging of an ancient lift, it is cluttered with bins of old papers. You don't expect to meet the Prime Minister there.

So, walking to the stairs just as a colleague asked me how many rebels would surface today, I flung open the door with a confident declaration. 'Sixty,' I said. And stared point-blank into Mrs Thatcher's eyes.

I felt myself blushing. What do you *say*? I was seized with an absurd desire to sing 'green bottles, hanging on a wall, sixty green bottles . . . – Oh! Good afternoon, Prime Minister. Fancy seeing you here!' . . . but suppressed it, and stood mute.

Mrs Thatcher glanced at me for a micro-second, and – almost on the instant – addressed her Parliamentary Private Secretary: 'Ah, Mark, I think it's one floor further down.' I heard her voice trailing down the next flight of stairs: 'It's *such* a labyrinth . . .'

She was on her way from casting her vote in the Comittee Room above.

Denis Healey passed me on his way there, eyebrows beetling famously: 'I want to vote in the Tory leadership election. Where can I apply to join? *You* should remember.'

I returned to the *Times* room. 'How would you have voted?' someone asked me.

I wonder.

Happy Ever After?

When, asked Neil Kinnock yesterday, would Mrs Thatcher see that 'this whole arrangement was a fairy tale from the start'?

He was talking about the community charge. The Fairy herself stood there, shimmering a little. She had left her wand at No. 10, in favour of more simple ornaments: green jade buttons and a gold brooch . . .

Once upon a time, children, there was a place called Hamelin in Germany. It was 'twinned' with somewhere called Westminster.

And, in this place, they had a terrible problem. An infestation of rates. Rates were everywhere: huge rates, rates with sharp teeth, slinking through people's letter-boxes and ruining their lives. The citizens begged their leaders to get rid of the rates; but the problem was, nobody could think how.

Then a man called Mr Baker with silver hair and a big smile came forward. He wore flashy wide ties and they called him the Wide-Tied Baker of Hamelin.

'I know a way of eradicating rates,' he said. 'Trust me. But if I do this, I want you to reward me. I want to be the next Leader of Hamelin.'

Not *everybody* did quite trust the Wide-Tied Baker but they were frantic to get rid of the rates, so they agreed to let him try.

He was as good as his word. He passed a law, saying that 'from 1 April, all the rates are abolished' and – hey presto! – they were.

But it was at about this time that the Wide-Tied Baker noticed that the people were unlikely to make him Leader. Frankly, the elders were not giving him the nod. Younger citizens were pointing at him and snickering about some of his other schemes, like Student Loans, GCSE and the National Core Curriculum.

And, though he continued to smile, the Wide-Tied Baker grew rather impatient and slightly bitter, for he was a clever man and had really meant well, underneath. Yet there was no sign that the present Leader was planning to retire and no sign that, when that day came, Baker would be the favoured one.

And a very evil idea came to him. He called everyone together. 'With the rates gone,' he announced, 'I'll take you all somewhere really fantastic. It's a magical mystery tour to the Polltax Mountains. Not an easy journey but it'll be great when you get there; and, to lead you, my young friend Christopher Patten will dance ahead and play sweet music all the way. You'll love it, honestly.'

At this, young Chris looked a bit nervous as he wasn't at all sure he knew the way, or that people would like it when they got there. But the Leader of Hamelin told him it was his duty.

And off they all set. The Wide-Tied Baker had detached himself, now, from the throng and sat on a rock at 32 Smith Square, watching them stumble towards the horizon. A thin smile played upon his lips.

'Have fun!' he called.

As night falls, and they still don't seem to be getting anywhere, and the ground grows stonier, the path steeper, and the wind colder, cries of distress fill the air. Yet still they stumble forward . . .

Children, there is a logical flaw in the plot of this story. Can you spot it? Yes – correct, David Wilshire. *The people didn't have to go to the Polltax Mountains in the first place. They still don't. They could just turn round and go home again.*

Do you think they will?

Cat on a Hot Tin Roof   *13.4.90*

As we go to press, a dramatic rooftop protest continues. On the roof of Number 10 Downing Street one of the most hardened inmates the place has ever known, a certain Margaret Thatcher, is still refusing to come down. We are looking at a desperate woman.

She came from nowhere in 1975 and scaled the perimeter fence of a crusty old political party. In a daring raid in 1979 she snatched the keys from 'gaoler' Jim Callaghan and stormed the country.

But then in 1981 she seemed to be cornered. Having laid waste large sections of manufacturing industry and with no relief in sight, a whole artillery of menacing opinion polls had Thatcher at bay.

How she gave them the slip, no one can quite remember but (like many a convict before her) she sought her fortunes abroad and distinguished herself in a foreign war. By 1983 there was no restraining her and she stormed the country yet again.

From 83 to 87 she laid low. There were a few hairy moments – most notably when she took on another battle-scarred street-fighter by the name of Scargill. But she saw him off. Indeed there were few who could stand up to her. One by one, the senior officers most experienced at dealing with this offender retired or were fired. 'Warder Willie' (who had talked her down from many roofs in his time) was transferred to a gaol down the road with red leather benches. 'Gentleman' Jim Prior was already there – as were two old lags from her foreign adventures, Carrington and Pym.

'Paddy' Jenkin joined them. Patrick had never entirely recovered from horrific wounds inflicted when she used him as a human battering ram ('Secretary of State' she called it) in her successful break-in at County Hall, London. In each of these attacks she had personally been triumphant, but each had taken its toll on her followers, and comrades-in-arms were usually mutilated beyond recovery.

One key comrade, a fellow they called 'Tarzan', noticed the fate of all who fought with her and did a runner. He grassed – turned Queen's evidence – on one of her worst capers. This had happened at a helicopter factory through which she smashed her getaway car. A passenger, now known on the Continent as 'Commissioner' Leon, was maimed; but the woman herself escaped. And again she stormed the country in 1987.

By now you would have thought that her appetite for adventure was satisfied. Not so. A shootout in the nation's schools was closely followed by a showdown with the nation's nurses. Then she attacked the doctors, took a swipe at some lawyers, flogged off a swagbag of water companies and pitched into some ambulance workers.

There seemed to be no stopping her. Yet again, there were costs. One of her oldest partners in crime, a man they called 'the Chingford Strangler', had already wearied of aggro, and hung up his jemmy in a late bid for respectability. Ken 'The Bouncer' Clarke won the GPs' and ambulance workers' scraps for her, but he won't bounce again for quite some time. And when 'Bully' Lawson quit – fed up with her habit of shin-kicking her own mates just for a laugh – she lost a heavyweight.

It looked bad to her followers too. She had started with a fair number of fans. The woman was a gangster from the start, but gangsters can be popular – when they're winning. Yet with every run-in she made new enemies. At first it didn't matter. But as nurses added to teachers, added to dons, added to civil servants, added to ambulance workers . . . the followers grew more ragged. And the team grew more ragged too. Nearly all the old fighters were gone and those who remained were wounded.

Yet at this point she launched her most outrageous assault of all. She picked a fight with half her own team, local authorities, householders across the nation, and tens of millions of her fans, all at the same time.

Battle has been raging now for more than a month. Our heroine is on the roof and chucking tiles in all directions. She is surrounded, at bay, and yet defiant. Megaphone in hand, she assails the crowd below with statistics, Biblical quotations and ritual abuse.

One by one her original army has deserted her. Some slipped quietly away before she emerged on the roof. Others have been talked down by teams of pollsters and political commentators. Only a few remain.

There is John Major – though some see him more as a chaplain and psychiatrist. There is Chris Patten – though rumour has it that he is as much a hostage as a willing combatant. There is Douglas Hurd – though he is suspected of being a law officer under deep cover, sent in to relay messages to and from the real world. There is Geoffrey Howe, and of course there is old Nick 'Scarface' Ridley, faithful to the end.

What are the odds? Roofs don't come hotter – yet this cat has nine lives.

My own guess? I'd say it was the eighth. The Prime Minister is on her penultimate roof.

(From the *Investors Chronicle*)

Hallowed Be Thy Name-calling   *21.6.90*

'Woollens, worsteds, flax and soft furnishings.' Eric Forth, junior minister in the industry department, looked an unlikely lift attendant. His interrogator, Frank Haynes, 'the snarling grandpa' (Lab, Ashfield), an equally unlikely Selfridges' shopper. Mr Forth straightened his tie. Forth was telling Haynes the (selected) good news about textile exports.

It was a positive moment in a rancorous afternoon. The rancour started as the echo of prayer died away in the Chamber.

Newspapermen are excluded from the religious ceremony. It is only after 'Prayers for the Parliament' in which Mr Speaker's chaplain leads the MPs at 2.30 every afternoon, that we journalists are allowed in. Crowding at the oak doors, pressing our ears to hear the murmured devotions, we might just pick out the words:

'Almighty God, the Fountain of all Goodness . . . by whom alone

Kings reign and Princes decree justice . . . we, thine unworthy servants . . . do most humbly beseech thee to send down thy Heavenly Wisdom from above, to direct and guide us in all our consultations; and grant . . .' Or so I recall.

'Questions to the Secretary of State,' the Speaker cried. All fell at each other's throats.

'. . . that laying aside all private interests, prejudices, and partial affections . . .'

'There are a number of unpleasant features about the hon gentleman.' Junior minister Douglas Hurd was referring to Labour's industry spokesman, Gordon Brown. 'Discreditable,' said Hogg.

'. . . the result of all our counsels may be to the glory of thy blessed Name, the maintenance of true Religion and Justice, and tranquillity of the Realm . . .'

'This arrogant little shit has not answered one question!' shouted Labour's George Foulkes (Carrick, Cumnock and Doon Valley). He was talking about Mr Hogg. Screams of protest rose from the Conservative benches.

'He will withdraw that word immediately. And do not repeat it,' said Mr Speaker, his colour rising . . .

'. . . the uniting and knitting together of the hearts of all persons and estates . . .'

'Which word?' Foulkes shouted back: 'Arrogant, little, or shit?'

'The last word,' snapped the Speaker.

'. . . in true Christian Love and Charity one towards another . . .'

Now it was Hogg's turn: 'This whingeing and whining from the Opposition benches is amusing and pathetic . . .'

'Further us with thy continual help, that in all our works begun, continued, and ended in thee, we may glorify thy Holy Name . . .'

'Humbug!' roared Nicholas Ridley, the Industry Secretary. 'Humbug!'

'. . . and finally by thy mercy obtain everlasting Life through Jesus Christ our Lord . . .'

The Chair has the last word, here, too. Amid the hurling of abuse, Mr Speaker rose, shaking his bewigged head wearily. 'Some rough things are said in this Chamber,' he sighed. 'That's what it's all about.'

'. . . Amen.'

Portillo Mk II Shines

When a new minister is taken out for road tests, it is a privilege to be among the observers.

Fresh from the showrooms, the air-cooled Portillo Mark II – 'Poll Tax Turbo GTI' – was driven round the circuit for the first time yesterday. Results were promising. A discreetly lively performance, road-holding good.

Over at the Department of Transport, the machine had been put through extensive trials as 'Rail minister', and reports were positive. The sleek Latin lines have, of course, been widely admired; but the Portillo's performance had been restrained. Backroom boys were impressed by this minister's information system; but the Portillo always seemed to be operating below design specifications. Answering for BR sandwich quality hardly tested this minister to the limit. This machine had still to win the hearts of the public and the plaudits of the trade press.

To do so under the 'Poll Tax' badge was never going to be easy. This is a troubled marque with a history of horrendous teething problems. Preceding the Portillo in this niche, the David Hunt (or 'Wirral Wonder') had been a smooth performer, but criticized as lacking kick. The challenge facing the Portillo was formidable.

They wheeled him in at 2.30. While a trusty Trippier raced up and down the tarmac at Question 1, final checks were made to the Portillo's paperwork and exterior trim. The minister was ready.

Performing the bump start at Question 2 was an able young mechanic, Tim Devlin (C, Stockton S). Devlin chose a safe stretch of track.

'Is it not remarkable that my hon friend has not received the promised policy paper from the Opposition?'

That was more than enough. The minister fired first time. Brm, brrm, brr . . . The Portillo was away.

'Yes, I think it is truly remarkable that they have not come up with an alternative . . .'

Into a gentle bend: 'They have no "reasoned policy document" . . .'

A touch on the throttle: 'There was no background paper.'

Easing up a gear now, needle creeping up nicely: 'Indeed, I suspect there was no background.'

On the straight – maybe a taste of burning rubber? 'Labour have no idea what to do about local government . . .'

'Hear, *hear*!' came approving growls from the grandstand. There was an angry whine of Opposition engines, revving in the pit. Their wheels – 'alternatives to the poll tax' – long promised from Walworth Road, had still not arrived. The Portillo purred past, first lap complete.

It was time for a fast run through the S-bends. Richard Tracy (C, Surbiton), an experienced race official from the back benches, flagged the Portillo away: would the government look at the standard community charge and the uniquitous suggestion by some local authorities that it must always be applied at the two-times multiplier?

'Of course I will look at the point.' The minister moved silkily up through the gears. 'This is an area where the government wishes local government to be local.' Rubber bit into asphalt now, as the minister tried a boost to the turbo: 'They can apply multipliers on the standard community charge up to a maximum of two.'

Chrome flashed in the afternoon sun as the minister coasted past the grandstand. The Portillo Mark II 'Poll Tax Turbo GTI' was making an auspicious debut.

Two Myths Are Born

12.10.90

The 1990 Tory Conference. . . .

Yesterday at Bournemouth we were present at the birth of a myth.

It was 16½ minutes of sweetly choreographed ecstasy. Eyes were filled with tears. Speeches were filled with standing ovations. Mrs Thatcher's hand was kissed twice. Prominent persons from the new Eastern European democracies were led to the rostrum to pay their respects to Mrs Thatcher, praise the Conservative party, and receive small plastic ornaments featuring Mr Baker's Tory flame of freedom, redesigned to look less like an ice cream.

While the video screens showed the Berlin Wall collapsing – and Mrs Thatcher – and Lech Walesa – and Mrs Thatcher – waves of emotion swept us all. A foreign prime minister saluted our own PM, a Polish professor kissed her hand and a smashing Czech brunette offered a personal thank you. Eat your hearts out, Labour.

So moving was the spectacle that we lost track of the reason for it. This was lucky, for the whole show was founded upon an illusion.

The illusion was outlined by a Mr Michael Teale, speaking (from the floor) about the flame of freedom which had burnt behind the Iron Curtain. 'It owed much to Mrs Thatcher,' he said. 'British resolve played a vital part during those dark hours.'

Mrs Jackie Nilsson was less grudging. 'Without your great leadership,' she told our PM, little would have been possible. Change, freedom, the fall of the Berlin Wall – 'We see proof in these miracles. Who did this? Margaret Thatcher.'

Too generously, though, Mrs Nilsson also gave a little credit to the foreign leaders on the rostrum: 'Kind gentlemen with beautiful manners. These are the people we need . . . so polite to Mrs Thatcher.'

If, before lunch, poor John Major had realized the scale of gratitude that would be offered to the PM after lunch, he would hardly have volunteered his own paltry effort. Indicating his ministerial team rather as a sultan might point to a posse of superior eunuchs, he turned to Mrs Thatcher. 'I'm grateful to you, Prime Minister, for giving them to me,' he said.

But it was otherwise his most accomplished conference speech yet, and the representatives warmed to him.

And it was gently done. I suspect that the Chancellor has been advised not to raise his voice, for his throat tightens to a strangled monotone, like a distant model aeroplane engine. He began, however, by shouting. About a third of the way in, looking more assured by the minute, he remembered to drop his voice and started to vary the pitch and speed. The speech improved immensely.

Mr Major tried one of his shy Princess Diana smiles: a great success. He dropped his voice yet further. The effect was stunning, but it was now becoming hard to hear what the Chancellor was saying.

The PM led the standing-up for his ovation. She then led the sitting-down. Mr Major's prospects are improving.

10.11.90

First Ballotah

The leadership questioned. . . .

Tory leaders used to 'emerge' but now we have democracy. Democracy among Tory MPs, as Julian Critchley has explained, is the system under which the common will is least likely to triumph. Events of the past week prove it.

Half the Tory backbenchers you talk to subject you to a private harangue about how much nicer it would be if Mrs Thatcher could be surgically removed and somebody cuddly put in her place quickly, before the next election.

'But would you vote that way?' one asks.

'On the second ballot, yes,' they reply.

'What about the first ballot?'

'Ah.'

Ah. We could summarize the problem as the 'first ballotah' dilemma. How to get from here to the second ballot without passing through a first ballot on the way. The crocodile has been goaded into the shallow water, but who is to stick in the knife? The first lunge might not kill; she might make it back into the deep water; her teeth are sharp and her memory is long. Legs could subsequently be bitten. So they all stand gingerly by the edge of the pool, muttering about 'loyalty' as the sharp-toothed one thrashes around on the mud bank.

Mr Critchley, I think, would like to go back to the old system, but nostalgia is pointless.

Nor is it reasonable to accept the existing system but ask the MPs to be braver. If they were brave they would not be MPs. An MP has been selected, elected and promoted for his circumspection. All his political life he has been punished for any tendency to say things that elements of his audience may not wish to hear.

My own proposals go with the Pavlovian grain. At present it is up to the prospective candidate to decide whether or not to stand. He 'lets his name go forward'. Why? That attracts unnecessary odium. Why not enter the name of anyone who has been proposed and seconded, regardless of whether he *says* he wants to run. We know he wants to run.

My second proposal goes further. Voting among MPs for the leadership is by secret ballot, and that is as it should be. You see who wins, then let it be discreetly known that this was your choice too, protected by the cloak of secrecy. Why, then, deny the candidate that cloak? Why can't Tories stand secretly for the leadership?

I can guess what you are thinking, but you are wrong. In the first ballot, MPs do not need to know for whom they are voting: they only need to know for whom they are *not* voting. The ballot paper would say '1: Mrs Thatcher; 2: Not Mrs Thatcher; 3: Another Not Mrs Thatcher . . . etc.' If No 1 did not gain an overall majority there would be a second ballot and numbers 2, 3 etc. (who would have been voted for randomly) would be invited to say who they were. If we hadn't guessed already.

Mild Turns to Bitter

14.11.90

Sir Geoffrey Howe resigns. . . .

All along the rabbit warrens inhabited by journalists at Westminster, a tannoy system crackles occasionally into life with urgent information. At ten to four yesterday came a warning his . . .

'Attention! Attention! In view of Sir Geoffrey Howe's personal statement, there will be no four o'clock.'

We looked at each other, incredulous. Our deputy prime minister (resigned) – the mildest of men – has never been suspected of so much as wrenching petals from a marigold, let alone hours from the day. Colleagues explained. At four o'clock, Bernard Ingham (Mrs Thatcher's press secretary) gives a briefing for lobby correspondents. They expected as much, yesterday, but it seems that Sir Geoffrey's personal statement to the House (scheduled for 4.15) had intervened.

It was only the first of Mr Ingham's disappointments.

'Oi! Bernard!' – one of the journalists, leaving the press gallery after Sir Geoffrey's speech, called across to the PM's press secretary – 'that certainly got *her*, middle stump!' Mr Ingham stormed forward, wordless, his face like thunder.

What a pity the word 'devastating' has been drained of meaning by journalistic overuse, for it was never so apt as yesterday. When can so much powder have been kept so dry for so long? Outsiders sensed, as much in the gasps of the packed Chamber as in Sir

Geoffrey's words themselves, how much greater was the impact on a House which knows the unvarying low-key style this man has adopted over the last twelve years. The urgency of feeling reminded your sketchwriter how seldom the quality of earnestness is sensed these days in the parliamentary performances of any but the mad, or impotent.

Mrs Thatcher started with a look of tense composure and a faint smile. The composure held, the tension grew, and the smile disappeared. As for her senior colleagues, they were trying to remain expressionless, often with difficulty.

John MacGregor, John Major, Kenneth Baker and Norman Tebbit were all to be seen with hands raised to mouths, chins, and (in Mr MacGregor's case at one point) eyes, too.

Michael Heseltine sat, strained, watchful. A gentle smile flickerd across Ted Heath's relaxed features, while Sir Geoffrey spoke of Mrs Thatcher's 'nightmare' vision of 'a continent positively teeming with ill-intentioned people, scheming . . .' Poor Mrs Thatcher could have looked around, across, behind her and above – and reflected that the nightmare was closer than Calais. And she was not dreaming.

That will teach her to take a fellow's country house away. If this wasn't Mrs Thatcher's Waterloo, then it was undoubtedly her Clapham Junction.

Hear Hear, Perhaps

22.11.90

One after the other they rose. Members of the party which, beneath the cloak of anonymity and in the shadows of Room 12 the evening before, had plunged in the knife, stood now in the light of the afternoon to congratulate their leader. With one voice they cheered her to the rafters as she entered the Chamber.

'Hear, hear, *hear*!' they bellowed.

One hundred and fifty open mouths in round faces; one hundred and fifty expensive suits; three score waistcoats covering three score plump stomachs; gold watch-chains, gold tie-pins, silk handkerchiefs billowing from top pockets . . . the Tory party was marching behind its leader, every shiny shoe in step. It was a magnificent sight.

Of course 'hear, hear' has a certain anonymity. 'Hear, hear' is a noise, not an undertaking. 'Hear, hear' is not contractually binding and does not constitute an offer. So there was no shortage of mooing and yelping and growling in Mrs Thatcher's support yesterday.

Getting up to speak is rather different. You are all on your own, then. You have stood up, and you will be counted.

So when the Prime Minister had finished her statement, reporting the CSCE summit in Paris ('hear, hear!'), what could be seen differed strangely from what could be heard. The usual crowd – the place-men, job-seekers and fair-weather friends – sat motionless. And in their place rose a small and eccentric platoon: the men still willing to be numbered in her company.

They are best not named, for there were some brave supporters, careless of their own advantage, but there were also fools, ignorant of danger, and creeps so inured to creeping that they have forgotten the purpose of sycophancy.

More depressing to Mrs Thatcher even than the sneers of her enemies must be to observe the calibre of much of the band that still count themselves her friends.

For each, the Prime Minister had a word of gratitude. If we had not known that she was facing political death, nothing in her manner would have suggested it. Dressed in a mustard suit edged in black and pinned with a brooch shaped like a panther leaping, Mrs Thatcher's own expression was not unpantherlike. She looked as ready as ever to leap.

She delivered her statement like a robot, as usual, but sprang to life under hostile questioning, most notably from Tony Benn about war in the Gulf. Mrs Thatcher has never been comfortable dealing with the new 'moderate' Labour party, and flew at this representative of the old, familiar enemy with practised passion. They would miss each other, if she had to go.

All is Safely Gathered in

The journalists' church of St Bride's in Fleet Street should hold an additional harvest thanksgiving service this week, for media people to offer gratitude for the windfall of the Tory leadership crisis.

What a bonanza! '*Potosí!*' as Spaniards exclaim – referring to a Bolivian mountain composed entirely of silver. This yuletide there will be turkey galore for us all.

If a leadership crisis did not exist, it would be necessary to invent one. Maybe we did.

Can we spin it out to a third ballot, do you think? Three more days of views, opinion polls and comment? Three more days of rumour and gossip?

'I've got some good stuff from the Major camp,' I heard one lobby correspondent greet another in a Westminster corridor last week, 'discreetly rubbishing Hurd. I'm getting back to the Hurd camp for something to balance it, discreetly rubbishing Major. Should make a nice little piece.'

In the predatory pack that we media folk constitute, these, the lobby correspondents, are the big players: the condors of the team. If some great political beast seems to be limping or breathing hard, these are the ones who first dart in for an exploratory peck, while the rest of us hover at a distance, watching.

Should the beast then stumble, should its herd not gather to protect it, the lesser predators move in. Mongrels from the tabloids, jackals from the Sundays, pedigrees from the quality magazines converge. Magpies from the diary columns squeak and dive.

The beast is down and bellowing. In this, the last stage of the kill, the beast's fellow-beasts have retreated entirely, trampling her with their own hooves as they gallop over the skyline in a cloud of dust.

And now ground and sky are thick with scavengers. Some of the front-line predators turn to snap angrily at lesser tormentors trying to steal a share of the action.

Others are bigger-hearted. One such, remembering my own Christmas, handed me a South African radio interview the other day. 'Here,' he said, giving me a Johannesburg telephone number, 'have this. Leadership crisis.'

For I am part of the second wave, as much scavenger as predator.

A sort of rook. Preening my glistening black plumage, I am conveyed in taxis from radio station to television studio to radio station . . . Microphone on? Red light. Cue? Green light. And we're away with our profound thoughts.

'Mrs Thatcher is in deep trouble.' How deep? 'Very deep.' Terminal? 'Possibly.' Green light off. £20 plus VAT. 'Ping,' goes the cash register. 'Taxi!' Off to the TV studio.

Cameras rolling? 'Mrs Thatcher is in deep trouble.' Ping! £50 plus VAT . . . Radio down-the-line telephone interview? Maybe; what time? 7.30 am? Do you pay? Ah, yes, well, I do have a phone by the bed. Give me a ring beforehand to wake me up, would you?

7.30. Ring, ring. 'Hello? What sort of man is Mr Major? Quiet, classless, blah, blah . . . Heseltine? Showy, presidential, blah, blah, vote-winner, blah . . . Hurd? Safe pair of hands, assured, blah, blah, establishment candidate, blah . . . Who do *I* think will win? Who knows? Ping! £15 plus VAT. Roll over and go back to sleep.

Lord, send us a new Tory leader, but not just yet.

The Tribe   *28.11.90*

The fall of Mrs Thatcher. . . .

There will be people who will portray what has passed in recent days as an embarrassing lapse. Such people speak of chaos and confusion, of panic and self-destructive anger. Soon they will be referring to these past few weeks as an awkward wobble, when the Tory party temporarily took leave of its senses, then recovered its nerve.

Nothing could be further from the truth. As in some tribal folk-mystery, the Conservative party has suffered a great internal convulsion, triggered as much by the collective unconscious of the tribe as by any conscious plan to contrive its survival. They have not, as individual men and women, known what they were doing, but the tribe has known what it was doing, and has done it with ruthless efficiency. The instinct to survive has triumphed.

Not that they were aware of that. All they knew was that they were heading for disaster. Each had his own opinion as to why. What they concurred upon was the imminence of danger; and when they concurred on that, the convulsion began.

At their conference in Bournemouth, a strange, flat despair gripped the occasion. We all noticed it, but none of us knew how to interpret it. Then they began to fight. They lashed out at the media, they lashed out at Europe, they lashed out at the Opposition, and they lashed out at each other. The tribe was in turmoil.

Michael Heseltine – as much, by now, a totem of dissent as a person – found members of the tribe dancing around him and chanting. He responded. The media took up the chant. Michael Heseltine started a teasing dance: was it a war dance? Nobody knew. He did not know himself.

At this point their leader took on the dervish character. Saddam Hussein said she was 'possessed'. In a series of sustained rants she stunned the Chamber, alienated half her party and scared hell out of most of us.

There followed a short silence, and then the murmurs began. They grew until an extraordinary thing happened. One of the elders of the tribe, Sir Geoffrey Howe, began to speak. He spoke almost in tongues: he spoke as he had never spoken. He poured down imprecations upon the head of the leader.

Around Mr Heseltine the dance now reached a pitch of excitement that demanded answer. He rose, took the dagger and stabbed her.

What happened next is folklore. With the leader now wounded, but still alive, her own senior tribesmen drew back with one accord and left her. Suddenly alone, she hesitated a moment, then staggered from the stage.

The tribe mourned her departure. Not falsely or without feeling, they wept. Then, last night, the final twist occurred. The tribe fell upon her assailant, Michael Heseltine, and slew him, too – with many shouts of anger. Real anger.

All drew back, and the new leader, already blessed by the old leader, clean, apart, and uninvolved, stepped forward. With cries of adoration, the tribe gathered around him.

It could have been done as a ballet. It had all the elements of a classical drama. Like Chinese opera or Greek tragedy, the rules required that certain human types be represented; certain ambitions be portrayed; certain actions punished. Every convention was obeyed: every actor played out his role. The dramatic unities of time, place and action were fulfilled. It started in autumn 1990, and ended in the same season; it started in Committee Room 12 at Westminster, and ended there.

It started with an old leader, who was assassinated as she deserved; then her assassin was assassinated, as he deserved. Then the new leader stepped forward; and here the ballet ended.

And the tribe danced. As I write, they are dancing still.

Mr Major Begins to Bore   *30.11.90*

A group of reporters and political sketchwriters sipped tea yesterday in a Commons cafeteria. Despair gripped us. It was 3.40, just after Prime Minister's Questions. One spoke. He voiced the mood of all.

'If people are going to be moderate, reasonable and fair-minded, they have to be got rid of. They are no use to us.'

Yesterday was John Major's debut.

Mrs Thatcher had arrived first, in papal purple.

Opinion divided sharply among the press corps as to whether she was early for Prime Minister's Questions (3.15) or late for Prayers (2.30). One faction among us noted that waiting until other MPs had arrived (and the public gallery had filled) guaranteed the cheers she got.

The other faction speculated that she would not have wanted her new life to start with devotions. Missing Prayers might arise from having been caught in her first traffic jam for eleven years. Now she knows what all those stationary cars are doing.

When she came in, Mr Heath's front seat was empty.

'Don't let Heath get that place!' came the helpful call from Labour's Dennis Skinner. Mrs Thatcher smiled and shook her head, occupying a more modest position near the back. She sat next to Mrs Elizabeth Peacock (Batley and Spen), a known second-ballot 'Heseltinista'.

Next, at 3.11, came Mr Heseltine himself. He strode in to scattered cheers from both sides and plonked himself down next to Chris Patten, who gave him an encouraging pat on the arm – as well might a minister who had just handed his successor 'an unexploded time bomb' (if Mr Patten's description of the poll tax is to be believed).

Then, thirty seconds later, in walked the Prime Minister.

There was a huge cheer from the government benches. Mrs Thatcher smiled – her face a tug-o'-war between pride and anxiety: like a gym mistress watching her young star pupil approaching the vaulting-horse in his new leotards.

3.15. They were away – with a planted question from Roger King (C, Birmingham, Northfield) of a type of which we all fervently hope Mr Major's fixers do not intend to make a practice.

And what, you ask, of the main event?

What indeed! It was dull. Mr Kinnock asked a routine question about the poll tax, Mr Major gave a holding reply about the need for 'refinements' and Kinnock (luckily for Major) did not enquire how exactly you do refine an unexploded time bomb.

A series of the usual crawling questions from the government benches, and the usual insults from the Opposition left both the strengths and the weaknesses of their target untested.

Apart from the intriguing hint of an underlying petulance, Major kept a cannily straight bat. He looked intelligent but nervous and sounded like the whine of a chainsaw in a distant forest. He does not, yet, command the Chamber naturally. Achieving that took Mrs Thatcher years.

'Resign,' shouted Labour hecklers at him, without enthusiasm. 'Resign,' came the returning shout back at Neil Kinnock from some Tories. From others, more interestingly: 'Don't resign.' It was, in short, a day like any other. If this was Thursday, that must be John Major. If this was Prime Minister's Questions, that must be the Prime Minister.

Both Sides of the Fence

16.1.91

War with Iraq looms.

Halfway across the barbed wire is neither a comfortable nor a dignified place to rest, but Neil Kinnock yesterday hit upon an alternative to sitting on the fence.

He jumped rapidly from one side of it to the other. It worked well. It gave an impression of intellectual vigour and lent pace and excitement to his speech. The Labour leader turned himself into an energetic and forceful blur.

But a blur is what it amounted to. Was he here . . . 'Sanctions alone were never going to be enough'? Or was he there . . . 'if there is any chance of achieving [Iraq's withdrawal] without reward and without war, that chance must be pursued to its fullest possibilities'?

It was, in its way, a magnificent performance. Intellectually shabby, morally ambivalent and politically adroit, it could be recommended to A-level students in party management. What Mr Kinnock was saying was that we should hang on a little longer, so that when we did attack every last doubt as to the necessity of this course would have been dispelled.

But that only takes 15 seconds. The Labour leader's speech took half an hour. At the last Tory conference, John Major's only really good joke was that the reason it took Mr Kinnock so long to conclude his remarks was that, having nothing to say, he found it hard to know when he had finished. That would be to underrate his performance yesterday, which had a purpose, and achieved it.

Sometimes, while you are attempting to reach a telephone extension, they play you gentle music. The Opposition leadership finds itself in just such an awkward interim. Soon, war may be declared and Mr Kinnock will be able to bury his scruples without dishonour. The military effort will be engaged: so, wise or unwise, patriots will support it. But we are not there yet; and the Labour left is getting restless. Hence the mood music. It was well done.

Pruning the Dead Lettuce
22.1.91

This was 'the first time since the invasion of Kuwait,' the Prime Minister said, 'for honorary members to express their point of view.'

The slip was instructive. Mr Major's style is that of the honorary secretary of a local residents' association, drafting (perhaps) a solicitor's letter to an outside concern causing (shall we say?) an environmental intrusion. It is a large residents' association he serves, of course (some 56 million residents in all); and the intrusion a highly offensive one. But it was hard to watch the PM in the Gulf debate yesterday without conjuring up the image of a young businessman from the Standard and Chartered Bank, commuting in from Huntingdon, and giving up his leisure time for the local community.

'Nor should we underestimate the time it may take to complete this matter.' A very considerable period is, I would anticipate, our current estimate as of now.

The United Nations' resolutions must be implemented, he said: 'Nothing more and nothing less will suffice.' Nothing *more* will suffice, eh? If Saddam Hussein were not to stop at quitting Kuwait, but lay down his arms, resign, and give away his private fortune to charity too, that wouldn't suffice then?

'There may well be times when we shall all need to bear bad news with fortitude.' Yes indeed – oh yes! We shall have to face the future with hearts and minds fully resolved to discharge our duties and face up to our obligations, bearing any burden, however great, with the courage and fortitude of a nation utterly determined not to shirk its responsibilities, however onerous, and I must emphasize that, and offer you finally and in conclusion the assurance of our best attentions at all times. Trusting that this finds you as it leaves me – in the pink . . .

Sorry. Back to the Prime Minister, who only said 'considerably' five times yesterday. 'Such broadcasts are wholly objectionable in every respect' – Mr Major was talking about the parading (for the cameras) of prisoners of war, something which was 'utterly deplorable and wholly unforgivable' – and, yes, 'I can absolutely reaffirm that point again,' for it was contrary to the Geneva Convention: something 'we shall hold them to', apparently, 'completely'. Mr Major was eager 'to register beyond doubt our views in this matter'.

Please understand that your sketchwriter questions neither the justice of Mr Major's argument nor the depth of his feelings. I only remark on his reluctance to express that argument or those feelings in language that is fresh or sharp. This speech was written beforehand and there was plenty of time for someone who was not preoccupied with running a war to cast an eye over the text and remove the dead lettuce leaves. It is one of the few practical skills the gilded Oxbridge youth who adorn our civil service do possess.

Action this matter soonest please, Mr Major. And have a nice day.

Dame Alabaster

23.1.91

Dame Janet Fookes (C, Plymouth Drake) is a very majestic dame. Almost statuesque, I would imagine, in a mist; even the harsh lights of the Commons Chamber glance helplessly off the dignity that is Dame Janet. Seldom does anything as coarse as a frown or as frivolous as a smile demean the serenity of her countenance.

If not the most senior chairman of committee on Mr Speaker's panel, Dame Janet is surely the most respected. Just the hint of disapproval in those well-bred accents is enough to stay the hand of the most intransigent of troublemaking coalmining MPs. Her chairmanship of the RSPCA struck terror into the hearts of badger-baiters, cockfighters and fox-hunters. She it is whose bill, now law, hammers the kerbcrawlers of Tooting Common.

Well do I remember when she and I were members together of the committee on a criminal justice bill to which I had proposed an amendment abolishing the imprisonment of prostitutes. Dame Janet (then plain 'Miss Fookes', but beneath that humble title there was already a dame struggling to get out) was one of the only Tory members of the committee prepared, with me, to meet a delegation of prostitutes that arrived by coach from Birmingham. We duly met them.

She listened intently to what they had to say, and, when they had finished, rose. 'I agree with the change in the law for which you ask,' she said, in tones calm but severe, 'and I will vote for it. But I must tell you that . . . *what* . . . you *do* would be,' (she paused) 'to me,' (she paused again) 'a fate worse than death.' And she sailed out. But she voted for reform. Little wonder that hushed voices in the Lady Members' Room whisper of 'Janet' as perhaps the first Lady Speaker. Let us hope so.

Yesterday afternoon, Dame Janet's dress – we should really say 'robe' – was a rich, dark, silk-and-jade affair. Her hair was burnished copper. The whole impression was of a minor but deeply respected Javanese sea-goddess. This was reinforced by the application, to sculpted cheeks, of powder so pale that the Dame appeared to be almost of alabaster. Her face was quite without expression. Her head, motionless, was held high. As if in a trance, Dame Janet seemed to contemplate, with dreadful tranquillity, man's terrible fall from grace.

In such company did we approach Question 7 to the Secretary of State for Defence, from Ian McCartney (Lab, Makerfield).

'Mr Ian McCartney!' called Mr Speaker. 'Question seven!' called Mr McCartney. Dame Janet was still, silent, staring forward like the figurehead from a great fighting ship of old. It fell to the junior minister, aloof and poker-faced Archie Hamilton, to answer.

'As my Right Hon friend announced to the House last year,' intoned Mr Hamilton – and launched into details of the navy's plan to decommission vessels in the Fleet. Still no sign of emotion from the Dame. But the sting was in Archie's tail. 'A number of older boats,' concluded Mr Hamilton, almost casually, 'including HMS *Warspite*' – Dame Janet flinched – are being decommissioned.'

After Mr McCartney she rose – not HMS *Warspite*, but Janet Fookes.

'Would he reconsider the wisdom of reducing the nuclear submarine fleet, in the light,' (and this she said sorrowfully) 'of the uncertainties of the world . . . ?'

But Mr Hamilton would not reconsider. Dame Janet sank back to her seat with such poise, and such grace, that her movement resembled the gliding passage down to the water of a great liner, after the launch.

Except, I think, that no mortal, not even royalty, would contemplate smashing a bottle of champagne across those stately bows.

29.1.91 # Tactical Baby Seals

Yesterday, Michael Heseltine told the House what Saddam was doing to 'fish, sea mammals, and shellfish'. MPs were the angriest they have yet been, in this war.

So far as is known, there are no baby seals in the Persian Gulf. This is a pity for Hussein. It deprives him of the ultimate weapon against the British public and its outraged House of Commons: to target Scud missiles on to seal nurseries. Short of this horror, all that is left to the evil Iraqis is to breed seals in one of their secret biological establishments and engage in low-level baby-seal-bombing, dropping their furry bomblets straight into the greasy sludge. To judge from yesterday's performance, the psychological blow here would be devastating.

None of the atrocities so far committed by Baghdad against humans has unleashed a thesaurus of parliamentary shock of anything like the intensity we heard yesterday. It was no particular expression (any of which, alone, could be justified) but the sheer scale of accumulated adjectival outrage which impressed.

'Abomination,' said environment secretary Michael Heseltine, 'outrage', 'calamity', 'catastrophe'.

This was mild. 'Monstrous,' thought the Father of the House, Sir Bernard Braine – one of those few with the grace to mention (in passing) the mass murder, by gas, of Kurdish people. 'Blackmail,' said Heseltine. 'Vicious,' (Jonathan Aitken), 'evil and reckless' (Peter Shore).

'Desperate act,' said Labour's spokesman, Ann Taylor, 'war-crime'. Each one of us, she added poetically, was the poorer for this. She did not quite say 'Any oyster's death diminishes me/Therefore never send to know/On whom the oil spills: it spills on thee . . .' But she nearly did. Mrs Taylor was concerned about the 'eco-system'. Or it may have been 'echo-system' – a reference, perhaps, to the Opposition's response to government policy in the Gulf.

Has military science yet developed a sea-cow-seeking missile? Such a weapon would give Saddam a key advantage in the war of nerves. There was concern at Westminster about the loss of human life: that was bad enough. But to threaten *sea-cows*!

'Absolute inhumanity of this repulsive regime,' was Gravesham's Jacques Arnold's phrase; 'despicable ecological devastation' came from Simon Burns (C, Chelmsford).

I wonder whether Saddam has considered taking a group of cormorants hostage? To judge from yesterday's anxiety, this would unnerve our elected representatives a good deal more than the holding of British journalists. I had not thought of cormorants as an endangered species, but yesterday, plummy voices – voices able to report the most harrowing of news at the tensest of cheese-and-wine parties, and still stay steady – trembled with horror. Even Mr Heseltine's grammar deserted him ('deliberate act of environmental appalling consequences') as he thoughtfully carved out for himself a post-war role in organizing a 'working party' for permanent international preparedness.

'Appalling and uncivilized' (Norwich's Patrick Thompson), an 'evil man,' thought Anthony Beaumont-Dark (Selly Oak), 'vicious and brutal' (Phillip Oppenheim, Amber Valley) . . . 'Eco-terrorism' was what Henry Bellingham (Norfolk NW) called it.

The Liberals' Simon Hughes wanted environmentalists to enjoy the same privilege as the Red Cross in war zones. Tony Banks (Lab, Newham NW) wanted to go there himself ('I'll go!' he shouted) to assist.

Nobody has yet tried 'Saddam Hussein ate my hamster' on the House. But they will.

8.3.91 Mr Speaker Ducks the Auto-tributes

Perhaps nobody in the world knows better than Mr Speaker how prone are MPs, at the drop of a platitude, to blow themselves into a gale of windy rhetoric. Any MP worthy of the title is ready at the slightest notice to dip into the inexhaustible well of sententiousness that lies beneath the Commons. Any excuse will do: a terrible railway accident; a victory in the Eurovision song contest; the outbreak of war, or scabies . . .

. . . Or even the retirement of Mr Speaker. Jack Weatherill knows, if anyone knows, the tributes and regrets which will at once flow unchecked from the bottoms of what pass as politicians' hearts. He knows there will be no way of telling from the words themselves, which are sincere. When the word 'tribute' occurs twice or more at Westminster, you might as well go home. MPs are on auto-tribute. All is lost.

So if, over the years, he has wearied of the same words, the same vapid sentiments, the same pious regards, every time a Boeing 747, a cormorant, or a sparrow, falls; every time a train, or a Barlow Clowes, crashes; and whenever a prime minister, or a tower-block, crumbles . . . then you should not suppose that Jack Weatherill's idea of fun is to hear them all over again, even if it is to him that they are now directed.

It was not surprising therefore, that he yesterday eschewed all ceremony, left the Leader of the House to mention that their Speaker is to retire at the next election, and tapped his Order Paper tetchily on the arm of his oak throne, as a string of MPs launched into their personal tributes.

Could there be, asked the Father of the House, Sir Bernard Braine, 'a very special moment' dedicated to tributes? Perhaps wishing that it could indeed be a moment, Mr Speaker confined himself to a restrained: 'I'm very grateful but I think we should now get back to the business for next week.'

Time will be found for this, said the House Leader. It is to be hoped that when it is, MPs on auto-tribute will remember that at the retirement of a Speaker you do not 'congratulate the emergency services,' nor does your 'heart go out' to the bereaved. For his part, Mr Weatherill will know which of those bearing tributes once wielded knives.

My own view is that if you are a kid in a remedial class in a rough comprehensive – looking to your class teacher as the fount of authority – then it is easy to forget how delicate is your teacher's position. Why, you wonder, does he not *discipline* the rowdier elements the moment they threaten order. Why does he brook even the hint of disrespect?

What you overlook is that the teacher has scant means of ultimate enforcement. Some of it is bluff; some of it is harnessing the natural obedience of a majority against the truculence of the minority. He is not so much a magistrate, outside the class, as a diplomat – part of it, and trying to keep everyone on board. This Speaker did keep everyone on board; and did so over a period when the Opposition parties came quite close to despair, elements could easily have rebelled against the Westminster system, and nobody would have known what to do.

Mr Weatherill's instinct has been – in the phrase now famous – to go the extra mile with troublemakers. The result has been that no Labour rebel has ever had a valid cause of any importance against this 'Tory' Speaker. His speakership is distinguished not by the little scraps which did occur, but the constitutional bust-up which never quite did.

Backseat Growls

The Budget. . . .

Dave Blunkett's guide dog, Offa, lay disconsolately on the carpet, staring up at the mace. Sir Nicholas Fairbairn's orange blazer and white trousers left this dog unimpressed. That Dame Peggy Fenner was attired like an Aztec sun-warrior, and David Ashby was wearing a violent green dickie bow, meant little to an alsatian-retriever cross. If Austin Mitchell's tie offended dogs as much as it did humans, Offa kept his opinion to himself. This might be the Budget, but to Offa it was just another day.

Mrs Thatcher, in a black suit with white Quaker collar, looked as formidable as the fellow on the porridge oats packet and rather less cheery. She was of more interest than the real prime minister to the gentleman beside me: my seat being right next door to the 'overflow' gallery used by government MPs who have found no room downstairs, I had the benefit throughout of growled Tory comment and interruption from my left. It enlivened a heavy afternoon.

Sitting on the carpet, Harry Greenway (C, Ealing N) had wedged himself up against the arm of Mrs Thatcher's bench. 'Look what she's got for a book end!' came the first growl, as Norman Lamont rose.

The Chancellor started by noting that recent polls showed him level-pegging with Desert Orchid for public recognition. Both had huge stakes riding on them.

'And neither of them has her on his back' – another growl from my left.

Speaking of last year's ill-fated boom, Mr Lamont observed that '. . . Some firms, and individuals, became over-extended.'

'Her, for instance.'

'. . . If I may confess it,' continued the Chancellor, 'I don't believe in miracles.'

'You'll say twenty "Hail Margarets" for that.'

'. . . This will assist those who give up safe managerial positions to set out on the rocky road of running their own business.'

'Poor John . . .'

My Tory commentators fell silent for a bit, while Mr Lamont

lobbed a little praise, gingerly, in Mrs Thatcher's direction: '. . . And this' (he meant the change in economic attitudes) 'was the lasting achievement of my right hon friend for Finchley.'

'Look at her!' I looked. Mrs Thatcher wore an expression of deep suspicion.

'. . . There will be tax relief for seafarers.' Ted Heath smiled. 'Relief will be given on gifts equipment to schools . . .'

'Especially Harrow.'

'. . . And I propose to alter the basis on which beer is taxed.'

'After it's drunk.'

Mr Lamont began to explain additions to the taxation of spirits. The bench of peers in the 'distinguished strangers' gallery suddenly emptied as their Lordships filed out.

'Where are the old boys off to?' Two minutes later, their Lordships filed back. Much giggling to my left. 'Went out for a quick drink before they put the prices up.'

In future privatizations, said the Chancellor, shares could be 'distributed directly to the public through high street outlets.'

'Ladbrokes.'

Raising tax bands, Mr Lamont explained, meant that higher rate tax should only begin to bite into income beyond £29,000. Chuckles all round: MPs earn £29,032.

'Good stuff, Norman. Just under the wire.'

Offa opened and shut one eye. I think he was winking.

Poll Tax: The Final Curtain
22.3.91

Any keynote speech, any poem, novel, story, *career*, of any consequence, turns upon a fulcrum. Somewhere concealed within it will be found a word, a passage, an episode, upon which the centre of gravity of the whole thing rests. In logic or in passion, every argument has a heart.

Yesterday's statement by the Secretary of State for the Environment was no exception. Michael Heseltine, though back on cracking form, could not escape a single phrase, buried in paragraph 40 on the fifth page of his long and closely argued statement. He had been building up to it for years. It lay there, waiting for him. He knew it was coming.

In a sense it was the sentiment for whose expression the whole of the Opposition had been cat-calling at Prime Minister's Questions, minutes earlier, when they shouted, 'Say you're sorry! Say you're sorry!' over and again.

It was the thing which every Tory MP dreads facing in the long months ahead at a hundred 'any questions' sessions and a thousand cheese and wine parties. It was the rock which scuppered Mrs Thatcher.

As his ship approached those straits, the minister's voice was lowered and the Chamber hushed. 'The public,' said Mr Heseltine, 'have not been persuaded that the charge is fair.'

'Say it again!' someone shouted. There was an enormous cheer from the Opposition. Most Tories grinned, foolishly.

The first half of Mr Heseltine's statement had been a gingerly approach to this sentence. What now remained was the painful climbing down which it entailed. He carried this off with aplomb. He almost seemed to be having fun.

For Labour, Bryan Gould had fun with his reply. To the gourmet of mixed metaphor, Mr Gould is a feast. He approaches the table of possible imagery rather as one who has paid a fixed price for a plate of salad under one of those 'all you can eat for £3.95' schemes and, starting with the potato salad, finds the sauerkraut equally attractive and the bean shoots hard to resist. The dinner loses coherence.

Mr Gould rose, and approached the table. This, he said, was a 'complete capitulation and a startling U-turn' as well as 'the most shameless abandonment of principle in modern political history'. It was a 'flagship, fatally holed below the waterline' but still 'afloat, the hulk a danger to shipping'. It 'refused to lie down and die'. It had taken the Prime Minister 'through the revolving door,' whereupon he had been 'bounced by a leak'. Still 'in thrall to the monster it had created,' it was now mutating into 'a pig in a poke' which 'put a price on the right to vote'. The pig in the poke was 'in the driving seat', a 'debacle', 'born of arrogance', and 'spreading its malign influence'.

But the pig, debacle, chauffeur, mutant monster or floating hulk, having completed its capitulation, shamelessly abandoned principle and accompanied Mr Major through the revolving door: and having then avoided the bouncing leak, refused to lie down.

It was, said Mr Gould, 'a bloodstained statement'. It was a pretty bloody reply, too.

Lego Man Takes on Bendy Doll   *27.3.91*

Wilde defined fox-hunting as 'the unspeakable in pursuit of the uneatable'. At PM's Questions yesterday, Mr Major, tackled again on the subject of the poll tax, gave a passable impression of the improbable in flight from the unsaleable.

There was another 'row' between Mr Major and Mr Kinnock. Lego Man meets Bendy Doll. If either of them had anything to say, it would matter less that neither has the gift of language. If either had the gift of language, it would matter less that neither has anything to say. Here were two men saying nothing, badly. It was unspeakable, uneatable, improbable and unsaleable.

Introducing Right Trusty George   *25.4.91*

A new archbishop takes his seat. . . .

A painful lesson, quickly learnt by sketchwriters, is that on any grand occasion you may confidently report a great man's presence but must never categorically state that he was absent. Maybe he had just nipped out for a cigarette: maybe you missed him. There are unlit corners, even in the gilded Chamber of the House of Lords . . .

So we are far from alleging that Lord Jakobovits, the Chief Rabbi, was not present yesterday afternoon for the introduction of the new Archbishop of Canterbury; and far from claiming that our foremost lay Catholic, the Duke of Norfolk, was absent. But they were not in their usual places.

Britain's most famous Presbyterian was there, though: not only there, but officiating on the woolsack. It is perhaps fortunate that Lord Mackay of Clashfern, the Lord Chancellor, has already been castigated by the Free Presbyterian Church of Scotland for attending a requiem mass for a Catholic colleague, or he might have been thrown out yesterday for his complicity in the incorporation of an archbishop into parliament.

Lord Mackay was wearing what appeared to be a large black Cornish pasty on his head: a three-cornered affair, unlike the four-sided mortarboards carried by three gentlemen in glasses who now appeared from behind the Throne. They wore black frocks with white slipovers, each with a flash of magenta at the neck. They stalked up to the table like bespectacled flamingos.

One of them knelt before the Lord Chancellor. This was the Archbishop: the remaining flamingos were the Bishops of London and Gloucester. Lord Mackay gave the arch-flamingo a piece of paper, which he brought back to the table.

From the government benches Lord Hailsham, with two sticks, looked on. The Baroness Strange (whose most recent escapade was to place a bowl of Easter eggs in the entrance lobby for her fellow-peers) had abandoned her home-knitted cardigans and wore royal blue and pearls for the day.

A secretary bird, taller and plainer than the flamingos, with no magenta flash, took the paper from the arch-flamingo. This was the Reading Clerk. The paper was a letter. The Reading Clerk read it aloud.

Humbler correspondents sometimes put (on the back of the envelope) 'From:' and their name. This missive, too, included a little modest information about the sender: 'Elizabeth II, by the grace of God of the United Kingdom of Great Britain and Northern Ireland and of Our other realms and territories Queen, Head of the Commonwealth, Defender of the Faith.'

After that, 'Dear Dr Carey,' would be an anticlimax. The letter addressed 'The Most Reverend Father in God, Our right trusty and well beloved Counsellor, George Leonard, Archbishop of Canterbury, Primate of All England and Metropolitan'. Not the District line? If the address was spectacular, the contents were plain. 'Greeting,' it said, commanding the flamingo's presence, 'waiving all excuses'.

George then took the oath in the pleasantly unassuming accents more of a primary school headmaster than a primate, signed the visitors' book, adjusted his glasses, and was led by the other flamingos to the bishops' bench. All three stood, spectacles flashing in the TV lights. They bowed, sat down, stood up again and took off their hats. Then they bowed, sat down, stood up again and bowed once more.

There were no tambourines, nobody clapped. Waiving all excuses, the flamingos stalked off.

Never Say Porpoise, John

10.5.91

I arrived at the Commons to find the Minister of Agriculture, John Selwyn Gummer, on his feet in a flight of passionate oratory on behalf of porpoises.

This minister should say 'dolphins'. There may be politicians who can pronounce the word 'porpoise' without looking funny, but Mr Gummer is not one of them. There is something horribly risible about the juxtaposition of 'Gummer' with 'porpoise'. His face and mouth form themselves almost automatically into the round 'o' of the dominant vowel. His little eyes bulge naturally with that hint of dignified affront conveyed by the very sound. There is a sense in which this minister's whole being, the dignity and majesty that is Gummer, invites a cheeky shout of 'porpoise'.

'And no one must be in any doubt about our commitment to the protection of the whale,' added Mr Gummer, for good measure. This was a mistake too, as it got Geoffrey Dickens going. Anything more like a whale you are unlikely to find on land. As always with the MP for Littleborough and Saddleworth, it was clearer that his heart was in the right place than that it was engaged to his brain. Dickens was on auto-bellow.

'Whales throughout the world are being slaughtered . . . and many species are getting rather low.' He paused.

The pause was a mistake. It let in Dennis Skinner's shout of: 'Declare your interest!' Mr Dickens wallowed on through waves of laughter, spouting: 'What can the minister do to reverse these dreadful trends?' Not much, it seemed, but share parliamentary outrage.

Shared outrage was what another minister, David Maclean, offered Harry Greenway (C, Ealing N). Mr Greenway famously rides British horses and equally famously wants to stop Frenchmen from eating them. 'We're in harness on this one,' whooped Mr

Maclean, to general groans.

The minister went on to agree that there was too much transporting of live animals in Europe and he would do his best to persuade the Europeans to kill them first. 'But I cannot dictate to consumers in what form they should eat their food,' he added, alarming us with the thought that continentals eat their animals alive.

On question eight, outrage peaked. North of the border (the SNP's Andrew Welsh, from Angus E, told us) 'the Scottish raspberry industry' is under threat. Scots are being engulfed by 'a flood of cheap imports'. MPs gasped at this vision of a squelchy red tide rolling in from abroad. Mr Gummer tried in vain to calm the House.

'I'm well aware,' he burbled, 'of the importance not only of the Scottish raspberry industry, but of the soft fruit market as a whole.'

Soft fruit as a whole? Why? Do banana wars loom behind the raspberry tide? Will melons roll in from all sides? Shall Campbells and MacGregors unite before a bombardment of peaches?

There is never a dull moment at agriculture questions. Where else would an innocent query from Bob Cryer (Lab, Bradford S) about free surplus food for pensioners, elicit from the minister, David Curry, the reply that he did not see why 'my noble friend, the Baroness Trumpington, or your friend Robert Maxwell' needed such handouts. Dividing up the entire beef surplus would amount to '$7\frac{1}{2}$ oz per pensioner'.

Lady Trumpington, a substantial baroness with a healthy appetite, excites unqualified admiration. I hope it is not impertinent to remark that $7\frac{1}{2}$ oz of beef is unlikely to make a difference to Lady Trumpington.

Let the Clichés Roll

24.5.91

A notice at the Commons press gallery announces that reporters 'may now wear shirtsleeves'. Playing safe and retaining my trousers, I went in. MPs were gathering in their playpen for a final romp before the spring break.

First came Douglas Hogg, minister of state at the Foreign Office, answering a debate on relations with Israel. In Mr Hogg a transformation has occurred. This Jack Russell of a minister now masquerades as a bonsai St Bernard.

Some say that God, looking down on mankind and seeing how short in stature some of his creatures were to be, made the small ones more aggressive, to compensate. But I think that, looking down on the young Hogglet and seeing how aggressive he was going to be, God made him small, to limit the damage.

Last year, even Mr Hogg was forced to recognize the problem. After a session in which he simply barked wildly at the Opposition for three-quarters of an hour, a Labour backbencher shouted 'Woof!' and the whole Opposition began barking. Something had to be done. Hogg took advice. Backstage designers got to work.

This year the New Hogg was unveiled. Serene, monumental, he fixes his eyes upon the common good, and never rises to the bait. He has become a man of gritty majesty. And it works. The small Hogg is now being taken seriously by all who do not know him. There was one regrettable lapse with Greville Janner (Lab, Leicester W) on Wednesday, but we shall not speak of that. Yesterday, statesmanship was resumed.

It was masterly. Opening the debate had been Michael Latham, the Conservative MP for Rutland and Melton who is giving up at the next election because he is fed up with politics. Latham has been a long-standing but not unthinking friend of Israel and made a fine speech, perhaps his last on the subject. It was, said the young Hogg (rolling the phrase round in his mouth), 'a contribution of unusual distinction'.

Nor was that all he said. He said that 'if we do not see peace then we face the prospect of war'. To this he added the wise thought that 'the first step to progress in negotiation is to get the parties to sit down together at the table'. The platitudes rolled. The minister was on auto-plat, full of dignity.

Impressively, this was done without notes. Looking down, I saw that he had no text, just a couple of handwritten jottings. A depressing feature of modern Tory ministers is that even their clichés need to be scripted, but Mr Hogg is of the old school and can reach into his own soul for homily.

Banquo's Ghost a Welshman?

11.6.91

Welsh question time yesterday was overshadowed by a phantom presence. It hung in the air like Banquo's ghost. Constant reference was made to it, each MP confident that he knew its opinion on every subject and was personally familiar with its habits. But nobody could agree what these were.

They called it 'the people of Wales'. Just when you thought it was safe to go caravaning there.

The 'people of Wales' were summoned at every question: as judge, jury, witness and final arbiter. Whatever you felt on any matter, that was what 'the people of Wales' felt, too. They would bear you out. If, however, your political opponent thought the opposite, why – 'the people of Wales' supported him, too. Seldom can a race have proved itself as fickle in its affections or unstable in its judgement as 'the people of Wales' yesterday.

'The people of Wales do not want market forces!' cried Alan Williams (Lab, Carmarthen) asking about hospitals. Junior minister Nicholas Bennett shot back: 'The people of Wales do not want the truth hidden!'

'The people of Wales are not going to be frightened' by Labour lies, thought the Tories' Kenneth Hind (W Lancs). But according to Alun Michael (Lab, Cardiff and Penarth) 'the people of Wales' were frightened already and 'have a *right* to be frightened' at having Mr Bennett as a minister. Cardiff's Ian Grist (C) agreed they were frightened, because Labour 'were going around trying to scare the people of Wales'. Hard, surely, to pin them down to scare properly, because (according to Bennett) 'the people of Wales are already moving around' to get their operations faster.

A disturbing picture was growing of this bewildered tribe: a worried people, anxiously chewing leeks, plucking harps and fiddling with daffodils as they rushed from hospital to hospital in search of operations while ducking the 'redundancies', 'raining down' (gasped Labour frontbencher Barry Jones) 'on the people of Wales'.

Or were they? Wyn Roberts (entering his thirteenth year as a Welsh minister, so he should know) advised that 'the people of Wales would prefer to listen' to an 'excellent' announcement on jobs: 'very good news for the people of Wales'. Barry Jones thought the Government's economic policies 'are hurting the people of Wales'. Said Bennett: 'He continues to misrepresent the facts to the people of Wales.' Will the real people of Wales please stand up?

The Vulcan and the Donkey

14.6.91

John Redwood, now Secretary of State for Wales, has unusual origins. . . .

The finest thoroughbred horses are often accompanied by a favourite donkey, goat or sheep. Some racehorses will travel nowhere without such a beast. Animal psychiatrists report that the pedigree is relaxed by the presence of its plebeian pal.

Sitting behind the junior industry minister, John Redwood, yesterday was his new parliamentary private secretary, David Evans (Welwyn Hatfield).

A PPS, who is unpaid, is a backbencher appointed to mind the backbench interests of a minister. The PPS keeps the boss in touch with feeling and acts as his eyes and ears in bars and tearooms where ministers do not go. If there are ruffled feathers, a PPS will let his master know. If a minister seeks to plant a question, a canny PPS will find the mug to do it.

It is up to ministers to choose. Redwood has chosen Evans. Not since Noddy and Big Ears has a more odd couple been seen.

Though Evans trades shamelessly on his humble origins, loves to play the buffoon and boasts of failing his 11-plus, he is no fool. A shrewd businessman and ex-chairman of Luton Town football club, Evans's braying interventions at PM's questions shock and delight. Beneath his superficially vulgar populism lies . . . well, a profoundly vulgar populism. To say that the member for Welwyn Hatfield is no intellectual is more than fair: it is your sketchwriter's best hope of avoiding a black eye. Yet the Evans family crest bears the motto *Ne me minoris face* ('do not underestimate me') – or would, if Evans could be doing with Latin. 'Watch yer step, sonny' says it all.

John Redwood could hardly be more different. Possessed of a

supersonic intellect, this slim young ex-investment manager with Rothschilds, philosopher of the new right and Fellow of All Souls, is a lean, mean thinking machine. But he is dry, apparently cold, and has an emotionless manner which sometimes spooks his colleagues. This column was the first to tumble to the fact that Redwood is not in fact a human being at all, but a Vulcan, recently landed from the planet of the same name, where merciless logic rules. Redwood now passes as human, engaged in the covert task of assembling a team of Vulcans to take over the Conservative party.

The plot thickens. Redwood has employed Evans. Why? Evans is human!

I shall tell you why. Colleagues have advised Redwood that his only serious bar to upward mobility is his apparent lack of a sense of fun: he should show more warmth, a more roustabout quality, towards fellow MPs. To see what they mean, he has tapped the words 'fun', 'warmth' and 'roustabout' into the secret computer package of 'handy phrases for travellers to Earth' they gave him when he left Vulcan, but it flashes up only synonyms, equally unfamiliar. How can he cultivate emotions alien to him?

'I know,' he has concluded, 'I'll get a PPS. Somebody with all these qualities, to act as a bridge between me and the humans. I'll key the words for every vulgarian quality into my computasearch program, and see which MP the screen throws up.' Tap, tap, tap . . . 'rollicking', 'rough', 'roustabout', 'rude' . . . finally, he presses EXECUTE.

Oh dear. 'Evans, David John'. The computer has overdone it. Human, yes. All too human, but there is no way a Vulcan can know that. Operating according to strict binary logic, the computer has produced the optimum solution. Reacting with utter rationality, Mr Redwood has accepted it.

The best of luck to both!

The Killer Cherry Speaks

27.6.91

An ex-Prime Minister enters the Eurofray. . . .

Resplendent in cerise, Mrs Thatcher seemed to bob upon a sea of dark-suited gentlemen. A glacé cherry in a bowl of prunes. This was the killer-cherry the Tory business managers had tried so hard to remove.

They even reorganized the afternoon to keep her off live television. A 'statement' was laid on, to postpone the Europe debate for 30 minutes: an expensive half hour, for the only statement they could think of was an undertaking by the social services minister to prepare for a unified age of retirement. Cost? A few billion? It might have been cheaper to give Mrs Thatcher the money to retire.

In one short speech she reminded those who had forgotten what firepower a former Tory prime minister of her calibre commands. As Mrs Thatcher sailed in, the Opposition front bench were on the beach at Dunkirk, all hope gone. She rescued them.

Douglas Hurd had made one of those speeches which remind us that the presence of intellectual content can still win an argument in the Chamber. It was elegant, funny and serious. Like some footsoldier, he said, in a battle described by Homer, his European negotiation would be interrupted from time to time as 'attention passes to the clash of fabled gods . . .' (Mrs Thatcher laughed) '– or goddesses –' (Mrs Thatcher did not laugh) 'in the heavens above his head. But when the thunder of the Great Ones dies away, those on the ground have to get on with the work.'

This he did, and only Paddy Ashdown tried seriously to spoil the fun, scolding him for quibbling about mere names.

'He knows all about changing names,' shouted Dennis Skinner at the Liberal Democrat, ex-Social and Liberal Democrat, ex-Alliance, ex-Liberal.

'Mr Ashdown,' retorted Hurd '. . . energetic and lovely . . .' Sadly he corrected himself: 'Lively'. Mr Hurd sat down to a cheer.

Gerald Kaufman made one of those speeches which remind us that the absence of intellectual content can still lose an argument. Mr Kaufman is sometimes spoken of as a frog (Kermit) and sometimes as a middle-aged mutant Ninja turtle (Geraldo). But all agree that there is something as amphibian about Labour's principal foreign affairs spokesman, as there is something ambivalent about Labour's policy on Europe. For months now, as the European battle between the Tory Great Ones rages above his pond, Kermit has been floating, quite still, just below the surface.

Yesterday he pushed a fraction too far. He thought he could get them with a speech describing disagreements between Conservative MPs, and avoiding any commitments of his own. Tory hilarity grew as Geraldo quoted Mr Heath, the *Daily Telegraph*, Mrs Thatcher, the *Telegraph*, Mr Major, the *Telegraph* . . . everything but Labour policy. 'What would *you* do?' The shouts became more insistent, his plight more hapless.

'We shall make positive proposals!' he finally cried. 'We have a list!'

Then he attacked Japan, said that he had voted against the Common Market, seemed to add that he had not changed his view, asserted that his doubts had now been reconciled, and scampered with relief to some observations about 'the Pacific rim'. He sat down. All seemed lost.

Until Mrs Thatcher stood up. By the end of her speech, Mr Major's smile had disappeared. Ted Heath was soon on his feet, doing his best to repudiate the anti-Europeans. But Ted can only gum his opponents. She still has teeth.

Malice Through the Looking Glass

4.7.91

'There's glory for you,' said Humpty Dumpty.

Mr Peter Brooke, the Northern Ireland secretary, came to the Commons to report that his talks had been 'brought to a conclusion'. He told us what had been 'achieved'. The talks had been 'a source of encouragement', and 'of value', showing 'common ground', proving that 'the time is ripe' for fruitful negotiation. You would not have thought he had come to report that his talks had collapsed. So why the glory?

'I don't know what you mean by "glory",' Alice said.

Or, as Michael Latham (C, Rutland and Melton) put it: 'If these talks were as robust, constructive, and made such progress as you say, then why can't [the participants] go on talking?'

'I mean there's a nice, knockdown argument,' replied Humpty Dumpty.

Peter Brooke implied that the Unionists had knocked down his Irish talks. A glorious success.

'But glory doesn't mean a nice, knockdown argument,' Alice objected.

Or, as a previous Labour Northern Ireland secretary, Merlyn Rees, put it: 'The bald fact is that the talks have broken down.'

Oh no, said Mr Brooke, 'I would not say they have broken down . . . they have run out of time.'

Ah. Run out of time. That was Pharaoh's army's problem, crossing the Red Sea: they ran out of time.

On he went. 'I do not regard this as a setback,' he burbled, raising a serious doubt as to what Mr Brooke *would* regard as a setback. It may be a useful quality in his job that you do not regard *anything* as a setback, but I thought of Emperor Hirohito's announcement, after Hiroshima: 'An event has occurred which is not necessarily to Japan's advantage.'

Was Mr Brooke making a fool of himself? Or was he (as his friends will be whispering) giving the Unionists a breathing space, to catch up with themselves? And were the Unionists, behind their triumphalist rhetoric, tentatively signed up for another stage of Mr Brooke's mystery-tour? Or were they laughing at him?

It was plain that he was talking palpable nonsense, but then he did not really pretend that he was *not* talking palpable nonsense. He seemed to think that if he talked sufficiently palpable nonsense then we would acquit him of dishonesty, shake our heads wisely, and assume that he had some deep purpose, rooted in Gaelic complexity, hidden by an Irish mist.

Thales, I think, enquired of the ancients whether it was possible to step into the same river twice. Wittgenstein wondered, darkly, whether it was possible to step into the same river once. Mr Brooke yesterday added the thought that if certain parties had agreed to rules and then not held to them, then though 'it would be right that they held to' these rules, it would not be wrong that they had not held to them. 'No blame' attached.

Yesterday Mr Brooke tested verbal formulae, one foot at a time, to see what weight they would bear. From time to time he glanced nervously across at the Unionists, arms grimly folded as they waited for him to trip. It was like watching Sophocles on trial before a parish council. There was something humiliating in the spectacle. David Steel used the word 'failure'. It was 'wrong' stammered Mr Brooke, to say his talks 'had failed. They were frustrated by circumstances'.

'When I use a word,' Humpty Dumpty said . . . 'it means just what I choose it to mean – neither more nor less.'

Mr Browne Sits on His Hat

16.7.91

John Browne (C, Winchester), deselected by his constituency association and soon to quit politics, flails before going under. . . .

Your sketchwriter's resolution has cracked. I am going to tell you about Mr Browne's black top hat. How else can I explain the fuss when he sat on it?

Every MP has a streak of the self-publicist. They learn to live with it as an addict may handle a drug habit: allowing just so much, exercising self-discipline over when to stop. Like all sinners, MPs are quick to censure in others the temptations with which they themselves struggle. Thus, when Harry Cohen (Lab, Leyton) told the energy secretary, John Wakeham, yesterday that 'the Tories are too bloody mean to be green,' immediate outrage followed. Cohen had broken an unspoken rule. Using rude words is not an acceptable form of attention-seeking in the Chamber.

Nor is wearing silly hats.

John Browne has had his personal troubles, but his enthusiasm for chosen causes remains undimmed. He has been trying to publicize the plight of three Grenadier guards who lost their legs during a training exercise in Canada. Of late, Mr Browne has taken to wearing a huge black silk top hat in the Chamber. He says he will not cease this dreadful practice until compensation is given to the guardsmen.

His stunt has met with fierce reaction from colleagues on all sides.

Backbenchers, whips, ministers, and Mr Speaker himself, are furious. They are determined to stop him getting even a scrap of the attention he seeks, for, in their hearts, each knows that he or she would *almost* consider wearing a silly hat in parliament.

Almost, but not quite: because MPs sense that, once a couple started wearing funny hats, everyone else would, too: or go one better, with a luminous vest or bells on their ears. Within days, Edwina Currie would be wearing an orang-utan chest-mask while Harry Cohen would be waving a huge plastic banana.

I think the real reason that the guardsmen remain uncompensated is that this would be taken as a victory for Mr Browne and his top hat. Every new cause would then attract a crop of MPs on trick cycles in clowns' costumes, and Opposition spokesmen juggling chainsaws at the dispatch box.

So the whole House is determined to take no notice of Mr Browne. Even the media have sensed this, and looked away. For weeks Mr Speaker has been trying not to see him. Obliged occasionally to let him speak, Mr Speaker has said 'take that . . . that . . . *thing* off first,' and Browne had obliged, doffing it as he stands, donning it as he sits.

This he did yesterday, during energy questions. Nobody can remember Mr Browne's question, for attention quickly moved to his hat. He had taken it off, hesitantly, to speak. And Harry Greenway (C, Ealing N), sitting next to him and perhaps conscious that this was a way of getting on to television, devised his own version of a 'Hello mum' placard, and waved Mr Browne's hat. Friends say he was trying to give it to Browne, who was actually addressing parliament at the time.

Finally, Greenway tired of the hat, and shoved it back along the bench in Browne's direction. Just as Browne began to sit down. In a desperate move, Greenway now threw himself towards the hat, attempting to snatch it from the path of Browne's descending bottom.

Too late. Mr Browne shot up like a scalded cat. The abused hat was retrieved. Mr Browne put it on again. Mr Speaker just groaned. Whether it has helped the legless guardsmen is an interesting question.

MacDours Rattle Begging Bowls

At the start of Scottish questions yesterday, there was not a single Scottish Tory backbencher in the Chamber. Eventually two turned up, to join a handful of embarrassed Englishmen herded in by the government whips. The occasion, which occurs once a month, has become a sort of purgatory for all concerned.

It seems that, to cut a figure back home, a Scots MP must stand out in two respects. First, he must complain longer, louder and in more violent language than the others that Westminster is not giving Scotland enough money. This lends a dreadful staleness to Scottish afternoons at the Commons.

The second distinction a Scots MP seeks is to be more insulting than the others about the ignorance of the English (and the government and parliament England dominates) towards the problems of Scotland. This adds to the staleness a special rancour. Whenever an MP who does not represent a Scottish constituency tries to speak, he is jeered at for interfering in matters which (the argument goes) are none of his business.

Emma Nicholson (C, Devon W and Torridge) endured this yesterday, before being rescued by Lord James Douglas Hamilton's remark that he had last seen her in Glasgow a few days ago, addressing a conference on hearing disability. And not before Miss Nicholson had been obliged to protest that she had 'Scottish blood going back 980 years'.

In a sort of malign pincer movement, two arms of the cancer – the rattle of the collecting tin, and the resentment of a small nation against a large one – now combine to drive away MPs from other parts of the kingdom. Every month Scottish questions get duller, more bitter and more parochial. Every month fewer MPs who are not dull, bitter or parochial care to join in: a vicious tartan cycle, the whole demeaning spectacle a fearsome argument (in your sketch-writer's opinion) against regional (or federal) assemblies which are not responsible for fixing the taxes or running the economies of their own territories.

They become begging-bowl parliaments. Scottish questions at Westminster, from which English MPs are now effectively excluded, provide a dire preview of a 'Europe of regions'.

Labour's Touch of Class

25.7.91

1993 is not the first time that Michael Howard (now Home Secretary) has faced Labour's formidable Tony Blair. . . .

Across the dispatch box yesterday, an entertaining battle took place between two rising stars. Both are young, both good-looking. Both are barristers, both articulate. And both are very, very bright.

Each speaks for his party on employment. Each is tipped as a possible PM. Neither is wedded to dogma, for these men are not crusaders or class-warriors: political pragmatism is another thing they share . . . Little comes between them: little except ambition, and party.

And background. For the battle was between a public school boy and a state school boy. The posh one, himself a barrister's son, lists two middle names in *Who's Who* ('Charles' and 'Lynton') and was educated at The Chorister School, Durham, and Fettes College in Edinburgh, whence he went to Oxford. The grammar school boy, a shopkeeper's son, lists no middle name and was educated at Llanelli grammar school, whence he found a place at Cambridge.

Anthony Charles Lynton Blair is Labour's principal employment spokesman. Michael Howard is the Conservative Secretary of State for Employment.

Howard was there to introduce his green paper on industrial relations law reform. With an eye to the coming election, this includes the citizen's charter commitment to give individuals the right to trigger injunctions halting strikes in public services. It includes a great deal more, whose details escape us, designed to draw approving growls from Tories and yelps of protest from the Labour side, and probably not much else.

Howard has been shrewd. He has been sifting through the ashes of the trade union reform battles of the 1980s: clinker from coals which once made a blaze before which Mrs Thatcher warmed her hands through three elections. The search has been for tiny lumps as yet unburned, or glowing still: a quest familiar to the skint through the ages.

So our scholarship boy came into the Chamber armed with a big sheaf of papers and a very long statement indeed. He had it to heart.

He knew all the answers. And he read it with the emphasis and hint of earnestness which are his hallmark, in accents unmarked by class or region, beyond a very slight Welsh edge. The Tories behind him cheered lustily and often. 'Ho ho!' the cheers implied, 'here's a good, well-tried stick with which to give Labour another whacking!'

What could Blair say? He was surrounded by TUC dinosaurs from mining constituencies. To please them with a thundering rehearsal of the glories of unreconstructed trade unionism would play straight into the hands of Tory Central Office. A quieter response would disappoint his own side.

Mr Blair pitched it just right. With the lightest of touches and complete self-confidence he sauntered through the green paper, grinning. He tweaked this, prodded that, inspected the teeth of a clause or two . . . and pronounced that it did not pass muster. It was all got up for the hustings. He gave examples, seemingly very learned examples, with the winning assurance of a likeable young swell.

His own side barely understood what he was saying, but loved it. Later, Mr Howard painstakingly picked it apart. But Mr Blair won the moment, and that matters in the Chamber. A certain swagger helps, and a public school education provides it. Class still counts for something in the parliamentary Labour party.

13.9.91 **A Dead Spider Reaches for the Skies**

The Liberal Democrat Conference in Bournemouth. . . .

Paddy Ashdown has four famous poses. His favourite is staring, commando style, flinty-eyed into the middle distance: hand to chin, one finger up the side of his face, three fingers under the jaw, with neck jutting forward. In a previous era he would have chewed a pipe. Male models like this used to advertise knitting patterns in ladies' magazines. 'Paddy looks to the future.'

He enjoys too his 'come into my parlour' pose. Looking the front row straight in the eyes, he leans softly forward on to the lectern and, resting on elbows, lowers his voice. 'Paddy tells it straight,' or the 'frankly, my dear' stance.

For the 'agony and the ecstasy' pose – careworn yet compassionate, eyes narrowed to slits with suffering – the face is raised heavenward as the Ashdownian features grow taut with pain and passion. Sometimes the arms are outstretched. 'Would that this cup were taken from me.'

Finally, the 'I see angels!' pose. Arms wide open but chest now thrown forward; and on his face an expression of powerful optimism. '*Believe* me, friends! Come into my world! If only you could see how beautiful it is!' Parachutists call this the 'freefall position'.

To these four poses, Mr Ashdown yesterday added a fifth. It is new: designed to accompany moments of intense and very personal conviction. For this the body is hunched slightly, the shoulders rounded, the right hand held out, tense, at chest level. Palm facing upwards, extended fingers and thumb are clawed into an upturned cage, cradling – as it were – some sacred flame, or pearl of unknown price. The face is racked with urgent certainty. 'O fellow Britons! This is wisdom! This is truth! What treasure have we here!' I call it the 'dead spider' pose.

It was a huge hit yesterday. As the Liberal Democrat leader rallied the faithful at the end of their conference and the beginning of their march to glory, I counted more than 37 dead spiders from the lectern: two for each page of his interminable speech.

It was a dreadful speech and most effective. It was corny, it was hammed, and we would never have tolerated it from Kenneth Baker – yet, perhaps because he has still to be undone by office, from Mr Ashdown we somehow do.

They say George Bush is plagued by an inability to rise to what he despairingly calls 'the vision thing'. Reviewing speech drafts, friends mutter 'where's the vision, George?' Paddy has the opposite affliction. His problem was the reality thing. The speech was *all* vision.

It was vision in paragraph one, vision in paragraph two, and vision right through to the end, at paragraph 270. Within seconds of kickoff and only moments after we had been confronted by 'a new spirit abroad' – this following 'a new era of democracy and liberalism and peace and democratic renewal in our continent' – it was, said Paddy, 'a time for optimism' (*dead spider*) and 'a moment for democratic renewal' (*freefall position*). Those of us who felt it might also be a moment for a cup of tea were dismayed to hear that now came 'the hour of the free citizen'. The *hour*? He wasn't exaggerating. Page three (and 14 pages still to go) found modern liberal democrats (like Martin Luther) concluding 'here I stand. I can do no other' (*knitting pattern pose*). Aagh.

By page 13 ('words are not enough!') words were too much. One grew desperate. By page 15 – (*frankly my dear stance*): 'I give the people of our country this clear undertaking' – one knew it must end. It did. Mr Ashdown swept upwards through the raked galleries towards the ceiling and the Bournemouth sky, allowing the populace to touch him as he passed.

'Let this,' cried Charles Kennedy, 'be a metaphor for the ascent of our party!'

After the agony. After the triumph. The ascension of Paddy.

1.10.91 <u>Shifty Ways to Lose Your Leader</u>

The Labour Party Conference in Brighton. . . .

Hardly had the breakfast marmalade on our ties congealed on a sunny Brighton morning, when we were hit from three directions: John Smith, Gordon Brown and Margaret Beckett.

Three Labour leadership bids, and all before Monday lunch! At a party where mentioning serious politics is now regarded as the height of bad taste, can there be anything left to talk about for the rest of the week?

The existing leader was there, in spectacles, looking intelligently interested. Mr Kinnock seemed all unawares of the small 'Thinks' bubble above the small head of Mrs Beckett, the medium-sized bubble above the medium-sized head of Mr Smith, and the big bubble above the large head of Mr Brown. The bubbles said: 'What if (heaven forbid!) we *don't* win the next election? He won't, surely, stay beyond the summer of 1992 . . .'

Neil Kinnock smiled and clapped. He has an unfortunate habit of clapping with fingers wide outspread, as a small child or adult gecko might. He should have a word with Peter Mandelson.

He clapped John Smith enthusiastically. The principal economic spokesman had just been on television explaining what 'Neil *meant*' when he had said that people paid enough tax already. Conscious of gossip about a leadership challenge, Mr Smith was taking great care not to fuel it.

So, apart from one small victory wave, which seemed to slip out before he could stop it, his speech avoided the 'vision thing': it was a quiet, end-of-year hon treasurer's report to Rotary, sorrowfully recounting losses occasioned by the folly of others. Even more adenoidal than usual, Mr Smith spoke of the binibub wage, pregnant buthers and the baxibub rate of BAT. He sat down to beasured applause as bight one who is bore accustobed to City luncheons at Bidland Bontague.

His ambitious sidekick, Mrs Beckett, was dressed all in yellow. She increasingly resembles a minor marchioness, except for the white plastic shells in her ears. She looked up at Mr Smith (in beak-nosed lament at the ineptitude of the Tories) as might an adoring canary contemplate a balding eagle in flight. *Thinks*: 'Now he and I – he from the right, I from the left – *he and I* . . .' only her dreadful earrings now stand between this capable woman and high office.

Her speech was a *tour d'horizon* of Opportunity Britain, with just a hint of Opportunity Beckett. Starting cautiously, she finally abandoned restraint as the vision thing, not unmixed with the ambition thing, entered her soul and swelled her bosom. Concluding, she advocated 'aspirations', 'directions', 'partnership', 'opportunity' and 'dignity', and much else.

Gordon Brown was powerful and funny: perhaps a shade too powerful and a touch too funny. He began launching things. On page one he launched a 'manufacturing investment programme'. Then, quite without warning, he launched a Satellite University on page eight. None of these wonders, he warned us, would come through 'the invisible hand beloved of free-market dogma'.

Then how would they come? Jaw working, the visible hand of Mr Brown twitched, impatient for office. The visible canary glanced nervously sideways. The visible balding eagle blinked. The gecko clapped.

10.10.91

The Lady's for Returning

The Conservative Party Conference in Blackpool. . . .

The appearance on the platform yesterday of the top half of Mrs Thatcher – mute and nodding, her smile too broad – was like those videos of hostages. Along with the audience, I wanted to storm the rostrum to see whether her legs were in irons, she had been forcibly injected with sedatives or Chris Patten was twisting her arm behind her back.

For days we had been promised by the Tory high command that they were going to show us Mrs Thatcher. We would see for ourselves that she was well treated and in good spirits. She would appear on the platform in Blackpool.

Appear? How? Wild speculation gripped devotees and the media. Roadside reporters were posted all around the hall but, as helicopters chopped the wind, rumour had it she might land from above. A story circulated about a tunnel: she could pop up from the rostrum floor. Others pictured a figure in an azure tutu, abseiling from the wings.

One Tory MP speculated unattributably that she might materialize in mini-hologram form, a tiny blue image shimmering, like Princess Leia in *Star Wars* on the chairman's palm, endlessly repeating the same message: 'There is no such thing as society . . .' The hall waited. Then the platform party parted like the Red Sea awaiting the most important Israelite of all. Leaving a 50 yard gap at its centre, ministers cowered to each side as though to receive in their midst a radio-active rod.

And she simply walked on, with Mr Major.

A conventional entrance, an unconventional welcome. The conference erupted, leaping to its feet. If there were any doubts for whom, the Prime Minister settled it: modestly bowing to the obvious, he stood, and clapped. Immodestly bowing to the obvious, she sat, and acknowledged it.

Now that everyone applauds everything, you have to cheer too. There was a huge cheer for Mrs Thatcher, she stood, waved, sat, stood, waved, and sat again. Shouts continued. But still she did not speak. Brows furrowed. Was she all right?

'Speech!' someone shouted and soon everyone was shouting '*Speech*'. This had not been scripted. The podium mafia looked worried. Mr Patten scowled. And on it went. '*Speech*'.

I cannot report that Mrs Thatcher shook her head, wrote a note, or did anything to indicate unwillingness to speak. Her face showed only rapture. But around her the men in dark suits were frowning and growling to each other. Suddenly the chairman took the initiative.

'I have received a message,' he shouted. 'I have received a message from Mrs Thatcher' . . . the crowd fell silent '. . . and she has asked us to continue with the programme.'

Had she? We looked at her, the Woman in the Iron Mask. Her face now was expressionless, the men in dark suits were smiling. Mr Patten pushed out his hand to stop the applause.

All through the debate she peered forward, sometimes smiling a little, sometimes clapping, but silent. At 12.30 they took her away. She was not dragged, but always there was a little knot of big men around her. Outside, helicopters beat the air, car engines revved and blue lights flashed. She was gone.

Rumour swept the press that she was to dine in the Palm Court room at the Imperial. We hurried thither, hopeful she might be able to speak to us. Her limousine arrived. She was hustled through the crowds into a waiting lift to disappear upwards.

'It has been decided,' we heard, 'that lunch should be in a private room.' They rushed her out of the Imperial the same way; bystanders tried to applaud.

'She does not wish to attend the afternoon session,' we had been assured.

But temporarily she escaped her captors and somehow broke into the Winter Gardens and made it to the rostrum halfway through a debate, startling Mr Heath. Her old pal, Ken Baker, who had supported her to the end, praised her in his speech, but as soon as he sat down the men in dark suits crowded round again.

The last time I saw her, it was only her blonde head, bobbing, helpless, as they walked her down a ramp. Apparently she broke free and attempted a walkabout in the tea room where party workers touched her and sobbed.

Four tall men took her away. Sirens wailed outside the Winter Gardens. The sealed train was ready.

Like a captive Mary Queen of Scots, they are incarcerating her in luxury. Forget the Birmingham Six! Free the Chester Square One!

Tiaras in Disneyland

The opening of Parliament 1991. . . .

There is a Disneyworld feeling about the Chamber of the House of Lords. Constructed at the same time as St Pancras station, its gold paint and pasteboard heraldry were hardly dry when the Midland Railway reached Derby.

Today, its mock-gothic grotesqueries provide a monster TV studio for an ancient pageant of which the ancients never dreamed, the origins lost in the mists of time, about 1911.

It is hard to avoid the feeling that, just around the corner, Mickey Mouse is waiting to sell you tickets for a space ride to the Enchanted Forest.

But the tiaras yesterday were something else. And not just the tiaras. 'There's a seriously expensive row of emeralds round her ladyship's neck,' said a colleague, pointing to Lady Cochrane of Cults. Lady Cochrane's tiara resembled a Sony Walkman headset, diamanté.

Across the floor the French ambassador shimmered like a pearly king in a garment of spangled brocade. Closer to me, Lady Palumbo sported a headborne stockade of pearls on prongs with opals dropped between them. 'Is she English?' I whispered to my colleague.

'No. Too beautiful,' came the reply.

Princess Margaret arrived in turquoise. In the galleries above, two peers' children played the scissors-cut-paper/rock-blunts-scissors game across the knees of their elegant mum.

Charles and Diana arrived, the prince's face set in a sort of frozen quizzicality, the princess forever the little girl in the front row of the school pantomime, cutely self-conscious about her fancy-dress.

I glanced at the official seating plan for ambassadors. 'Bolivia – in wheelchair,' it said. Two black ladies – ambassadors' wives –

swathed to their ankles in brightly coloured cotton and looking like illustrations from *Uncle Tom's Cabin*, whispered.

Not far from the Throne stood a man I used to know as Mr Waddington, carrying a shower cap mounted on a broomstick. The Queen came in. She looked completely unimpressed. There followed a long wait while Black Rod summoned the Commons. The Queen stared round, wearily.

Then, from down the corridor, grew the sound of distant chatter, as though a charabanc of vulgar picnickers was approaching. It was. At least this time Norman Lamont had shaved. The Lord Chancellor handed the Queen her speech and teetered backwards down the steps.

Every year the Gracious Speech sounds more Graciously Perfunctory. An oration which starts 'I am looking forward to visiting Australia,' goes on 'My government will, with our Community partners, pursue the successful conclusion of the Uruguay Round of multilateral trade negotiations,' and climaxes 'A bill will be introduced to provide for a Cardiff Bay Barrage,' could in truth be summarized: 'My government will whistle for the wind for a few months more.'

Over in the Commons, the Prime Minister and the Leader of the Opposition duelled with all the skill of that party game where the two combatants are blindfolded. They call: 'Are you there, Moriarty?' then lash out, stumbling, at each other.

'Are you there, Neil?' *Whack*. Missed. 'Are you there, John?' *Whack*. Missed again. Thursday staggered from one ludicrous ritual to another.

Mr Speaker Is Shell Shocked
19.11.91

In its most serious public relations blunder to date, 10 Downing Street yesterday bungled the release of Terry Waite. What are things coming to when the whole majesty of our Foreign Office is unable to get this man kept in captivity for a couple more days – so his return elbows Mrs Thatcher's Euro-outburst from the next day's headlines? For the first time in her career, Canterbury has passed up an opportunity to queer her pitch.

Mrs Ann Clwyd made a spectacular if doomed bid to upstage Waite. Pulling out all the stops, Labour's overseas development spokesman gave an emotional speech on the plight of the Kurds, then brandished a foot-long brass shell at Mr Speaker.

'It's shells like these,' she exclaimed (as though providing the breathless voice-over for video pictures in a TV documentary), 'that are being used on the Kurds.' With this, she rummaged in her extensive woolly Welsh cardiganry and pulled from somewhere a big brass rocket-like object.

'I want that thing taken out of here,' said a visibly alarmed Mr Speaker, barely keeping his voice steady.

'What, this?' cried Mrs Clywd, waving that thing in front of the cameras.

'On a point of order,' said the Tories' bow-tied Michael Morris, '*I* was apprehended when I brought an *orange* into the Chamber'.

'I want it removed,' insisted the Speaker. Old Frank 'Snarling Grandpa' Haynes (Lab) disarmed Mrs Clywd. It must be the first time in history Haynes has defused rather than inflamed a parliamentary moment.

'I'm sorry you're all so squeamish,' came Mrs Clwyd's lilting Welsh pout.

She misses the point. There is a good reason why standing orders prohibit MPs from bringing visual aids into the Chamber: for there would then be no stopping them. Each would seek to amuse or shock more violently than the others.

Enterprising young Tories would wave in front of the cameras patent kitchen gadetry in whose manufacture they had an interest. Anti-hunt Liberal Democrats would toss the remains of mauled fox-cubs across at the Tory front bench. On the comic side, there is no telling what sorts of unpleasantnesses Mr Tony Banks (Lab, Newham NW), who loves to intervene facetiously during discussions about raw sewage outfalls, would use as props. On the tragic side, I ask you only to imagine one of the Commons's frequent debates on abortion, without Mr Speaker's wise prohibition. It would not be long before MPs were demanding that *Hansard* be printed with colour photographs. . . .

Prescott on a Flyer

'It's a peculiarly frightening thing,' said Sir John Cope (C Northavon), 'to have an accident in a tunnel.' There was a shaking and rumbling from John Prescott's seat on the benches opposite.

'Hear, hear,' murmured MPs. A train crash in a tunnel was frightening indeed, but they knew something even more frightening: to meet Mr Prescott in a tunnel. This was an accident they dared not even contemplate. Yet such a thing was about to happen, and the House knew it.

Labour's transport spokesman was building up a head of steam. Coal-fired, as are most of the Opposition, he was stoking the boilers of his anger.

Like a lime-scaled kettle coming to the boil, the member for Hull East shuddered with a hiss of escaping steam and many a small ping and pop. His eyes blazed: his jaw worked: his cheeks puffed in and out. It was, if Sir John will forgive us, peculiarly frightening, for Mr Prescott crashes all on his own, with random timing and in no particular direction.

Whoever happens to be by the trackside may be injured in the break-up but it is not meant personally: in no sense is Mr Prescott *directed* at anyone. Malcolm Rifkind watched, fascinated. I should like to report that the transport secretary seemed to be in the driving seat: but Mr Rifkind reminds us more of a clergyman train-spotter.

Elements of this Scots political phenomenon can be glimpsed from the pew, and elements can be seen from the trackside at Clapham Junction: but in this minister they strangely combine into a sort of railway Jesuit or ecclesiastical steam buff.

True, the clerical collar was not quite visible beneath his anorak. We couldn't actually see the fur-rimmed hood, the row of sewn-on badges or the Thermos of tea.

But Mr Rifkind's mild-mannered eccentricity – his wild eyes, crazy hair and jerky intensity – whisper that here is a man of the cloth, the notebook, and the photographic memory for Great Railway Accidents of the World, of which Mr Prescott regularly provides us with examples. Would yesterday bring us another? It was not to be, but we had to wait to find out.

First came the transport secretary's statement, which passed without incident. There was an angry muttering from Mr Prescott, but he did not rise after the statement, leaving the initial questions to others.

These were fatuous. Nobody, said Mr Rifkind, yet knows what caused the Severn tunnel crash in December 1991 ('two trains in a tunnel!' shouted Labour's Peter Snape) so there was little to say.

To Ian Grist (C, Cardiff Central) Mr Rifkind (remembering 'the wrong type of snow' and narrowly avoiding a mocking headline of his own) regretted that the emergency services were late because they had approached 'from the wr . . . *inappropriate* end of the tunnel'. Robert Adley (C, Christchurch) called for more red lanterns and less high technology.

By this stage the red lights on John Prescott, who is a low technology, were flashing dangerously. There was a steamy snort. He rose. Building up speed from a slow start, he congratulated the emergency services, moved gently into a wide curve, missed a signal and derailed.

It was signalling failure, he snorted. 'BR accept responsibility.' It wasn't the Martians, then? Mr Rifkind peered across at him, fascinated, and scribbled something in his notebook.

Repossession on the Mind

18.12.91

A preoccupied John Major spoke to MPs at Westminster yesterday. Home repossessions were on his mind. One case in particular was worrying him.

To you or me it was just an ordinary house, not (at first glance) unlike a million others: a mid-terrace property of plain, Georgian design, recently redecorated. Conveniently situated in central London, close to all amenities and local services, the property is a stone's throw from the local park and five minutes from three Underground stations (Northern, Bakerloo, District and Circle lines). Many local buses – notably numbers 3, 11, 12, 24, 29, 53, 77a, 88, 109, 159, 177, 184, 196 and 511 – run virtually past the front door, and Victoria, Waterloo and Charing Cross railway stations are within a mile. Restaurants, theatres and galleries are within walking distance and the neighbourhood is well served by local churches.

The property enjoys a remarkable, elongated garden. An interesting feature is the original outside loo, which has now been incorporated into the main structure. Though there is no garage, extensive car parking is available on a disused parade ground nearby. A security system, which has been installed to the highest standards, has recently been upgraded further by the construction of some interesting wrought iron gates at the entrance to the cul-de-sac.

The house has new curtains. Another curiosity is a trapdoor to what appears to be a sophisticated warren of bomb and radiation-proof underground accommodation. The property is well patrolled and comes with an en-suite policeman.

The house, though of modest size, boasts an imposing staircase, a number of gracious reception rooms, an extended dining area and a magnificent view of the Foreign and Commonwealth Office. On the top floor is a granny flat occupied, until last year, by a granny. We are assured that, after a tussle, vacant possession has been obtained.

A comfortable family home, the property also enjoys the benefit of a well-appointed office and study. We are advised that 30 years ago extensive work was undertaken, at some expense, to remedy a problem with dry rot. The owners state that full guarantees were obtained at the time from the contractors (the Property Services Agency) and remain in force . . .

How coldly the estate-agent's blurb reads! For this is a human story. This inventory of bricks and mortar conceals a looming personal tragedy. The present ocupiers, if they go, go unwillingly.

Housing distress knows no bounds of class or profession. Living there have been a couple – to you or me a quite ordinary couple – comfortably off but far from wealthy. A year ago, an unexpected promotion encouraged the breadwinner, who had been working as a successful accountant, and his quiet wife, to move up a notch in the residential market. His new job seemed secure. Little threatened a long freehold tenure at the new address.

So they moved in. Probably the last couple in Britain to benefit from Mrs Thatcher's drive for home ownership – and certainly the last she intended to help in this way – were John and Norma. Even as Norma paced out the room sizes and chose the new lampshades, the 1980s economic boom which had taken John so far in his career was fizzling out.

His position worsened by the day. Struggling to keep both his new job and his new home, John keeps making promises to those who put him there. Every week the promises are more extravagant, his hopes of fulfilling them less realistic . . . A steepening slope, familiar to debtors through the ages.

John has been given until July at the latest. At the door of the home he and Norma love stand two other frustrated couples, waiting in the housing chain. Neil and Glenys, stuck in Walworth in South London, have dreamed since their childhood in Wales of this West End address. Paddy and Jane, more modest in their ambitions, have a form of shared tenancy in mind, and say they would share as happily with Neil and Glenys, as with John and Norma. But, frankly, for John that's not an option. There are cheques to be honoured by July, or it is cardboard city. As a worried Prime Minister yesterday faced Mr Kinnock's taunts over repossessions, John – and Neil – knew that.

Don't Take No for an Answer

29.1.92

Neil Kinnock: 'Will you put up VAT? Yes or no?'

John Major. 'No.'

Neil Kinnock: 'Why can't you give a straight answer?'

I paraphrase, but not much. Yesterday Mr Kinnock asked the PM for 'a categorical assurance that he will not impose any increase in VAT'. Mr Major had 'no plans'. This did not satisfy the Labour leader: 'Why can't the Prime Minister give a straight answer to a straight question?' That was what Mrs Thatcher always used to say, he complained. A more categorical statement was required.

Mr Major gave it. Government spending plans, he said, meant there was 'no need' to put up VAT. 'There will be no VAT increase,' he said.

'It's time the Prime Minister came clean,' said a flustered Leader of the Opposition. He was clearly angry, but with whom? With the advisers who had proposed this as his choice of subject for the afternoon? Poor Mr Kinnock was now stuck with a duff script and a set of useless supplementary questions. Your sketchwriter, who sits directly above him, could see them, neatly typed out, with little underlinings here and there. Pity to waste them, really.

First Cuckoo of Swing

28.2.92

As any child knows, people who hear the first cuckoo in spring write to *The Times*. Well yesterday, at 3.27 pm, I heard the first cuckoo in the election campaign. Nicholas Winterton (C, Macclesfield) supported the government.

The song of the Macclesfield Cuckoo, or *Cuculus Maccles-fieldiensis*, is a rare one. The bird is often heard in the Chamber, but almost never in song. Its familiar cry is a scolding sound, a sort of angry screech, for this bird has been in a continuous rage against the government for as long as anyone can remember.

From its customary perch below the gangway it rises, week after week, its silvery-yellow plumage ruffled in irritation, the area round its beak pink with fury, and pecks angrily at whichever unlucky minister is on duty. Month after month, the Macclesfield Cuckoo has squawked its displeasure at the decline of manufacturing industry, the disarray of the government's 'care in the community' policy, and any one of a number of subjects known to outrage this senstive bird. But it never sings.

Never, until yesterday.

Heaven knows, we had warning. When Ted Heath wears his light blue socks, we know something is up. When Dame Peggy Fenner (C, Medway) arrives in full Aztec war-goddess's robe, we know it is serious. But when Nicholas Winterton compliments his own front bench, we know that this is it. We have lift-off. The general election is upon us.

Cuculus Macclesfieldiensis first began to bob up and down on its perch during a question from Ted Garrett (Lab, Wallsend). The bird's agitation was odd for Garrett is one of the most popular MPs in the House. His question, about the threat to British shipyards from German subsidy, reflected concern on all sides, and Mr Major, replying, appeared to agree. Besides, the question – technically speaking – was 'whether the Prime Minister will visit Wallsend'.

Wallsend is nowhere near Macclesfield. So what bothered the Cuckoo?

Mr Speaker noticed the fuss and called the bird to speak. 'On his way to Wallsend, will the Prime Minister visit Macclesfield where he will find . . .' MPs prepared for a rant.

But no. The Cuckoo began to warble 'an area ready to respond to the sound foundations of the economy which he and I know the government have established . . .' the Cuckoo paused. It was not unknown for this bird to preface its attack with a soft note or two. Four hundred MPs waited for the inevitable '*But* . . .'

No But! This was all. The Cuckoo sat down. From the bench in front, Anthony Beaumont-Dark leaned over and with his Order Paper fanned his colleague, who had gone pink. Mr Winterton smiled.

The most tremendous cheer arose. The whole Commons, Conservative and Opposition parties together, roared, as much in shock as acclaim. Youthful Tories who had never heard Mr Winterton praise the government, looked across, wide-eyed, at the phenomenon. The occasion reminded your sketchwriter of his boyhood in Swaziland, when, one winter, it snowed for the first time in living memory, and people ran in fear and wonder from their huts to marvel. Have stars collided? Will lions walk in the streets of London?

Only upon the faces of Mr Major and the chief whip beside him, did a note of alarm register. Winterton was on board: where had they gone wrong? 'What shall we, then, say to these things?' wrote St Paul to the Romans. 'If God be for us, who can be against us?'

Indeed, thought the chief whip, but if *Winterton* be for us. . . .

5.3.92

The Day I Saw a Sphenodon

Comparing politicians with their animal likenesses offers hours of fun. Mrs Thatcher's partridge-like walk, for instance – diving forward in a series of tiny, hurried steps – is, once likened, never forgotten. To have seen Ted Heath as a grumpy panda is never quite to see him as the Rt Hon Edward R G Heath, MBE, again.

Norman Lamont is much better viewed as a sharp-minded but edgy pekinese than as a Chancellor of the Exchequer, while you will never entirely understand John Major until you have noticed the similarity with a quiet, earnest, grey beaver in glasses, patiently nosing twigs and logs into place, year upon year, as his secret design slowly takes shape. Kenneth Clarke, the Education Secretary, may be rather substantial for a butterfly, but the political sunbather in him, gently opening and closing his wings in the warm rays of his backbenchers' approval as he perches on whichever ministerial portfolio the summer breeze last blew him to, is unmistakeable.

And if Alan Clark is not a bird of prey reincarnated (unconvincingly) into a defence procurement minister, then I am not *The Times*'s political sketchwriter.

But I have never quite got Gerald Kaufman right. In early sketches this column protrayed him as a frog in a lily pond, blinking and waiting to be kissed. Later we remarked on the comparison with a middle-aged mutant Ninja turtle, and christened him Geraldo. Neither image was spot-on, yet neither entirely missed its mark. Both, of course, take their analogy from the world of reptiles.

And it was from this world that, looking down on Mr Kaufman at foreign affairs questions yesterday, a new image leapt to suggest itself. I had been reading, that very morning, a letter from a traveller newly returned from New Zealand. He had described to me a most unusual Antipodean lizard, and the word-picture stayed in my mind. My friend had seen a sphenodon.

Suffice it to say that those hooded eyes, neck craned a little forward, head held quite still, the impression of frozen movement broken only by an infrequent, lightning-swift blink . . . all were familiar. This was the first lizard ever to represent a Manchester seat.

'South Africa would face . . .' said the lizard. I craned forward, eyes peeled, searching for that little triangle of shiny skin pulsing, just below and behind his ears . . . No, the angle of the lighting made it hard to see . . .

'South Africa would face a period of total international isolation.' Actually, Mr Kaufman is facing a period of domestic isolation himself. They seem to have taken him off the screen, and he has not yet appeared on any of Labour's new posters, so it was good to be reminded of this clever but strangely disconcerting presence.

Minutes later he leapt with sudden passion to the cause of the

Greek Cypriots in their conflict with the Turkish Cypriots. Momentarily surprised by this, one remembered that there are more Greek barbers and chip-shop proprietors in the marginal con- stituencies of North London than there are Turkish baths.

Tristan Garel-Jones, Foreign Office minister of state, thought the same. 'The Right Hon gentleman has been rushing up and down the country courting Greek Cypriots and Kashmiris,' he complained. The thought of Mr Kaufman courting a Kashmiri was arresting.

Kaufman seemed to think so too. As Garel-Jones spoke, the lizard held himself absolutely still, staring at the minister. Then he moved his head ever so slightly to one side . . . and – yes! There it was! Just below and behind his ear. I caught it. A freeze-frame picture, except for this: a tiny triangle of bare, waxy skin, throbbing, urgently, in the televison lights.

The sphenodon was listening.

13.3.92   Paradise Lost in Bear Garden

Weep, Tories! Wednesday was not a bad dream. The fruit-and-nut cases really have decided to call a general election now. Starship *Westminster* has moved into its terminal phase before they pull the 'destruct' lever at Buckingham Palace.

Over in the House of Lords, peers whiled away their final hours discussing the merits of hard-boiled eggs, while in the Commons there was a development of the direst sort. Our representatives moved into after-dinner mode. MPs were saying goodbye.

Hon members started quoting Great Men and Women of History. The PM quoted Shakespeare. The Leader of the Opposition quoted Thatcher. Sir Bernard Braine quoted Burke, Andrew Faulds quoted Andrew Faulds, and Harry Ewing quoted the House of Commons barber.

I have thought hard before writing this. I have asked myself whether there is anything, *anything*, so noble as to justify comfortable, congratulatory speechmaking by elderly men. Sadly, I have had to conclude that there is not. 'Sadly,' because there can be no higher object of a sketchwriter's admiration than our retiring

Speaker, Bernard Weatherill; and it was Mr Weatherill whom MPs came to Westminster to praise yesterday.

First, just for old times' sake, the Chamber enjoyed a 15-minute orgy of throat-busting, tonsil-ripping uproar. It was their last question time. They would send their Speaker away with a rollicking example of what he will miss next year, as he dandles the little grandchild-Weatherills on his knee.

Labour barracked so nobody could hear Mr Major; the Tories howled so nobody could hear Mr Kinnock; and anonymous miscreants made squeaking noises while Dame Elaine Kellett-Bowman (C, Lancaster) tried to speak.

Mr Speaker gazed, lovingly and a little misty-eyed, at this paradise garden in which he now took his last stroll, and which he must soon leave: 450 grown men and women stabbed their fingers in the air and yelled fit to bring the rafters down, and I should like to record that tears of nostalgia rolled down Mr Speaker's cheeks, glanced from the woolly skirts of his full-bottomed wig, and splashed on to his tights . . . but I cannot. From where I sit, I could not see.

Little passed of note. Mr Ashdown has been agitating recently for a televised debate between himself, Mr Kinnock and Mr Major. Yesterday Ken Livingstone put the proposal to the Prime Minister. Replying, the PM ruled it completely out. At this point there was a rush of enthusiasm from Mr Kinnock for the idea. Why wouldn't the PM agree?

We were perplexed, later, when the Father of the House, Sir Bernard Braine, paying his tribute to the Speaker, said: 'I sometimes wonder what a rabble this would be, were it not for you and your predecessors.' I sometimes wonder what Sir Bernard calls 'rabble'.

'I think it was Edmund Burke who said . . .' mused Sir Bernard. When a speaker says this, thinking people rush for the doors.

Though that would have been to miss Andrew Faulds (Lab, Warley E). 'So impartial have you been,' he told the Speaker, 'that I have never been able to tell whether you admire and approve of me . . .' Mr Speaker's face was a mask of impartiality. 'Or consider me a total berk.' A hint of a smile played on those forgiving Weatherill features. The House roared its assent to the second of Mr Faulds's proposals.

The Lady Sails Proudly Away

17.3.92

Mrs Thatcher attends the Commons for the last time. . . .

After years of making personal remarks about the former prime minister, perhaps I am permitted to say that yesterday she looked lovely. She wore very dark green with black collars and a diamond star on one lapel. She seemed quite composed. John Major was absent. Mrs Thatcher made for the government front bench, which was empty. What, we wondered rather nervously, had she in mind?

The table on which the dispatch box sits – where she had stood so many thousands of times – was littered with papers. Mrs Thatcher walked up and tidied the mess. She put the documents together into neat little piles, glanced at her handiwork, and left.

I remembered how, when she was Leader of the Opposition, she would climb on to chairs to check for dust on top of the picture frames in the shadow cabinet room. 'Its the way a woman knows that a room's *really* been cleaned,' she once told us.

MPs tropped off to the Lords to hear the prorogation. Neil Kinnock being absent, Mrs Thatcher paired up with Frank Haynes, the retiring Labour MP for Ashfield. His booming and good-natured interruptions have always made her laugh.

When they returned, it was time for Mr Speaker to send us home. It was his final duty. 'I have to acquaint the House . . .' he began – and read out the completed bills: 'Still Birth Definition Act, 1992, Traffic Calming Act, 1992 . . .' Then 'by virtue of Her Majesty's command', he prorogued the Commons.

Mrs Thatcher, who had sat with her long-time supporter and friend, Gerald Howarth (C, Cannock and Burntwood), was almost the first to say goodbye. To a huge cheer she walked down the gangway, shook Mr Speaker's hand, and sailed proudly out. It was sublime.

Spot the Difference

The General Election begins. . . .

Yesterday, Labour launched their manifesto. Minutes later and not five hundred yards away, the Conservatives launched theirs.

On rainy days when we were young, my favourite from the child's puzzle book was 'spot the difference'. There would be, apparently, two copies of the same picture, depicting (say) a cat up a tree. Firemen with a ladder would be rescuing puss. The challenge was to find the tiny, hidden differences between the two pictures. A twig here perhaps, a whisker there or a fireman's bootlace, would be missing in one, present in the other.

Much the same puzzle now faces the electorate. True, in one corner of Labour's picture John Smith has drawn a terrier dog, Budget, ready to sink its teeth into the ankle of the scowling plutocrat in the top hat. The Tory picture shows no terrier, and the plutocrat is smiling. Any child can spot the difference. It was one of the few.

Both ceremonies were punctuated by the pop of a hundred magnesium flashes. Both were smoothly packaged. One had music but I forget which: the real music was the whirr of television cameras. To avoid obstructing one another's views, cameramen now go all-fours on the carpet, a whole pack crawling like hungry strays around the podia on which the Great Ones sit.

And the manifestos? Once, a reliable way of distinguishing a Labour manifesto was the appearance of the world 'socialist', used approvingly. Yesterday a journalist asked Mr Kinnock where 'socialist' appeared in his new manifesto. It doesn't. Tippex in one hand, Mr Kinnock is erasing the things that aren't also in the Tory picture.

Others asked about privatized industries. But, crayon in hand, Mr Kinnock has been colouring in, on his own picture, all the privatizations he can find in the Tory one. Already he has spotted a privatized telephone pole, aeroplane, electric light, and gas main, and popped them hastily into the Labour scene. But he had left out the privatized water pipe. Yesterday he noticed it. In a trice it was sketched in, almost as privatized as the Tory water pipe. This competition is now closed.

Over at the Tory unveiling, John Major declared that 'we must be more ambitious about our future'. He mentioned street lighting. There would be 'more street lighting' under the Conservatives, and a huge party in the year 2000 'to mark the Millennium'. There was a bold commitment to the 'Parish Path Partnership' and the care of canals. A journalist rude enough to query the solemnity of the pledge to 'introduce a Hedgerow Incentive Scheme' was mildly ticked off by Mr Major. Hedges mattered.

As did, for instance, the manifesto commitment to 'promote the use of the English language' (page 2). This from the party which gave you gobsmacked, porkie, whammy and bummeroo!

Such were the issues. When someone asked what place there would be in a classless democracy for a second chamber filled by patronage or pedigree, Douglas Hurd, sitting beside Mr Major, roared with laughter. It is a mark of good manners in the British establishment to classify every important question as a lapse of taste, or a joke.

The PM waved his new manifesto. It was like the Labour one, like the Liberal Democrat one. It was full of limp sentences, stale abstract nouns, sly sub-clauses and shiny paper. It was entirely without warmth. Nothing important was put in and nothing trivial left out. No homily was spurned, no cliché unrehearsed.

Somewhere – somewhere beyond the soft lights and pastel carpets of the conference centre where we sat – fifty million real souls were moving. This document was for them but not addressed to them. It was crafted to move through them without touching them: never confronting, never insulting, never estranging, never quite embracing. It was evasive, but not unusually evasive. It was like a thousand other political manifestos.

Cuddly Green Mammals

20.3.92

'To be Green in Britain in 1992 . . . is like being a small mammal watching the last two dinosaurs engaged in a struggle to the death. On the one hand, there is a deep inner sense of personal fragility. On the other, there is a deep inner confidence that the future does not belong to the dinosaur.'

That prefaces the Green party manifesto, launched yesterday. The small mammals had gathered in a modest burrow near Covent Garden. The hounds of the press had gathered to bait them. The London Ecology Centre, 21 Endell Street, lacks the pretensions of a great conference hall. Squeezed between Johnsons' outfitters ('Closing Down') and the Carrie Awaze II Deli and Sandwich Bar, a simple room awaited. At one end was a table with a green tablecloth and three chairs.

Into the three chairs filed a mouse, a grey dove and a rabbit. The mouse was called Richard Lawson: a small man with a kind, slightly anxious face, and very bright eyes. The grey dove told us her name was Sara Parkin. She had a finely chiselled beak and, though quite young, striking grey hair worn long and unadorned. There was a sort of handsome serenity about her, like a Quakeress. The rabbit, Jean Lambert, was a little shorter with round face and nervous movements. Fur and feather neatly brushed, the small mammals had come to present their survival plans.

Manifestos were distributed. There were two. One was called *The Path*, the other *The Policies*.

The grey dove spoke first. The double manifesto was 'a special treat' for us. She and her fellow mammals were 'in very high spirits'. They were 'the fastest growing political movement the world has ever seen'.

Some Greens from Czechoslovakia had come to stay with some of the Green candidates here. 'Greens from Prague to Portsmouth are inspired by exactly the same concerns.' The grey dove urged the dinosaurs to stop 'fiddling with a penny on income tax, while the planet burns' and handed us over to the mouse. The mouse made an arresting speech, in an offbeat sort of way. Peering intensely at us with his shining little eyes, he took a risk for a Green: he adopted a military analogy.

He and his fellow mammals were, he said, a tiny posse fighting huge and brutal invaders: the forces of extinction. The dinosaurs, Tories and Labour, seemed blind to the threat and collaborated with the wreckers of our planet. The Liberal Democrats were 'wimps'.

Green politicians deal in a different sort of prediction from the forward figures for interest rates or GDP. Last week Mr Lamont said the economy will grow by 1 per cent. This week, Mr Smith said the recession would continue, under the Tories. Yesterday, the mouse said that humans will end up alone on the planet except for cockroaches and rats. The householder canvassed in quick succession by all three parties may need a stiff drink.

Outlining the 'five screaming injustices' of modern politics, the mouse called Mr Kinnock 'Tweedledum' and Mr Major 'Tweedledee', and sat down. The rabbit told us it was acceptable, even desirable, to have no children. Pressed on this, she admitted that Greens are not proposing to legislate for it. She quoted Gandhi, proposed a tax on packaging, and denied that Greens were 'anti-car'. Their manifesto undertakes to cancel road-building schemes and offer 'incentives to those able to use the canal network'. The rabbit did not expand on that.

Finally, the mammals took questions from the hounds. The mouse got into a muddle about why the apparent £75 billion cost of his scheme for a basic wage was an exaggeration, and the grey dove inveighed passionately against the word 'other'. Greens object to the way pollsters lump their supporters under 'other' parties. In Sweden, she said, Greens sue people who use the O-word.

The hounds of the press restrained their savagery. These little creatures seemed to believe their own message and care little what we make of it. Small mammals which roll over on their backs and offer the jugular are confusing to scavengers. The mouse, the grey dove and the rabbit were not playing our game. We left: by taxi, there being no canals.

Time to Dig the Dirt

24.3.92

This, they said, would be 'the roughest election in living memory'. Rough? So Jack Cunningham and Michael Howard interrupt Sue MacGregor and have a rant at each other on the wireless – you call that rough? So John Major gets jostled in Bolton – wow! So a Militant supporter in Liverpool drops a piece of excrement near the election agent to Liberal candidate Rosemary Cooper – hell, it didn't even hit the agent, let alone the candidate.

Paddy Ashdown (to another Militant yob): 'Hiyah, friend.'

Yob: 'I'm not your friend.'

Ashdown: 'Well, you might be.'

Is this the sort of savage exchange expected of a democracy where candidates used to run for their lives, chased by screaming mobs? In his memoirs, *Blood on the Walls*, published next week, Willie Hamilton writes of his 1945 campaign in East Fife, 'the Communists were howling like a pack of wolves . . . and as soon as I began [they] started to rush the platform . . . too late, they realised the strength of our supporters, especially the women. The women were terrific. The laid into the Commies with fists, legs, and tongues . . . Our 1950 election campaign was even dirtier . . .'

Which brings us to dirt. Where *is* the dirt? The 1992 election was going to be the 'dirtiest ever'. I was looking forward to it. For years I have vainly hoped that Sir Geoffrey Howe might be a secret transvestite. One longs to discover that Gerald Kaufman keeps a troupe of dancing girls in Manchester for his private titillation . . . so where's the big affair, then? The Ashdown shock boded spendidly, and then . . . phut! Nothing. Ten days' campaigning, and still nothing. I'm sorry, but one back-bencher in a bush on Hampstead Heath won't do. The nation is so hungry for scandal that even a dalliance between John Gummer and Dame Elaine Kellett-Bowman might amuse but, sadly, no word of such exotica reaches us. Either they're all clean, or politicians have decided to leave that sort of thing out. This is desperate.

This, they said, would be an electoral road strewn with banana skins. Neil Kinnock would make some monumental blunder – suffer a brainstorm and revert to Labour's 1983 manifesto in an interview with Brian Walden, or do his Bug's Bunny impersonation on *Newsnight*. During a walkabout, Mrs Thatcher would flip, suffer the delusion that she was PM again, and start raving 'rejoice, rejoice!' No such luck. Mr Kinnock has turned into a right little sober sides, and Thatcher is sticking to the bottle-green twin-set she reserves for periods of intense self-restraint.

I have nothing to report to you from Monday. There was no rough, no tumble; no slap, no tickle. No jiggery, pokery, cloak, or dagger. On Monday there were press conferences, Dirtiest? Roughest? Funniest? We've been conned. This election isn't at all serious, and it isn't even slightly funny.

Poppets of Battersea

Mirror, mirror on the wall, who is the *nicest* of us all? At dawn yesterday, in two south London bathrooms, two perfectly charming middle-aged gentlemen stared into their shaving mirrors.

Butter would not have melted in their mouths. One of them was John Bowis, Tory parliamentary candidate for Battersea and previously their MP. Mr Bowis would not harm a fly.

The other was Alf Dubs, his Labour challenger and until 1987 the Labour MP for Battersea. Mr Dubs would not only help an old lady across the road, he'd offer her a polo mint too. Your average cuddly toy is a brute, by comparison with Mr Dubs.

Fate had decreed that these two complete sweetie-pies face each other in mortal combat, in one of London's most marginal seats. The Tory majority was 800 last time.

'Of course, Mr Bowis is a nice chap,' I said to one of Dubs's staff.

'That's our problem,' she replied.

'Alf's a nice bloke . . .' I said to one of Bowis's helpers.

'That's our problem,' she said.

'Mind you, John's the only really, *really* nice candidate,' said the chairman of the Battersea Tories. This was the battle of the nice guys. Picture a duel between Mother Teresa and Florence Nightingale. The first event of the day was the arrival of Neil Kinnock. At a press conference on health, the Labour leader had been bullied mercilessly by the press, but stepped now into a new world. A little boy rushed up, threw his arms around Mr Kinnock and exclaimed: 'I love you.' Such is the Battersea spell woven by Bowis and Dubs.

I followed Bowis into a rough council estate. 'Enemy territory,' I remarked. 'Ah,' came his mild rebuke, 'we'd never make it without the many friends we have here.' Mr Bowis resembles a favourite teddy bear. Lage, kindly and bland-featured, one feels quite certain that if one lifted him up by his feet or pressed his stomach gently he would emit a friendly growl.

I followed Dubs to a meeting with old folk at the Garfield Community Centre. Surrounded by kiddies' rocking horses and plastic dogs on wheels, he sat in front of a poster entitled 'Five Speckled Little Frogs'. 'Alf,' said a wrinkled old lady, 'I've heard that under the Tories pensioners will be thrown out of nursing homes.'

'Oh, no Lily,' said the honourable Dubs, 'I don't think that's the case.'

Care-worn and kind, Mr Dubs resembles one of those exotic dogs you see at Crufts whose faces are completely crumpled due to an excess of skin. 'You and I will have to have a little chat about this, Lily.'

'Mr Bowis, there's a lady who's disabled at No 31,' advised an earnest Tory helper. Bowis lumbered over. Actually the lady at No 31 was not disabled, but her father-in-law had diabetes and angina. 'Anything I can do to help?' asked Bowis. The lady at No 40 had the husband who was blind. Mr Bowis fondled the guide dog: 'Let me know if I can help.' At No 22 the man was on crutches. 'Does the weather affect you much?' The chap with the neck support at No 29 might not be voting for Bowis. 'Never mind, I'm here to help you anyway.'

At No 26, 'My dad's very ill with pancreatitis, diabetes and agoraphobia; my daughter's asthmatic, I'm seeing the social worker but my GP says I'm to be rehoused due to my own mental health and my mother says she can't stand no more of it. And my daughter can't settle at her school.' Mr Bowis stared sympathetically at his shoes.

'Let me see if I can have another go for you with the council.'

'You know me, here,' said Alf Dubs to the ring of old ladies around him. 'All I want to do is go on helping you.'

'Bye, bye, Alf,' they called as he left.

'Bye, bye. Bye, bye, Lily.'

Whoever wins this constituency on 9 April, by 10 April, Battersea will have an absolute poppet of an MP.

Real Men Are Called Dave   27.3.92

When Denis Healey arrives in the West Midlands to play the piano in an old folk's home, something must be amiss. When the seat is one which Labour had held by a comfortable 6,000, something is badly amiss. When they send Roy Hattersley, too, there is a real problem.

And when party workers are diverted from the winnable Tory marginal next door, the problem must be serious.

I went in search of the problem yesterday. All over Coventry South East, posters told me where to look. I found the problem in a snowstorm at the Rolls-Royce factory gates, haranguing the workers through a megaphone, while his supporters rattled collecting tins and plastic buckes. 'I play the piano, too,' said Dave Nellist. 'But I haven't had time to practise like Healey.'

Coventry suits Nellist. It is a hardbitten city. There is something raw about the place. 'People talk about "hard" and "soft" votes,' Nellist's agent told me. 'Well, our hard vote is hard. Very hard.' The agent turned to one of his helpers: 'Dave, take this man to the Rolls-Royce factory gates, where Dave is.'

When Dave and I got there a journalist from the *Socialist* called Dave was interviewing Dave. 'Why is everyone on the hard left called Dave?' I asked. 'We were all christened Quentin, but we changed it,' was the reply.

The Dave, Dave Nellist, has been the local Labour MP since 1983 but has recently been expelled from his party, ostensibly for refusing to denounce Militant. Fashions among Labour have changed while he has not. Nellist has been beached by a receding tide: ideological driftwood, but still a log to be reckoned with: no fool and no slouch.

So, standing against an official Labour candidate, Nellist styles himself 'a Labour independent for a Labour government'. He will support Labour whether Labour wants him to or not. He lives in the adjoining constituency whose own Labour MP has been Geoffrey Robinson. 'I've put Geoffrey Robinson's posters in my windows but Geoffrey spends his mornings touring *my* constituency in his chauffeur-driven Jag asking my constituents to take *my* posters down.' And whose posters were in Robinson's window? 'Geoffrey lives in a Lutyens mansion in Surrey, mate.' It was time for his speech to the workers emerging for their lunchbreak. 'Come over and hear Dave Nellist!' shouted an assistant through a tinny megaphone, 'a workers' MP on a worker's wage!'

Nellist, who has always refused to draw his full MP's salary, looked worn and tired and unusually strained. He exudes an anger which beats its breast to the heavens rather than intimidates the hearer. There is something of the martyr about him, waiting to be stoned. He treated a small crowd of workers in a biting wind to a litany of the woes of Coventry. Snowflakes glanced from his face. Nellist looked skyward and began to enlarge on the evils of Toryism. The rank grew, the volume swelled. The snow stopped. A burst of pale sunshine lit his grey face and wispy beard.

Later, Nellist was to address workers at the Hare and Squirrel public house, but for now he had finished. The workers began to drift away, and the rain started.

In the face of an oncoming party machine stood a real man, a real candidate – all at odds with history. Real passion, real argument and a real campaign: an increasingly rare thing, these days.

(*He lost narrowly.*)

Tory Faithful Cling to Maggie's Ark   *28.2.92*

In a few days, someone is flying to America. She has had time to canvass only for the Tory hopefuls she likes best. A UK map showing the constituencies visited would chart what Mrs Thatcher regards as dry land: hilltops of sanity poking their heads into the Thatcherite sunshine while the rising vapours of compromise lick all around.

The ex-prime minister's campaign voyage has been a fastidious progress from beacon to beacon, a Thatcher visit bestowing the lady's Good Housekeeping seal of approval. Departing a rally in support of her soulmate, Michael Forsyth, in Scotland, Maggie's Ark sailed south. Watchmen on the bridge peered through the Majorite mist . . . was there *any* dry land left in England? Yes, upon the hills of Cannock and Burntwood, home of her friend Gerald Howarth she went ashore yesterday and then onwards . . .

'Land ahoy!' It was North Warwickshire, an Ararat of no-nonsense Toryism awaited the blessing of her landfall: the domain of that dry young prophet of fiscal rectitude, Francis Maude.

Mr Maude is thirty-something with a majority of two thousand and something. An honourable man, an intellectual, and honest, but not one of nature's baby-kissers, Mr Maude is already financial secretary in the Treasury. He has ahead of him a highly promising career . . . or not. It depends upon the voters.

It depends, for instance, on the electors of Shustoke, a village near

Coleshill, where I caught up with him canvassing on a bitter afternoon. It was 2.30. Maggie's Ark had already been sighted on the horizon, and radio messages received. Mrs Thatcher was to come ashore at Coleshill at five. 'Mr Maude,' his office told me, 'will be canvassing until three. At five he will be awaiting Mrs Thatcher.'

And from three to five? 'He will be preparing himself for Mrs Thatcher.' I had visions of the thin and ascetic-featured Mr Maude in a hairshirt in the Coleshill churchyard, being birched by monetarists for two hours, in preparation for the honour of her touch. First, though, there was Shustoke to be canvassed. I followed Mr Maude from house to house.

'North Warwickshire' sounds blissful. In fact, it is a land of electricity pylons and humming power lines: old pit villages overshadowed by cooling towers and skirted by 1950s dual carriageways. In the night you can hear the roar of the motorways, never far, and always the orange glow of Birmingham in the western sky. Brick houses, mostly detached, are china-dog and porcelain-horse territory. Neither rough nor poor, North Warwickshire is not quite smooth and not quite prosperous.

Its electors are not really socialists and not quite Tories. 'He says he voted for the Social Democrats last time, and for the Liberals the time before that,' reported one of Mr Maude's door-knockers as Mr Maude himself approached the house. 'He says he votes whichever he thinks is best for the country.'

'Good of him, a kind concession on his part,' smiled Mr Maude thinly, his face completely blue with cold. At the next house an old gentleman *would be* voting Tory – out of sympathy. 'I heard you on the wireless. Clare Short was yelling at you,' he said. 'She's a big woman.' But it was time for Mr Maude to prepare himself. He left.

I found a cafe in Coleshill in which to prepare myself. In the streets of the town, for fully an hour before she was due, the people of Coleshill began to gather in knots, preparing themselves.

Whispers ran round. 'What's she doing?' 'Where's she going?' 'Why's she coming?' Labour supporters gathered in huddles to oppose, a sense of solidarity and purpose missing since November 1990 returned to their lives. She swept up in a black Jaguar. Francis Maude was waiting to lead her to the door of a new home in which a newly married couple were to dwell. She was to meet them.

Crowds pressed at the barricades. 'I'm not a Tory at all,'

whispered the lady next to me, 'but she's – well – *someone*, isn't she?' Mrs Thatcher, in a navy-blue suit with white piping, like a sea-captain's uniform, bore down on her. 'How *are* you? This is my *fourth* constituency, and *everyone* is in good heart . . .' She passed on, still talking.

'It's like the Queen,' said the lady beside me. Francis Maude stood in the doorway, smiling and wringing his hands.

(*Mr Maude lost his seat.*)

We Want Dial-an-Argument

30.3.92

'Is Neil with you?'

'Neil who?' asked the candidate.

'Neil Kinnock. Is he outside?'

At first the candidate was baffled, but then we realized the explanation. This voter's only experience of modern politics was of candidates from opposing parties having rows with each other on radio and television. The broadcasting rules of 'balance' dictate that you almost never get more than about 30 seconds from one party's representative without an immediate rejoinder of similar length from one, or two, of his rivals. The candidate's constituent had now had a full four minutes of this candidate who was about to depart. Something was obviously missing. He had assumed that in real life politicians travel around in pairs or trios, yelling at each other, just like on TV.

Well why not? Could this be the way to breathe new life into an old tradition? Could the discerning voter not demand that, rather than watch edited exchanges on TV, candidates bring the real thing to his doorstep? I have it in mind that constituency campaigns might include a travelling roadshow featuring all three (or more) candidates, the entire trio arriving at your door to have an argument for you there and then, on demand.

Voters could be asked what they would like the candidates to argue about: the NHS, defence, single mums . . . and the candidates would oblige. You might even be able to telephone in advance, as you can for a pizza delivery, and order your own special combination. Instead of cheese and tomato (deep pan) with anchovies and olives, it might be Tory, Labour and Liberal Democrat (no holds barred, please), with an SNP candidate thrown in, having a row (small, medium or large) about foreign affairs, family values and rural bus services. They could be round on scooters within 10 minutes.

For the national campaign, the party leaders should pool transport and occupy a specially constructed triple decker bus, one deck to each entourage. Every half hour the three men would join each other on the platform and have a blazing argument for the cameras and journalists. Edwina Currie and Peter Snape could follow behind in a taxi, pouring drinks on each other's heads.

Where the bus actually went, or whether it moved it all, would be, I suggest, a matter of little importance.

Hubris

2.4.92

Labour holds a rally in Sheffield. . . .

It is at times of retreat that an army's strengths can best be observed. It is in moments of triumphalism that we first see the seeds of its downfall. It was when Margaret Thatcher employed a train-bearer to carry her gown that we knew her day was done. It was in the slick, sick, cynical image-manipulation of Labour's spectacular at Sheffield last night that we first sensed the contempt into which they too must come.

'Any dream will do,' sang the children, as Neil Kinnock played king of the kids in a Leeds school yesterday. He was preparing for the Sheffield Arena. He took their song to heart. Any dream would do.

Something about the very instructions printed for backstage operators last night chilled the soul. It was entitled 'Running order for Mega Rally'. *17.30: Doors open: party bus; band, etc, arrive. Street entertainers will be working the audience outside.*

The days when candidates would have worked the audience themselves, treading the streets in person, are gone. The candidates were in helicopters.

18.00: Dave Blunkett does welcome. DB to Royal Box. 'Will Mr

Blunkett sing?' asked a reporter, 'And is it true his guide dog's gone sick? Will he sing "How Much Is That Doggy in the Window?"' *Regional contingents with banners and bands. 18.42: Neil Kinnock's arrival in helicopter shown on video screen.*

After speeches by Roy Hattersley and John Smith came the *first endorsement, 2 mins.* 'That's Mick Hucknall of Simply Red,' said the aide. 'No, he won't actually be there. He's in Marseilles working on his next LP. He'll be signing his postal vote and singing "Something's Got Me Started" and this will be intertwined with his message. The message will say (and she began to dictate): "On 9 April I'll be voting Labour . . ." (she paused for us to take this down). "It's time for a government that invests in skills . . ."'

And we were promised 'Sarah Jane Morris, ex-of the Communards'. Now of Democratic Socialards. I expect. This item was to appear in the *Top-Slot, 15 mins* preceding the *second endorsement* after which came *Opera-Slot, 15 mins,* except that it wasn't opera, but a lady singing 'Summertime'. Normally, as John Cole observed, 'You know it's over when the fat lady sings,' but this was a thin lady and it was far from over: for next came *20.05: NK speech.* This was printed in advance. It was entirely devoid of content. *20.35: NK finishes; 20.40: Jerusalem; 20.45: finale, NK and Shad Cab leave. 20.55: All out, Goodbye music.*

I spoke to a press photographer who has been following the Kinnock campaign. Photographers are normally mute and I have no reason to think this one was a Tory: his frustration was professional. 'The manipulation has been crushingly successful,' he said. 'This has all been done for television: it goes against a video cameraman's instincts to show the props holding things up and all the minders marshalling the crowds.

'All we're shown is Kinnock with smiling kids, Kinnock in hospitals – happy faces, young children . . . the image control has been total. The TV bosses need a few minutes of Kinnock every day to balance their few minutes of Major and if all he gives them is sanitized pap, that's all they can use. That's all anyone sees.'

As an ideal matures into a crusade and a crusade translates into a government, there comes a point when, throttled by the very apparatus set up to project it, the ideal begins to choke. This point has come early with Labour. Last night in Sheffield, image throttled intellect and a quiet voice in every reporter present whispered that there was something disgusting about the occasion. Those voices will grow. Peter Mandelson has created this Labour party and, on last night's showing, Peter Mandleson will destroy it.

'We will govern,' Neil Kinnock said, opening his speech, 'as we have campaigned.' Oh I do hope not.

Energetic Ashdown Passes the Initiative Test

7.4.92

Bumping into Paddy Ashdown at the BBC yesterday – he was about to be interviewed by Jimmy Young – I had the impression less of a politician on the stump, and more of an ambitious military recruit attempting in double-quick time a series of bizarre stunts designed to test his drive, ingenuity and physical stamina.

If, after landing an interview with Mr Young, his orders had been to cycle to Brighton and back then abduct five penguins from Regent's Park Zoo, it would hardly have seemed out of keeping. Such is the aura which has surrounded his campaign drive.

I watched him in Liverpool. If the ambition was to shake more hands in fewer seconds while saying more 'Hiyahs' than any glad-hander in history, then he was winning. If the challenge was to beat a liftful of journalists travelling up to the ninth floor of a squalid tower block by running up the stairs, then he succeeded. If his orders were to get himself photographed remonstrating with a Militant heckler, with a revolutionary poster as a backdrop, within six minutes of arriving in Broadgreen, then Captain Ashdown obeyed these, too . . . and the big yellow coach moved on.

Unlike the other leaders, Mr Ashdown has been in charge of his squad, not its mascot. He makes the running. His team just tries to keep up. He seems to love it.

His campaign technique mirrors his approach at party conferences. It could be adapted for audio presentation and marketed as *The Ashdown Method – a course in six cassettes*. Its essential components are 1. an impression of huge self-confidence, 2. correct breathing and posture, 3. rapid movement through a series of 'freeze-frame' poses, 4. five minutes' intense meditation before breakfast during which the students repeatedly chant 'I really do love each person I shall meet today', ringing a small bell between this and 5. the alternate chant: 'My party and I are friends: they are on my side.' Ting-ting. Oh – and 6. two portable autocue screens and three speeches. Thus forearmed, Mr Ashdown sets forth. So far he has never faltered.

It is important to identify the strengths and limitations of *The Ashdown Method*. It works. It would not do so, I suspect, without a strand of sincerity, and a strand of deceit. I believe Paddy Ashdown really does like people. In most politicians, years of exposure to bores, bigots and sleeve-tuggers breed a cold reserve. Mr Ashdown casts it aside with gusto. He gets a kick out of teamwork, and though with most of us hail-fellow-well-met wears thin after three weeks, with him it does not. This cannot be faked.

But soon, he will have to stop running, sit down, and answer cool and insistent questions. It is the success of his campaign so far which has brought him to this happy but awkward moment. I watched him yesterday being politely grilled by Jimmy Young, and noticed, for the first time, an intellectual raggedness, even panic, beneath the bravado.

An impression of rapid movement is vital to *The Ashdown Method*. But when the music stops, the contestants have to sit down, and there are not enough chairs, the game moves to a new phase. It should prove interesting.

Underdogs Get the Bone
13.4.92

The Tories win. . . .

'This pig does not weigh as much as I believed,' an Irishman once observed, 'but then I never thought it would.' This General Election, too, has turned out contrary to what we predicted: but then we rather thought it might. The losers have won. The day of Floppism has dawned.

You raise an eyebrow? Let me explain. Floppists maintain that the nation will vote for the party it believes most likely to lose. The Floppist analysis was vindicated last Friday when the party everybody had expected to triumph flopped. The party everybody had expected to flop triumphed. The pundits found this surprising.

But the lady in the newsagents opposite Wilko's in Matlock did not find it surprising. 'Never take anything for granted,' she said, smiling like a sphinx. Back in my kitchen I pondered that smile. My mind moved to three self-evident truths.

First, it is undoubtedly true that the nation had no desire for another Tory government. Second, that the nation did not want a Labour government. Third, that nobody wanted a coalition with the Liberal Democrats.

Whichever outcome, then, emerged as the most likely was the one that would fill the electorate with the most horror. Special hatred settled upon whomever began to look like the winner because, the prospect being more immediate, it was more odious. No party being admired, the sight of *any* of the three possible victors cock-a-hoop with certainty of impending victory was sure to prove especially detestable.

Picture each in that condition. Picture, first, a Labour party so confident that John Smith could summon us to an oak-panelled room and, standing in front of a big bowl of roses, unveil his 'budget'; so puffed up with importance that Jack Cunningham could discuss his forthcoming Queen's speech with commentators while yobs pelted Mr Major with eggs; so vainglorious that, before the mere formality of Thursday's vote, Labour could stage the biggest political rally since Nuremberg, at which the poor of Sheffield paid £1 each to sit in a stadium and watch a video of a pop star in the south of France telling them to vote Labour, and another of Mr Kinnock, getting out of a helicopter. Yuk. From that point the polls began to slide towards a hung parliament . . . so . . .

Picture next a boastful Paddy Ashdown prancing before us and telling us who might, and who need not bother to, 'pick up the phone'. And after the passion, the piety. Mr Ashdown stares tenderly into his autocue and confides the intimacies, the dreams, the little hopes and fears of Liberal Democracy. We can almost feel the manly stubble pricking on the pillow beside us. Ugh. Over breakfast on Thursday, the needle edges a little further towards . . .

. . . Yes. Picture, finally, not the Tory party we saw, but a Tory party that had realized it was winning easily. That smug look on Mr Major's face, the tongue-in-cheek Princess Di smile, the braying

Timothys and shrieking Amandas, the champagne and laughter, the young men who hardly need to shave, the triumph of vanilla, the jubilation of the jelly babies. Picture the two-fingered gestures from the honking Porsches making a quick circuit of the nearest council estate, the portable phones, the wine bars, the wing collars and the clutch of Kinnock jokes zapping round the computer network of the Square Mile. Spare us.

. . . But of course we *were* spared. The Tories never did believe it, so they behaved. Instead of triumphalism, we saw a poor chap on a soapbox, jostled and shouted down, a coach that went to all the wrong places, and the bungling of 100 photo opportunities. I heard that women were rushing from the pavements and flinging their arms round Mr Major, telling him never mind and not to be sad, poor lamb. He looked completely harmless. Naturally we voted for him. His winning margin came from votes intended to console him for losing.

Does John Major realize, even now, that it was the *failure* of his campaign that took him to Downing Street? That the cock-up that caused his final victory rally to miss *The Nine O'Clock News* saved him from defeat? Does he know how lucky he is that, when he said he was winning, nobody believed him?

Father's Day and Mother Speaker   28.4.92

The new parliament. . . .

Was it the changeability of an April day, or providence, which sent a sudden beam of sunshine through the windows of the Commons yesterday to bathe Sir Edward Heath in light as he took the Chair for the selection of a Speaker?

Sir Edward's great day had arrived. His smile said it all. 'I'm still here. She's gone! Yippee!' Few of us in our lifetime will see again a look of more profound pleasure spread across an old gentleman's face. If there had been any way, within parliamentary rules, for Sir Edward to climb on to the table and, breaking into a schoolboy chorus, chant in the general direction of Finchley: 'I'm the king of the castle . . .', then he would have done so.

Heath is now 'Father of the House'. 'I hope that includes "Mother of the House",' observed a sultry Gwyneth Dunwoody (Lab, Nantwich), temporarily ruffling Sir Edward's serene self-image.

Heath's arrival, as chairman, had been perfectly executed. He made a formal entrance in full morning dress, bowing three times in unison with his clerk as he approached the Chair. Sir Edward looked as though he had been practising all morning: the bows were just so: not too deep, not too perfunctory; each impeccably timed, each undertaken with slow dignity and gruff expression. He resembled Edward Bear doing his stoutness exercises in front of a mirror.

Black Rod's entrance was more flustered. We have a new Black Rod. The last one was very grave, but the problem with this one is that he has a sense of humour and a voice which, like an adolescent's at puberty, keeps jumping into a falsetto trill. 'I am commanded,' he announced, inadvertently yodelling on 'commanded' and then pausing fatally to smile at a wisecrack from Dennis Skinner. This afforded Skinner his second shot. 'If yer stand 'ere any longer yer'll get yerself nominated as Speaker,' growled the MP, to general mirth.

It was true. MPs were there to receive nominations for Mr Speaker. The electors of Bolsover having returned Skinner to us, there is no more a vacancy for Mr Heckler's post than for that of Mr Deputy Heckler – for Bob Cryer (Lab, Bradford S) is back. But now that Anthony Beaumont-Dark is gone, I nominate Lady Olga Maitland (C, Sutton and Cheam): Madam Rentaquote.

Though Mrs Currie returns to her post as Madam Limelight, Gyles Brandreth (C, Chester), who *on his first day* walked straight into the prime TV 'doughnuting' space, directly behind the PM, and sat down, is already mounting a challenge. Norman Tebbit having quit, nominations for Mr Polecat are open, while Dave Nellist's narrow defeat has left the Commons with no Mr Class Warrior. Finally, since Leith has lost Ron Brown there is a vacancy for Mr Knickersnatcher. I could name half a dozen challengers for the post of Mr Deputy Knickersnatcher . . . but I won't.

The Chamber, more crowded than I have ever seen, settled down. Sir Edward rose. For the election of a Speaker, he said, 'it may be helpful to describe the procedure . . .' There was a great, rueful laugh. Nobody could understand the procedure. It struck your sketchwriter that it might have been more helpful not to have an election at all, but to ask the parliamentary clerks to set the candidates for the job a short test: 'describe the procedure for electing a Speaker in not more than 500 words.' The first able to do so would be given the post automatically.

Imagine a Sunday school class faced with the decision whether to go to Blackpool, Morecambe, Skegness or Cleethorpes for a treat. Such a decision (you might think) could be taken by taking a vote on each and choosing the most popular. That is not parliament's way. They would toss a coin, propose a resort, and dare anyone to propose another. If anyone does, they vote on the *alternative*. Those who didn't want either are confounded. Luckily Betty Boothroyd – very much the Blackpool vote – enjoyed a natural majority.

Her posse were a varied lot. The Tories' best intellectual, John Biffen (proposing her) advanced, in the cause of our one-time Tiller Girl, not one but two constitutional hypotheses: the doctrine of 'constructive myopia' and the concept of 'fraternity in suffering'. Tony Benn as 'the Uncle of the House', praised her candidature as untainted by Labour and Opposition whips. 'The usual channels,' he added, 'the most polluted waterways on earth'.

Macclesfield's Nick Winterton (C) berated those 'who come to this House merely seeking ministerial office' whereupon the whole of the government benches started pointing at the Opposition and the entire Opposition pointed at the government benches. We could have pointed at both of them.

Betty Boothroyd spoke well: graceful but confident. The vote over, John Biffen and Gwyneth Dunwoody enacted the ritual of dragging her, unwilling, to the Speaker's chair. Frankly, Miss Boothroyd did not look unwilling. Mr Biffen, a rather slighter figure than either of the ladies and holding Miss Boothroyd by the hand, looked like a little boy being helped over the road by two lollipop ladies.

Mr Major quoted a previous Speaker – 'I'm tired, I'm weary, I'm sick of all this' – and wished Betty Boothroyd better luck.

So do we.

Defying Gravity with Gravitas

7.5.92

The Queen's Speech is delivered to parliament. . . .

In the Commons a spring chill has blighted the roses. Labour lapels were bare.

Over in the Lords, a quick tiara-count suggested that the recessionary chill blights even peers. Economic slump has taken its toll upon headgear. Diamonds were smaller. My *Guardian* colleague saw green shoots of recovery among Lady Wakeham's emeralds; but the Baroness Strange's tiara had shrunk from last year's TV aerial diamanté, to a small lozenge on her big blonde bun.

Lady Porter, of Tescos and Westminster, combined the commercial and the dignified aspects of her career by appearing as a large Easter bunny, her blue hat dwarfed by an enormous pink bow.

The men were duller, but the ambassadors' paddock offered relief from the wastes of ermine. One Arab envoy wore a sheikh's robes over what appeared to be an M & S woolly. The French ambassador, who resembles Maurice Chevalier, appeared in a waistcoat of gold brocade and looked ready to entertain us with an old-time song-and-dance act. The peers' wives' benches – all stoles and lorgnettes – put us more in mind of the props department of an amateur dramatic society; the diplomats' wives – saris, turbans and sarongs – of a Nigerian Sunday market.

But it was Lady Renwick who drew all eyes. Well, *parts* of Lady Renwick. An attractive middle-aged woman, hers was the lowest neckline I have ever seen in an upper chamber. Her tiara went quite unnoticed. She could have been an extra from *Fanny Hill*. With black cloak tugged insecurely around shoulders as she leant low to talk to Lady Granville of Eye, the effect upon the press was of fascination tinged with alarm. At any moment something dreadful could have happened. We might have another Wimbledon – a first, surely, during a Queen's Speech? Physics textbooks illustrate a London bus tippling sideways on a special machine to determine the point at which gravity takes over. Could a simulated peers' bench be constructed, then tipped progressively forward with the ladies buckled in, to establish when containment fails and catastrophe strikes?

It never did. I moved my gaze to the new Lord Cecil, Lord Salisbury's son, who was Viscount Cranborne until last week. A 'writ of acceleration' has transformed him into a peer capable of sitting in the Lords while his father is alive. Looking suitably accelerated, noble ermine flattened against noble chest by the force of 3G, he chatted animatedly to Lady Strange. Lord Waddington, now subjected to a writ of deceleration and sent to be governor of Bermuda, reminds us that velocity in politics is a wayward mistress. Over in the Commons, Andrew Mitchell (C, Gedling, Accelerating) was preparing an excellent speech. Kenneth Baker – a case of sudden velocity-loss – was to speak with him.

A trumpet fanfare disturbed the reverie: and in came Her Majesty.

It was a dull speech. There was a moment of tension when the Queen's remarks about monetary convergence prompted Lady Renwick to breathe heavily and slip her cloak, but without mishap. Field Marshal Lord Carver, a soldier of severely practical intellect, looked forbearing rather than ecstatic in his role as The Sword of State. The sword was heavy, the speech long. After it, The Cap of Maintenance (Mrs Wakenam christened him John) bumped into Silver Stick in Waiting (friends call him Jeremy), which is not surprising as both were walking backwards. Has it struck peers that forwards is quite a good way to walk?

No Smokie without Fireworks *13.5.92*

Yesterday saw peers in uproar. Keen-eyed Lord Campbell of Croy had spotted a threat to civilization as we know it. The Arbroath smokie is under attack from Europe. The Upper Chamber turned from lesser issues to confront the danger.

Seldom have we seen their lordships so aroused. When MPs panicked over the Falklands, peers stayed cool; when miners struck, peers were calm; when salmonella hit the parliamentary kitchens, peers stood aside from hysteria. War, insurrection, pestilence . . . peers can handle these things.

But this was too much. 'Having defended the British sausage and Scottish mince,' cried Lord Campbell to Lord Fraser of Carmyllie, what assurance could the minister offer 'for the future of the Arbroath smokie?' A great moo, the cry of aristocratic despair, arose from all sides.

It had been a pretty bloody afternoon. Lord Hatch of Lusby had been tormenting their lordships over carbon dioxide emissions, to which Hatch himself has made a notable contribution. He had goaded Lord Strathclyde into a verbal tangle with what sounded like 'Catholic converters', and a brush with 'sulphur scrubbers'. There were giggles.

Lord Strathclyde has not been himself since a Whitehall press release appeared last week, decorated with a cartoon dog and headed 'Lord Strathclyde launches national Scoop the Poop campaign.' The French, who simply rounded up their aristocrats and guillotined them, were kinder.

So when the House reached Arbroath smokies, peers were jumpy. The EC (said Lord Campbell) wanted to impose crippling expenditure upon manufacturers of these smokies. Though existing practice, time-honoured in Arbroath, produced 'no ill effect', Brussels wanted to replace wooden poles with steel. There was mooing.

A tricky moment. Lord Fraser handled it with aplomb. The minister knew about smokies. He lived 'five miles from Arbroath'. There were murmurs of approval. Smokies were 'a great delicacy'. EC measures were meant to boost hygiene. This was too much for Lady Carnegy of Lour. Smokies hung in pairs, she said, tied with string. Did it matter whether the pole they hung from was wood or steel? This kind of thing 'brings the EC into disrepute!' More mooing.

Dozens tried to join in. Others, embarrassed at the fuss, shouted 'next question!' Lord Marsh told us that Europe was looking increasingly silly. There was a short discussion on the extent of 'the contact of the fish with the poles', which peers insisted was minimal.'Few people know the correct way cook them,' opined Lord John-Mackie.

Lord Fraser summed up the debate so far. 'An Arbroath smokie is an Arbroath smokie,' he declared. Encouraging grunts from all sides pushed his lordship, next, into an indiscretion. There were people, he said darkly, who 'confused a smokie with a kipper'. This was 'an abomination'. Too late, Lord Fraser realized that some people might think he had described kippers as abominations. He struck out wildly for the other shore: 'I like a kipper just as much as the next man,' he stammered, forgetting to add 'or woman', 'but a kipper is not a smokie.' More moos.

Lord Hooson now raised the philosophical issue. Was this not a matter for national governments? Lord Hailsham, the great constitutionalist, rumbled to his feet. This was a question of subsidiarity.

'That's a big word in Arbroath,' cautioned Lord Fraser. Lord Carmichael rose to paint a frightening picture of a future in which only Scotsmen in breathing apparatus would be allowed to enter tiled huts of smokies, where the fish hung on aluminium poles. 'The mystique will be lost,' he wailed. No, said Lord Fraser, not aluminium poles. Steel.

But there was no reassuring them. Lord Marlesford was on his feet, Lady Saltoun struggling to be heard. The main debate of the day was forgotten as peers grappled with this threat to their lifestyles.

Slow Death for Labour

The Labour Party is cursed by its history, cursed by its roots, cursed most of all by the undying loyalty of nearly a third of the British population: a millstone round its neck.

Nearly a third. They are the literally millions of voters who will never, ever in their lives vote anything but Labour. They are the trade unionists, the blue-collar hard core: it is an army, augmented greatly in talent if not in numbers, by hundreds of thousands of convincedly egalitarian middle-class intellectuals whose Labour idealism will never be shaken and who will work tirelessly to keep the machine running. These people stand, a formidable barrier against failure, a total obstacle to success.

Labour is shackled to a sort of helpless, hopeless survival. It is only dying very slowly. Mr Major is recruiting them only by the handful. They absolutely guarantee John Smith an honourable result next time. Labour's Britain sustains the party's body, rotting its brain. The party does not know its peril.

And so it sits: a great cuckoo in the nest of opposition; a great barren weed of a party, its roots deep and strong, its branches bearing neither fruit nor blossom, poisoning the land and choking every other seedling. Last week's local election results confirm it; this is the beginning of a long, sad story with no ending.

(From the *Investors Chronicle*)

My Word! Did I Really Say That?

22.5.92

As the new parliament heads for a break, here are verbatim extracts from a speech by John Prescott in the House of Commons earlier this week. In the right-hand column is the official version of what he said according to *Hansard*.

They tried to make up for the loss of income British Rail in their financing by on the one hand sacking personnel at 6 and 7,000 a year which had the consequences on those that remained in the employment of British Rail of working in a rather exhausted way. Indeed the signalman in Clapham as it came out in the enquiry was working months on end without a day off because there were fewer left to do the job after you'd cut back on the manpower requirements.

British rail tried to make up for the loss of income by sacking 6,000 or 7,000 personnel, which resulted in those employees who remained having to work very long hours that left them exhausted. According to the enquiry, the electrician at Clapham who made that fatal mistake had worked for months on end without a day off because, manpower requirements having been cut, fewer personnel were left to do the work.

I accept readily the argument the Secretary of State says that 1 per cent of road transport is a small

I accept the Secretary of State's argument that a 1 per cent growth in road transport is a amount to the kind of growth we see that it will always be about 80 per cent of the traffic but that 1 per cent represents hundreds of thousands of lorry movements which is important down in the South-East [if you haven't got a decent rail network to take you to Europe our roads in the South-East are not going to be able to take that traffic and even if you was to double their capacity would not be able to take that kind of increasing amount of capacity].

small amount, compared with the overall growth in road traffic. However, that 1 per cent represents hundreds of thousands of lorry movements which will be relevant in the South-East if it does not have a decent rail network to Europe. Even if the capacity of roads in the South-East were doubled, they would not be able to take that traffic.

And even in the gas and electricity he talks about governments and Treasury particularly have always imposed a kind of energy tax on them, forced them to charge more through the external financial limits the negative role he talks about which is a tax on those industries.

The Treasury has always imposed a kind of energy tax on the gas and electricity industries, forcing them to charge more through a negative external financial limit.

The Heathrow Paddington seems to be falling about because British Rail can't get the money for the 20 per cent required to get in with the private sector. The Olympia & York now seems to be in serious difficulties because of possible bankruptcy situations in these matters and can't raise the money.

The Heathrow to Paddington link is collapsing because the government cannot get its 20 per cent with the private investment that is required. Olympia & York appears to be bankrupt and cannot raise money.

I mean that's an example of this government that believes in the private sector and is in fact

The government's insistence on private sector terms has damaged the public sector.

damaged the public sector's handling within the public sector in a number of these areas and you can go on with them in another areas.

So I think the basic point that it is necessary in order to have private capital in our industries to get the extra resources that we do want, that you have to be privatized is not borne out by the facts in other countries and neither we should we have it here also and if he's any doubts about that go and have a look at the reports that talk it.

This passage is not reported at all. *Hansard* gave up.

A Pillar of State

11.6.92

Mr Heseltine becomes a president. . . .

My favourite retired African statesman is ex-President Jean Bokassa. He ruled a country called the Central African Republic, with only one real town (Bangui), no roads to speak of, a few dismal huts, and many trees.

Not long after coming to power, it occurred to Bokassa that his position lacked status, considering his merits. So he renamed his country the Central African Empire and had himself crowned emperor. The coronation, planned and supervised personally by Bokassa, was based on that of his hero, Napoleon. It was by all accounts a magnificent ceremony. His small son, the heir to the imperial throne, was drawn through the potholed streets of Bangui in a golden carriage shaped like an eagle and pulled by six white horses. The coronation consumed one quarter of the nation's gross domestic product.

Arriving at the Commons for industry questions and finding this item replaced by an event called 'Questions to the President of the

Board of Trade', I guessed at once. Sometimes a man is just too big for his office. Something has to give. If the man will not contract, the office must expand.

Nevertheless there was bewilderment among MPs as to what the Board of Trade *was*. Keith Hampson (C, Leeds NW) asked whether this mysterious body might meet, so that we could see it?

The President rose, shook his majestic blond mane, and said: 'The Board of Trade has not actually met for many decades, except for a celebratory occasion to commemorate 200 years of success. If it were to meet,' he added, 'it would be attended by the Archbishop of Canterbury . . .'

Further clues to the President's unfolding plans came thick and fast. A junior minister, Edward Leigh, announced that his supremo was not just President of the Board of Trade: soon, when Britain assumes the EC presidency, he is to become President of the European Trade and Industry Council, too. The question arose (though none dared ask it) whether the President is to be referred to in the singular or the plural; and whether, when he is speaking in both his presidential capacities, himself, or themselves, as 'we'?

It was plain that the President is not, in the ordinary sense, a cabinet minister at all, but a pillar of the state, the holder of a great and ancient seal, a key part of the constitution.

Ordinary jobs like home secretary, or prime minister, sound vulgar, workaday, by comparison. And why was he only wearing a lounge suit? A uniform should be designed, with epaulettes.

In keeping with his new dignity, the President did not actually speak yesterday – no more, anyway, than a few words, mostly describing his office.

He was simply a *presence* on the bench: his lieutenants, the junior ministers, fussing around him with pencils, files and civil service briefs, and answering the tiresome questions that come from backbench drones. In answer to one complaint, Richard Needham (a minister) actually gave a Labour MP (Newport's Paul Flynn) his telephone number! Can you imagine the President doing that?

As I left, John Bowis (C, Battersea) was asking about 'trade in artefacts of torture'. A junior minister began a list: 'leg irons, shackles, gang-chains . . .' Across the President's august features, the beginning – just the *beginning* – of an interested smile rippled, and was gone.

12.6.92

Led by the Blind

Some robust reinforcements for the House of Lords, new rows looming over Maastricht, and the Earth Summit at Rio, lead me by different paths to the same question.

The new peers are a mixed tin of biscuits. Milords Gilmour, Parkinson, Walker and Howe will slip comfortably into the ermine – the ponderous courtesies, the 'your lordships may care to reflect on this . . .' and '. . . deferring to the noble baroness's long experience of that . . .' falling from their lips with instinctive ease, while Merlyn Rees has seemed to imagine himself in some sort of Upper Chamber for years. But Baron Ridley and Baron Tebbit could prove a positively gothic combination, while Lords Lawson and Owen may bring a welcome whiff of the unpredictable.

Were we not taught at school that, while elected MPs in the Lower House were swept hither and thither on tides of populist prejudice, peers, who feared no ballot and were appointed for their expertise and experience, knowledgeable, brave and unpartisan, sat challenging the judgements of the people's tribunes and daring to venture into original thought?

We were. And it's bunk. I've kept occasional watch on their lordships for more than a decade. Each is indeed an expert – but an expert frozen in time: caught, so to speak, at, or a little after, the summit of his influence, three, five, 30 years ago. Each one of them knew all about it – once. Ennoblement is a sort of formaldehyde.

There are, it is true, peers who remain leading minds in their chosen spheres but, with few exceptions, such men and women are rarely seen at the Palace of Westminster. We get prudence and caution from Britain's Second Chamber, but rarely original thought. The Lords is not a place to think the unthinkable. It is not really a place to think at all. An intellectual staleness hangs in the air there.

Which leads me to the question which is my theme. Where, outside government, in our legislature is the brain? Where is the mind, the intellect, located? Who is doing the thinking? Who is doing the study?

Take Rio. As I write, 651 MPs are leaping into judgements on the US position on global warming. Many are finding they feel passionately about the ozone layer too. Most of them don't even know what the ozone layer is or have any idea what it does. Not one in twenty could argue out the case on CO_2 emissions in better than O-level terms.

Casting my eye over the whole House, only Tam Dalyell springs to mind as an obviously expert advocate of the apocalyptic school, while only Teresa Gorman speaks with any intellectual grounding for the sceptical school. This is one of the great debates of our era, yet so few MPs rise to the debate.

Do you realize where most MPs get their opinions on 'earth' issues? They get them from the press. The press reports that 'scientists are concerned', so MPs express concern. Then the press reports that 'MPs are concerned', so MPs *know* they are concerned. Under pressure, now, ministers make statements, drafted by civil servants who don't know much but have 'taken advice'; and by now the public has the impression that everybody is unanimous in their alarm. So naturally the public becomes alarmed; whereupon MPs sense that there are votes in it, and redouble their concern . . . Perhaps it's all to the good, but do not imagine that your elected representatives know any more about Rio than you do.

Or Maastricht. A simple quiz on the content and effects of the Treaty would – I'll wager – reveal that most MPs prefer to rely for their opinions and information on . . . the press. If the Lords as a body is mainly contemplative in function, the Commons is reactive, and to secondary sources.

On some of the gut issues, and in the more straightforward problem areas of economic and commercial life, the two British Houses of Parliament retain their intellectual grasp and can approach policy with the creativity – and the scepticism – that intellectual self-confidence engenders. But, as it drifts towards the end of the century, Parliament sees whole swathes of modern government and administration opening up which it must – or will – funk.

I trust there *is* a hole in the ozone layer. I trust the seas really *are* rising to engulf us. I hope *somebody* has read the Maastricht Treaty. Because if there isn't, or they aren't, or nobody has, don't imagine the Lords, or the Commons, would know. Unless they had read it in the papers.

(From the *Investors Chronicle*)

Major Wields the Little Stick

17.6.92

A new, rather brittle John Major marched up to the dispatch box to take questions yesterday. The style was summary, almost tart. Mr Major was not lofty or grand, nor visibly angry. He lacks pomposity. But he can be starchy and coming home from Rio to find the House in disarray has been a shock. There has been a breakout from the nursery, the children are fighting among themselves and some of the younger ones have soiled the continental soft furnishings so lately acquired, and torn the Belgian lace. Discipline was needed.

This, Major administers not with rifle-butt as Lady Thatcher would, afterwards kicking her victim's head but with a flick of the cane on the soft part behind the knees, followed by a consolatory squeeze of the shoulder. Where Lady Thatcher would have chosen a rolling pin, Mr Major prefers a whisk. It works. Backbench Tories seemed subdued. Mischievous grins had vanished. At first, no Tory dared enquire about Europe.

Labour's Kevin Hughes (Doncaster N) took shelter behind a question about the depletion of a peat bog in Yorkshire. Mr Major was having none of this. In a *slightly* severe voice, he told Mr Hughes (in so many words) to ring his office with the details.

Barry Field (C, Isle of Wight) thought humour his best refuge, and tried an oblique approach, via mad dogs, rabies and the Liberal Democrats. The Liberals, Mr Field told a bemused PM, wanted to use the Isle of Wight as a test-zone for a rabies-vaccination campaign. 'Mad dogs and foreigners' must be kept out of Britain, he said.

We wondered where Mr Field's question was leading, but the next stage only confused us further. Liberal Democrats, he continued, have been defeated in the polls. What could this mean? Oh, he added, and border controls between EC countries were to remain. Nobody has the slightest idea what he was talking about.

So, concluded Mr Field, pink-faced as his logical destination hove at last into view: could the PM 'give this House an assurance that the government will continue the controls which prevent both these terrible diseases?' Mr Field sat down.

A Vet Writes: Liberalism and rabies are not often bracketed in this way. Most people regard Liberalism as far more dangerous, and certainly the effects of the malady upon its victim are more dramatic. The rolling eyes, foaming mouth and inclination to bite are more marked in the Liberal Democrat than in the dog, and there is no guaranteed inoculation against the political affliction, though a happy home life, regular meals and a proper job can help. There is no known cure for either disorder.

Still the Same

25.6.92

In the summer of 1974, Sir Keith Joseph MP made a speech which effectively ended his hopes of leading the Conservative party. Yesterday in the Upper Chamber, nearly two decades later, his voice quavering a little with age, Lord Joseph returned to the theme: rather sadder, infinitely more tentative, yet still insistent, still sure it mattered, still with that moral and intellectual courage which mark him as author of the Thatcherism she never understood.

As usual, the debate he hoped to provoke hardly got going. As usual, his speech was awkward. As usual, he was careless how his words might be twisted. As usual, he found no mind to engage with his. The occasion brought him full circle from the early years.

You may remember that first speech in 1974. Joseph drew attention to what he saw as a dangerous birth rate among parents least likely to bring up children properly. Within hours, his enemies were representing this as a call for mass sterilization. Though he went on to deliver the Tory leadership to Mrs Thatcher and become industry secretary and education secretary in her government, he never really recovered.

Now Lord Joseph approached, again, the rock on which he wrecked his career. Family problems could be found in every class, he said, but were more common among the less privileged. 'Careless procreation' was not to be encouraged. Young women should be discouraged from seeing 'childbirth as their only fulfilment'. We should not shrug shoulders at 'young men who breed irresponsibly'. A key to this was stigma.

Stigma. That was what he said, referring honestly and by name to a concept absolutely central to Western moral reasoning: a psychological breakwater behind which half a century of flabby liberalism has sheltered while turning its eyes from the sea. What the neighbours say should matter, he explained. It is a measure of the abject level of English jurisprudence that the sentiments sounded so odd.

For Labour, the Baroness Blackstone read a speech about the level of child benefit, completely missing the point. Keith Joseph looked, as he always has, disappointed. Lady Blackstone had brought us back to the red leather, gold leaf, and evasion.

Tory Rats Desert ex-Leader

30.6.92

Some of us suspect that John Major's positive attitude towards Europe may be prudent. Some of us suspect that Lady Thatcher's sudden attack of Euro-collywobbles is pretty rich, coming from her.

So what are we to do? Yesterday saw the rats on the Tory backbenches turning on their Queen. Logic demands that we support them; good taste cries out that we dispose of them.

Rodent after rodent rose from the Tory benches. Whiskers twitching, scaly tails slithering from the green bench behind and shifty little eyes glancing furtively round, the rats took nips at the woman who used to be their leader.

Each vied with the rat who had gone before for the sharpness of his bite, the novelty of his taunt. Scavengers who, two years ago, squeaked her praises, now squeaked support for their new King, urging him on to ever more extravagant attacks on the old lady . . .

'Would he not agree' this? 'Would he not point out to her' that? 'Would he not deplore' the other? Would he not put Lady Thatcher in her place? It was, as the *Daily Mirror*'s columnist, Cassandra, once put it, 'enough to make grown men long for a quiet corner, a handkerchief, an aspidistra, and the old heave-ho'.

Curious that I should have moved among them for seven years as a colleague, and never noticed, from some of those who spoke yesterday, the incipient enthusiasm for Mr Major's idea of being 'at the heart' of Europe. All the while, I now realize, there was this secret, powerful undercurrent of dissent.

Nobody, I now accept, liked her at all. All the while my colleagues were organizing resistance to the lady's folly – and I alone failed to notice.

Yesterday it surfaced. So let us cry, in a tongue now a little more fashionable than before: *Quel courage! Bravo!* 'Rat', I think, is the same in both languages.

Toupees Tipped to Barefaced Teresa   *2.7.92*

Halfway through questions to the Foreign Secretary yesterday, just as Mr Hurd tiptoed gingerly through a minefield of a question about Maastricht, Teresa Gorman appeared at the door, and hovered. It was her first public appearance since admitting on Radio 1 that her eyebrows were tattooed.

Hearts went out to Mrs Gorman. It was a brave admission. One thinks of all the male MPs who wear toupees, not one of whom has come out as a baldy. Peter Mandelson (Lab, Hartlepool) sports a Victorian stage villain's moustache which few believe to be genuine; Jerry Hayes (C, Harlow) is widely suspected of Afro-perming his famous blond beehive; and I know one secretary of state who was spotted queueing at Boots in Victoria Street for Grecian 2000. He bought two bottles. Wild horses would not drag from me his name. And nameless shall remain the Tory whose photograph in *The Times Guide to the House of Commons* showed an almost completely bald MP. He returned after an election with a full head of hair.

Women politicians, who are on the whole less vain than the men, are perhaps less coy about personal artifice. Barbara Castle recounts with candour the story of how, when social services secretary, she rushed at dawn to the scene of an old people's home, gutted by fire with terrible loss of life. Such was the urgency of her mission that she had time only to tip out of bed and pull on clothes, shoes and a wig. Picking her way through the cinders, the end of a trailing cable hanging from a rafter caught her wig and held it, suspended in the air. She grabbed the wig and planted it back on her head, sideways, unfortunately.

Lady Castle's diaries record her dilemma. Should she get out her vanity mirror and arrange the wig, standing in the rubble? Or should she complete her tour and arrive at a press conference with wig askew? She took the right decision: the second one.

But Mrs Gorman's honesty is the greater, for nobody had threatened to 'out' her over her eyebrows. She could have taken her secret to the grave, but volunteered it, to rouse interest in the subject of tattooing. Removing unwanted tattoos, she told the House, costs the NHS millions. A tattoo is so easy to acquire, she said; so painful and expensive to remove.

'Hear, hear,' replied her colleagues. Don't they just know it! 'I love Margaret' was tattoed all over the bodies of hundreds of them. From 1979 to 1990 it was the motto every Tory craved. Entwined with hearts, roses and cherubim, her name and theirs were linked in every constituency speech, every election address, every second parliamentary question of the decade. Spin doctors at Conservative Central Office are doing their best to change 'Margaret' into 'Maastricht', but the result is a mess.

Towards the end, 'I love Michael' became the fashion among a few. Conspicuously able Tories emblazoned the Tarzan motto across their chests. How David Hunt (banished to Wales), Emma Nicholson (locked out) and Edwina Currie (threatened with Kenneth Clarke) long to remove the unwanted tattoo!

Now 'I love John' is all the rage. Tattooists (who at Westminster are called *Hansard* reporters) are doing a roaring trade in getting that message down in indelible form, beneath a hundred names, no matter how tasteless the wording, how lurid the ink. Slow to learn, they should listen to Mrs Gorman.

A Midsummer Day's Dream

3.7.92

Lady T makes her first speech in the Lords. . . .

It was mischief: but it was delicate mischief. 'As gently,' said Lord Callaghan, 'as any sucking dove.' The sucking dove, in blue and pearls, smiled, her talons sheathed.

Callaghan put it best. She had sung sweetly to her new audience, he told us. Patronizing her, as he did in those far-off seventies when he was PM, he advised her that their lordships do not take kindly to being hectored, so she had been wise to avoid the histrionics. Observing her, he added, he was reminded of Bottom. Lord Callaghan paused.

Eyebrows raised. Callaghan explained. In *A Midsummer Night's Dream*, he said, Bottom says to his co-conspirators 'I will roar . . . but I will aggravate my voice, so that I roar you as gently as any sucking dove; I will roar you as 'twere any nightingale.' Peers chuckled.

The nightingale had been there from the start, looking nervous. From time to time she fiddled with a sheaf of notes, conscious that she was being observed. When the Earl of Onslow (something of a card) rounded on a nervous, bespectacled junior viscount, Lord Goschen (who was defending the government's record on homelessness) and told him that spending £96m on 464 'rough sleepers' was extravagant – 'it would pay my Lloyd's losses several times over' – she took care not to smile. When Baroness Chalker, foreign office minister, rose, Lady Thatcher took her glasses from a small black crocodile-skin case and put them on.

Lady Chalker spoke of 'the vision of a wider community that I know my Right Hon friend [Lady Thatcher] so much shares'. The dove took off her glasses, impassive. When Chalker, in episcopal drone, sailed into a peroration about 'special events' in the British presidency, 'a theatre, arts and business programme . . . wide range . . . full agenda . . . whole community . . . busy and interesting . . . firm basis for success . . .' Lady T fumbled in her pocket, pulled something out, and popped it into her mouth. A mint? Or a painkiller? She took off her glasses.

Roy Jenkins spoke before her, offering John Major 'my un*way*vawing support' but explaining that he would have to leave for dinner by 8.15. Prodding Lady Thatcher gently, he advised her not to pull her punches. Prodding a little more, he warned that the European vision was not a meal to be taken à la carte, picking through the menu. Lord Jenkins looked in lip-smacking form, and ready to sign up for olives, canapés, all six courses, pudding, savouries, cheese, biscuits, port and petits fours – and then to await the cigars. Lady Thatcher, lips pursed, looked ready for a small green salad. Before sitting down, Lord Jenkins was kind enough to read extensive sections of his Jean Monet lecture delivered in 1974, to refresh our memories.

The nightingale rose. She thanked Jenkins, complimenting him on his speech, which she took à la carte, approving (she said) of 'parts of it'. She looked forward to the tranquillity of her new nest 'after 33 testing years before the mast'. The humour worked, and, when she reminded their Lordships that 214 of them had been sent there under her premiership, they decided to take it as a joke. She was sorry to come so early to controversy, she said, but she simply couldn't wait. They took that as a joke, too. Behind her, Geoffrey Howe, who knew it was no joke, lowered his head like an irritable bear.

Lady T then treated us to a light skip through the meadows of her scepticism. 'I had some *great* budget battles in my day,' she breathed, 'I *always* found that the most *effective* weapon was No.' A chilling smile. 'And sometimes No, No, No.' Lord Howe gripped his jaw in his hands.

And soon the sucking dove finished her serenade, and yielded to Lord Callaghan, who yielded to Shakespeare.

But he did not finish that quote. After promising to start as a nightingale, Bottom arranges to meet his pals again, in a wood . . .

'And there we may rehearse more obscenely and courageously. Take pains. Be perfect. Adieu.'

The dove's lieutenants, crowded at the door to watch, understood.

Leading Rifkind a Merry Dance

8.7.92

With the future of the European Fighter Aircraft on our minds, we turn to *Hansard*. A Labour spokesman had asked for a statement.

Minister: '. . . Making good progress. It is expected to fly early next year . . . the jobs of 15,000 to 20,000 are involved.'

Backbench Tory MP: 'Will the minister confirm that this is a highly sophisticated and versatile aircraft, capable of both a nuclear and a conventional role? Will he denounce the unpatriotic activities of Labour members [in opposing it]?'

Minister: 'They can only damage the export possibilities of a fine aircraft. Orders have been placed by the RAF.'

Later, MPs questioned the Prime Minister himself about the fighter. One of them commented that 'the aircraft industry is a leader industry: its continued support is vital for the technological advance of the nation'. The PM concurred: 'My hon friend is right.'

The year was 1963, the Prime Minister Sir Alec Douglas-Home, the minister Julian Amery, the Tory stalwarts Gerald Nabarro and John Eden, and the Opposition doubters John Stonehouse and Eric Lubbock. The fighter aircraft was called the TSR2. It was cancelled the next year. Almost everybody would now agree that it had become a white elephant, though at the time many Tory backbenchers blamed its demise on a CND plot.

Yesterday, nearly 29 years later, Defence Secretary Malcolm Rifkind pirouetted gracefully through the opening scenes of this familiar classical ballet. The movements are well choreographed and have been danced by countless ministers before him. Rather the same thing is going on with the Maastricht treaty at present and European monetary union. The project is plainly doomed, the vessel sinking: but as a matter of honour and political self-interest, British ministers must stand saluting on the deck until the water is almost up to their ankles. By then, other nations will be heading for the lifeboats and we shall gratefully follow. Nobody will be able to call us rats.

But we are not there yet with EFA. It is early. In this scene, Mr Rifkind begs his German counterpart to stick with the project. Herr Rühe declining to do so, as everybody knew he would. Next, Rifkind beats his breast, declares himself more than ever committed to this marvellous enterprise, assures industry and the trade unions of his undying support, and promises the House to do his best to persuade the Italians and Spaniards to carry on.

Of this, of course, there is no prospect. One by one, they fall by the wayside (these scenes occur later this year) but Mr Rifkind dances on, serenaded by a full orchestra of defence researchers and developers, who are still being paid for the planning stage of the project (£5bn down, several billion to go).

As remaining dancers and chorus quit, the minister's doggedness begins to look eccentric. Even those who urged him forward in the early scenes are making other plans. Still, he did a jolly good job, all agree.

In the last scene (perhaps as late as 1993) when the whole thing is finally called off, a tearful Mr Rifkind is comforted and thanked by all for his unstinting efforts. Connoisseurs of this dance form will know that the curtain is coming down, as we speak, on the Ravenscraig ballet, with Scottish Secretary Ian Lang dancing the lead role while the steelworks crumble. Meanwhile the orchestra warms up for an obscure work starting next year (*Privatization of British Rail*) and a lengthy piece: *Trident Independent Deterrent*.

But back to EFA. Rifkind is dancing with great energy. Any doubts that the aircraft will never be built evaporated within minutes of his sitting down: the Opposition parties are supporting the project. All is lost!

Kinnock's Sun Sets with Dignity

15.7.92

Astronomers may know which suns and stars were colliding in distant constellations yesterday: for within a few hours Neil Kinnock made his final appearance at Westminster as leader of the Opposition; Denis Healey, the nearly-leader, took his seat in the Lords; and Geoffrey Howe, whose knife in his leader's back installed our present PM, depriving Mr Kinnock of the ultimate prize, joined Lord Healey, in ermine.

It is always a poignant moment when a Labour MP goes to the Lords. With apologies to J M Barrie, I suspect that every time a socialist becomes a baron a little fairy somewhere dies.

I know nothing of Denis Healey's principles and do not think him treacherous: but still I was put in mind of a poem by William Kean Seymour, written long ago.

> Let me be thankful, God, that I am not
> A Labour Leader when his life work ends.
> Who contemplates the coronet he got,
> By being false to principles and friends;
> Who fought for forty years a desperate fight
> With words that seared and stung and slew like swords,
> And at the end, with victory in sight,
> Ate them – a mushroom viscount in the Lords.

Over in the Commons, Neil Kinnock was squaring up for his final spat with the Prime Minister. This was the Commons' last PM's Questions before the recess.

After this Saturday, a new Labour leader will be installed.

As usual at Westminster when the moment is solemn and the mood dignified, something silly happened to spoil it. The something silly was, in this case, John Bowis (C, Battersea), first to question Mr Major.

It is not that Mr Bowis is inherently silly. He is a capable chap whose girth has grown with his growing Commons reputation. Nor was there anything inherently silly about his question. It was the marriage of *this* question with *this* questioner which caused mirth.

'Does my Right Hon friend agree,' said Mr Bowis, his tummy seeming to swell with the importance of his enquiry, his buttons almost popping, 'that real and lasting growth . . .' I fear he got no further: not audibly, anyway. Laughter overtook economics and a rueful Mr Bowis stepped back to survey the wreckage of what he had intended to be a helpful disquisition on the need to keep inflation – retail price inflation, that is – in check.

Then came Neil Kinnock. He rose. Jocular shouts of 'resign!' The mood changed. Mr Kinnock wanted to know where the economic recovery that the PM had promised had gone.

It was a simple, serious question, simply and seriously put. It was one of his best. It struck me that asking a serious question, without 'spin', is one of the few tacks Mr Kinnock has never really tried. He has tried gravitas, which is quite another thing, and inspired only giggles. He has tried humour, and provoked only scorn. He has tried long questions, and been mocked for long-windedness; and he has tried short questions, and been dismissed as gimcrack. But yesterday he indicated to the PM what everyone knew was a real problem, and played it straight.

Mr Major commenced his reply with a graceful tribute. 'Generous,' the press will call it, but of course it costs a PM nothing and goes down well. It was nicely done. John Major is a foxier fellow than at first we knew.

Kinnock replied that it had been an honour to serve his country in this way, and repeated his question about the economy, reinforcing it with examples. Major remarked that he and Kinnock shared common goals but differed as to means. By now the goodwill was becoming tiresome. MPs fidgeted.

Kinnock reminded Major that he was equally sincere, and Major gently suggested that at least they could agree about that. MPs began looking towards doors and windows for escape routes . . .

And it was over, very dignified. Nothing became his office like the leaving of it. One remembers with similar affection Mrs Thatcher's marvellous exit. Like a glorious tropical sunset, a resigning politician is a beautiful sight.

Of Parrots, Ostriches and Old Dogs

16.7.92

As the summer hols approach, MPs grow careless with their metaphor. In a debate on shipping and the merchant fleet last week Mark Wolfson (C, Sevenoaks) called for a level playing field. And yesterday afternoon, Phillip Oppenheim (C, Amber Valley) became so excited about the privatization of Parcelforce that he launched into a complex bird metaphor, getting his birds mixed up.

'Why,' he asked, 'do the dear old Labour party persist in burying their heads in the sand, parroting tired old formulae?' Mr Oppenheim might like to buy himself a textbook on tropical ornithology.

But he had a point. Let us move the metaphor from birds to the canine world.

Her Majesty's Opposition increasingly resembles a half-deaf, near-sighted, arthritic old dog, dozing in the summer sun. It is too lazy to nose around any longer looking for things to chase, and too stiff to follow them if they run. It has lost interest in fighting with other dogs, having been badly bitten four times.

But it can still bark. Rather a feeble, rasping old bark, but the instinct lingers, the last to fade.

It barks – this Labour dog – at anything that moves. The sense of smell, once keen, has gone, and our canine friend has lost the wit to distinguish between movements that represent a threat and those which are welcome. In the farmyard within its range of vision, any obvious, deliberate movement at all causes the old dog to lift its weary head, yellowing teeth half-bared in the remnants of a snarl, growl a little, in a token sort of way, and emit a routine woof. Old habits die hard. Movement in the yard yesterday was provided by the proposed privatization of the Post Office's parcels service.

The old dog simply registered the fact that the Tories were *changing* something – from public to private sector – and started to bark. 'Public sector good! Private sector bad!'

One Labour backbencher asked how it could be possible that a company should provide a public service *and* aim to make a profit.

Thus the Labour party gazes, half-stupefied, at modern Britain and barks at any sign of movement. But the bark has no meaning any more. Too far gone to move and no longer able to bite, the Opposition's higher brain functions have shut down. Only the breathing, the eye-movements, and a sort of undirected snarl remain. Only the reflexes, only the bark and howl, are left.

Putting a Toe in the Water

15.9.92

The Liberal Democrat Conference in Harrogate....

Lubricious! cried Robert Maclennan; then, excited by his only reference to Miss de Sancha and the tabloids, and voice all a-quiver, he said it again. 'Lub*ric*ious'. He moved on. Trust the Lib Dems to choose as Fun spokesman the only man in Britain who would not stoop to a Mellor joke. It would do Mr Maclennan no end of good to have his toes sucked, if necessary by force, one toe (this-little-piggy-went-to-market style) for each of the ten letters in *lubricious*.

Here at Harrogate, disbelief stalks the conference centre. At Brighton in three weeks it will stalk the promenande. At Harrogate, Liberal Democrats shake their heads in disbelief that they did not win. At Brighton, Tories will shake their heads in disbelief that they did. Liberals know that they are a band of saints and are amazed that the country does not see it. Tories know they are a cartload of monkeys and are amazed that the country has not found them out.

Thus failure bruises a Liberal but does not crush him. At Harrogate several thousand indestructibles are picking themselves up and vowing to carry on. Maybe next time? Of course Paddy promised it *last* time, but is greeted now as parents greet a little boy who said he was running away to America, and got 30 yards. 'Well, Paddy, how was America – or didn't it quite work out?' Fondly he is received back into the Liberal bosom.

Paddy, meanwhile, has a new venture. He is going to try being ordinary in different locations all over Britain, to see how it feels. He is to discover the people.

Yesterday morning he decided to be ordinary in a building site for 20 minutes and discover some construction workers but by some ghastly mischance (Heaven knows how this happened!) a press release got out beforehand. It is hard to be ordinary with 20 cameramen following you round but Paddy tried. Wearing a white helmet (he loves helmets) Paddy narrowed his eyes to those familiar statemanlike slits and peered, rapt, at a lump of reinforced concrete. Nearby, some other ordinary people discussed with me this phenomenon. They were navvies . . .

'Who's 'ee when 'ee's at 'ome then?'

'Wunerthem SDPs, innee?'

'Big booger, innee? Bigger than on TV like. Wozeedooinneer?'

'Lookin' fer votes, innee, like all the resterthem!'

Sad, isn't it, to find our countrymen so cynical? After a magnificently shameless pretence that the presence of journalists was a matter of regret to him, Mr Ashdown ceased being ordinary and was driven away in a big Mercedes-Benz. Seeing what it is like to be an ordinary German business tycoon.

18.9.92 ## Lib Dems Rise to Beith's Occasion

Mr Beith's speech coincides with Black Wednesday. . . .

Alan Beith, MP, is a small, cuddly man with spectacles. I know too little of bird genetics to be confident that you could mate an owl and a penguin, or cross a waddle with a shuffle, but if you try to imagine an owlguin in glasses, walking with a kind of wuffle and wearing an expression of suprised wisdom, then you have Mr Beith.

He's a rather unlikely modern Lib Dem: more in the mould of Methodist Sunday school teacher, a dying breed these days in the party. Marching for gay rights or penning himself into a battery cage is not Mr Beith's style. His politics are cautious, conservative, and his platform performance donnish. Beith has no truck with the sound-bite.

All these qualities make him an ideal Treasury spokesman, a portfolio he handles with quiet assurance. He would be a natural chief secretary in a coalition cabinet. Unlike many Lib Dem MPs, you can actually imagine Alan Beith in government.

Which is perhaps why a party of protest does not warm to him. Beith's careful speeches have seldom wowed Lib Dem conferences. He distrusts the vision thing. His party distrusts the action thing. So not for Mr Beith the rapture of standing ovations. Polite applause, furrowed brows and the sound of delegates scratching their heads is his normal conference fare.

That is why yesterday was so remarkable. With currency markets in turmoil and the real Chancellor flat on his face, even Liberal Democrats recognized the need to look up from their conference agenda and confront the crisis. They called for Beith. Beith was to make a statement. Delegates crowded into the hall. Silence fell. Beith rose.

Somehow the drama of it all had got through. Beith waved his arms. Beith derided the government. Here, he said, was another fine mess they'd got us into. Beith mocked. Beith advised. Beith warned. Beith lashed out. Beith did something almost unheard of in his decades in politics: he looked up from his notes. Finally, his blast finished, he prepared to leave . . .

But wait! A strange sound assailed his owlish ears. Could it be . . . *applause*? Loud applause. *Sustained* applause . . . and what was this? A delegate was standing up in her place. Another joined her, then another, then another. Soon, the entire conference was standing. It was – oh yes – it was a standing ovation for Alan Beith.

He raised his eyes and blinked. Then the owlguin began wuffling towards the steps. Something lit his face. On anyone but Mr Beith you would have called it triumph. Danke, Deutschland.

Sniggering MPs Denied Their Fun

26.9.92

David Mellor makes his resignation speech from the back benches. . . .

The fun – *Mr Mellor: A Personal Statement* – was scheduled for 11 am: a civilized time for a lynching.

Just before 11, Mr Mellor arrived for his ritual humiliation. Tory numbers had doubled. They had come for the usual show: pale figure of minister – head bowed – old school tie – restrained regrets concerning own folly – delicate references to nature of folly – heartfelt thanks to colleagues for support during difficult time – sit down – 'hear-hear' from all sides – shoulder-pattings from pals – dignified exit, to kindly buzz of 'poor David', 'there but for the grace of God . . .' etc from outwardly mournful, inwardly sniggering colleagues.

By 11, the Tory benches were full: a charcoal waste of Tories, one of whom has a new wig.

From back benches where he was a stranger, Mellor rose. Something within him said 'stuff the lot of you'. The speech was not an outburst: more a shrug of the shoulders, a brave grin, and two fingers fidgeting to make a rude sign.

'Having become heartily sick of my private life myself,' he said, 'I cannot expect others to take a more charitable view.' It was an eccentric statement, by degrees chatty, defiant, funny, menacing and bitter: but devoid of self-pity. His colleagues had come to reward a show of regret. But of regret there was little, so sympathy was tinged with bemusement.

A fortnight of total cock-up ended yesterday with just one resignation: a man agreed on all sides to be good at his job.

Minus a Seal, the Circus Carries on

29.9.92

The Labour Party Conference in Blackpool. . . .

Welcome, says my brochure, from *Tower World*, 'to Blackpool's newest, most exciting day out!'

It started yesterday morning with a rip-roaring speech from Labour's economics spokesman, Gordon Brown. I hardly heard a word of it. I was too absorbed by what he was doing with his tongue.

Have you watched him on TV? What do *you* think is happening inside his mouth? My own theory is that he is juggling two or three heavy ball-bearings on the end of his tongue. Where a Tory spokesman may speak with a plum in his mouth, it is fitting that Labour's man does it with ball-bearings.

'Why should *millions* of *pounds* . . .' (Brown is beginning to jerk his head to emphasize words in that turkey-like head-butt which Neil Kinnock made famous) '. . . go to a *few* of the world's *richest* men?' His style is sulky-angry, jowls a-quiver, sub-Lawson. You can hear the ball-bearings colliding. But then he stops, momentarily, for air.

Watch. He gulps, mouth agape between sentences. Tongue makes a sudden dart forward, curling down over bottom teeth and plumbing the space between lower gum and lip. Is this man perhaps itching to stick his tongue out at you but aborting the gesture? Is he repositioning the ball-bearings for another juggle? Taken as a conference speech on the economy, Mr Brown's performance yesterday is agreed to have been splendid. Taken as a championship display of oral juggling *while* making a major statement on economic policy, it was breathtaking.

Audience Fade Away at Blackpool   *1.10.92*

Here at Blackpool, Labour are facing a serious case of premature evacuation. The press have left.

The climax of the conference came far too early, almost before the occasion was under way. With the leader's speech on Tuesday, the conference peaked. The main event now over, those who remain hammer away with a simulated conference, but everyone knows it isn't the real McCoy. Nothing is really happening but nobody likes to say so.

If the platform party would only tell the floor party they aren't enjoying it any more, then the floor party could admit to the platform party that they aren't either. Both would rather be somewhere else, but each is grinding on in the belief that the other wants them to. By Friday, we shall all be completely exhausted and none the better for it.

But it was David Blunkett's final gesture that somehow summed up the futility of it all. He was concluding the session on health, after which a session on trade union links, block votes and the like, was to begin. 'All those in favour please show,' said Blunkett. 'All those against?' he paused. I swear his dog barked no signal of any kind. 'Carried overwhelmingly!' he grinned.

And in a flash the solution to the problem of premature evacuation dawned on me. *Nobody* needs to stay. Let the conference continue, with platform empty, press and delegates on the homeward train, and seats occupied by cards indicating the block votes of the trade unions. Post-climax, we could all go home. I always did prefer a nice cup of tea.

The Lady in Yellow

2.10.92

There are two drawbacks to sitting on the floor of the Winter Gardens Ballroom at Blackpool. One is the lack of visibility; the other is the smell.

My view of the stage is partial. Yesterday, while a show of hands was being taken, I stared up at the ghastly grey backdrop across which is written the slogan AGENDA FOR CHANGE. The delegate a few seats in front of me raised a slim arm.

She held it there, interposed (in my vision) between the first and the remaining letters of Labour's 1992 slogan. Thus I read: A GENDA FOR CHANGE. Labour, I speculated, was running a campaign for transvestism. The speculation was more interesting than the debate.

In the foreground, Margaret Beckett, the deputy leader, rose to take the microphone. The backdrop is a canvas painted with lines and triangles in different shades of grey. From ankle level on the floor (and from the vantage point of the TV cameras, too) the podium is positioned so that it presents the speaker's head at the thin edge on a wedge of light. It appeared as though a lighthouse beam was emanating from the top of Mrs Beckett's hair, piercing and illumating a world of grey shadows.

Mrs Beckett herself was dressed all in yellow, with big yellow stars in her ears. She was wholly self-possessed and held her head perfectly still. Her eyes blazed, her lips were full, glossy and red, and her teeth dangerous. Each colour of the V-neck of her sharp-cut jacket was emblazoned with a bundle of three strong bars, ascending. The plain yellow silk blouse beneath was decorated at the nape of the neck with a motif of two parallel, vertical lines, plunging towards the bosom. The whole effect was distinctly post-Fascist.

You felt, as she spoke, that there was absolutely no danger of Mrs Beckett's departing from her text, her brief or the official line: no possibility that she would add or subtract so much as a comma upon any whim of her own.

Tories try to present Mrs Beckett as a leftist monster masquerading as a moderate but waiting to throw off her disguise and guillotine all the readers of the *Daily Mail*. They recall her record as a minister (under the name of Margaret Jackson) in axing grammar schools, and insinuate that she is some kind of Stalinist. They are half right, and completely wrong. Mrs Beckett *is* a Stalinist but in the bureaucratic sense, not the ideological one. She simply does whatever needs doing for Labour. She is the perfect deputy. Mr Smith needs a competent counterpoint and Mrs Beckett is it. They make a lovely couple.

Tories should stop wailing about Margaret Beckett. If John Major had Stalinists of anything like her mettle in his cabinet, then next week would not look the nightmare it threatens to be.

Heckles Raise Hackles   7.10.92

The Tory Party Conference in Brighton. . . .

If a town's spirit is sometimes captured by its graffiti, the gist of a party conference is sometimes best expressed by its heckles. So it was in Brighton yesterday.

When elderly gentlemen in blazers barrack the Foreign Secretary, you know the Tories are in a tight spot. When a peer and previous chairman of the Conservative party beats up the Prime Minister, to rebel roars from the back, you know it's serious. But when Dame Elaine Kellett-Bowman heckles the lady mayor of Brighton, what is the world coming to?

Problems had begun early. The two hymns had passed without incident (a triumph for the word-police at Conservative Central Office: only 'distress' and 'feeble' in 'Praise My Soul the King of Heaven' slipped through the net) and Mrs Angela Rumbold looked tenderly at Mr Major as she sang 'All lovely forms declare his loveliness'.

But the New Testament reading had scolded the Euro-sceptics ('Oh ye of little faith!') and, rendering 'Sufficient unto the day is the evil thereof,' as 'Today's troubles are enough for today,' had annoyed Brugesists, many of whom believed that the Revised Standard Version results from a European directive.

Then came a barbed, ungracious speech of welcome from a lady in a hat: the Labour mayor. It goes against the Tory grain to heckle anyone in a hat, but Dame Elaine, the redoubtable MP for Lancaster and parliamentary equivalent of a gunboat, fired off three broadsides at the Worshipful the Mayor of Brighton, Cllr Mrs Gill Sweeting, all but knocking her hat off in the onslaught.

Mrs Sweeting began by saying she had hoped to welcome a Labour government to Brighton. Dame Elaine grew restive. Then Mrs Sweeting started to complain about the town's West Pier for which funds were needed. 'This is a party political broadcast!' shouted the dame, from the floor. Platform heads spun her way. Next, Mrs Sweeting explained that Brighton had applied for assisted area status. 'I hope you don't get it!' yelled the dame. On completing her speech, the mayor was handed a bunch of flowers. The conference chairman bade her farewell adding, chivalrously: 'May I thank you for your presence.'

'Why?' called Dame Elaine. Mrs Sweeting left hastily, hat in place, clutching her bouquet lest the dame leap on to the stage and grab it back.

Elaine Kellett-Bowman had meant to be helpful, but to the consternation of the platform party, her example spread. During the European debate that came later, your sketchwriter sat at first next to a Tory MP with a minor job in government. He shall remain nameless. When a speaker from the floor attacked Mr Major's

Euro-policy, my MP friend began growling – a sort of 'hear, hear' noise, but without moving his mouth, so that no one could see.

When the speech was over, he joined the clapping enthusiastically, but kept his hands under the seat-back, so that this would not be visible to the cameras or to the platform party. He is rather short-sighted, and said to me 'Is the Prime Minister looking my way?'

'No,' I said. At this point he raised his hands above the parapet and clapped even louder.

The next speaker was in favour of Maastricht. Our destiny lay in Europe, she said. 'Never!' somebody shouted from the back. The whole hall tensed up. You simply don't heckle at Tory conferences. But now somebody had, and it somehow broke the ice. The PM, continued the speaker, had 'halted the advance of federalism'. 'Rubbish!' came another shout from a different part of the hall, louder and more confident.

Then followed a speech asserting that 'the EC is moving towards becoming a free-trading, outward-looking bloc'.

'Bollocks!' – two or three shouts, this time, in unison. The Essex faction had arrived. There were giggles.

From then on, shouts of 'rubbish' came thick and fast. It is something I never thought I should see at a Tory conference, and something we did not see at Blackpool last week. It was a real debate.

Santa Margarita

9.10.92

Even the sea was calm, the streets hushed. Pennants hung motionless in the still air. Dawn crept up silent, in windless suspense – 'breathless', as Wordsworth says, 'with adoration'. Brighton was waiting for Baroness Thatcher.

There were police *everywhere*. At every corner and on every rooftop, trained marksmen, there for her protection, scanned the horizon. Some looked out to sea, in case it should part to reveal her. Some looked up into the sky, lest the lady Lieutenant-Colonel of The Parachute Regiment should come that way.

When would she arrive? How? Nobody knew. Wild rumours swept the town. One story had it that she had cancelled and left the country; another that she would helicopter in with a barnstorming speech; yet another that she was already in Brighton – had been here all week under deep cover – by day, in disguise, with Elvis Presley, battering haddock in a fish-and-chip shop – by night plotting with Lord Tebbit. Everybody had his own theory. Your sketchwriter followed the most timid and accepted that she might arrive as mortals do, in a car, at the main entrance. Along with 50 other journalists, I waited there, from breakfast. Uniformed men with guns lined each floor of the car park opposite. 'You'd think with all those marksmen someone would have got her,' quipped a passing MP, not a million miles from the government, to me. A cynical bunch, Tories.

As we scanned the waves of arriving representatives, new rumours spread among us. One was that she had negotiated permission to deliver a speech of four sentences. Press men speculated . . . 'No. No. No. No.'

We discussed a theory that Lady Thatcher was helpless, out of touch, and a prisoner of desperate men 'using' her for their own political purposes; and another – that she had herself started this rumour to distance herself from measures she must take. Or were her friends just trying to shift the blame? As we argued over her true nature, the real woman sank beneath the vapours of claim and counter-claim. Lady Thatcher approaches the status of Eva Perón, Mother Teresa or Buddy Holly. A faction will never believe it when she dies. A faction believes she already has.

As we argued, we noticed a change in the type of representative arriving. Gerald Howarth, her friend, stationed himself at the door. Tall men with bulging pockets strode up. And then Pharisees surged through the security-search – a wave of Chanel-and-pearls women and men with silk handkerchiefs. Suddenly the barriers were dragged aside, a small car tore through, four big men leapt from it, and a Jaguar swept up in its wake.

She emerged. She was in black with a new diamond brooch – dagger-shaped – must have cost a fortune – all of two speeches to Japanese businessmen. The media went wild. A ragged line of furry microphones advanced like lancers. She smiled and moved forward in her partridge-walk, quick little steps. 'Are you being disloyal, Lady Thatcher? *Mrs Thatcher*,' (under stress we revert), 'are you being disloyal?'

No reply. The little steps came even faster. The partridge was almost in flight. 'Is that blood on your teeth, Lady Thatcher?' – this, *sotto voce*.

And she had escaped. Up the stairs. Word ran around the hall, where a debate on employment was in progress. Lady Thatcher was waiting in the wings.

Through the blue velvet which curtains the door to the platform, a female hand reached – and was withdrawn. Mrs Shephard promised to abolish May Day, and consult on a new holiday. 'Thatcher day,' someone cried. Everyone was waiting. The upper balconies of the hall were secured with safety nets – lest she should try to fly down?

But she walked. Her entrance, when it occurred, filled the hall with a kind of moral panic. Many went crazy with acclaim. Others stood out of courtesy. A large minority stayed seated. A handful refused to clap. There were boos. A few walked out. It was not like last year.

Like Santa Evita, Santa Margarita's cult is secure for ever, and grows every year more intense. But the mainstream is turning away.

Lamont Lost for Words   *13.10.92*

Poor Mr Lamont. In a revealing moment at the Treasury select committee interrogation yesterday, someone quoted his press critics at him. Lamont's candour got the better of his grammar. 'They seem,' he said bitterly, 'to be extremely out to create a bit of problems here and there.'

You saw his point. We admired him simply for getting there. These days, if Norman Lamont asks a taxi driver to take him to Victoria station, the cabbie will probably make an intelligent guess and assume he means Waterloo. Picture breakfast at the Lamonts' . . .

'Shredded Wheat, Norman?'

'Yes please, dear.' Mrs Lamont reaches for the Coco Pops.

'And after your cereal?'

'Sausages, please, Rosemary.'

'Are you *sure*? Very well. Egg on toast coming up. Do you think it will rain today?'

'Absolutely not, Rosemary. Clear and sunny all day. Never been more certain of anything in my life.'

'Your mackintosh is behind the door, and the umbrella's in the hall.'

Who would be Chancellor of the Exchequer? Yesterday, milkmen rose early to sell an honest pint and collect a cheery 'Good morning' along the way. Widget manufacturers were proudly inspecting their widgets, doctors were tending to the living and vicars praying for the dead. Norman Lamont, meanwhile, rose and was taken to a place where he was asked by Brian Sedgemore MP whether it was not the case that: 'You're a dishonest person who gets civil servants to fake statistics for your own political purposes?'

The Chancellor blinked, his expression suggesting that Mr Sedgemore had a point but had perhaps overstated it. 'Can I say that's not correct?' he ventured.

His questioner repented of his discourtesy and tried what was, for the bear-like Sedgemore, a gentlemanly approach. 'Don't you agree that your judgement is probably the last judgement on Earth that anybody's going to believe?'

'How can we trust you?' added Giles Radice. Mr Lamont muttered that this was 'cheap'. '*You're* cheap,' said Mr Radice, in a conversational sort of way – but others were waiting for a chat too. Alan Beith wanted to tell him that he was in a hole. Dark-skinned Diane Abbott had broached the subject of Black Wednesday, signalling that the phrase was not, after all, politically incorrect: and Nicholas Budgen wanted to follow up his kindly suggestion that Lamont was telling lies. On these occasions, Budgen (C, Wolverhampton SW) becomes contempt made manifest.

The Cheshire cat may have left only its grin behind but, with the Wolverhampton cat, the last thing to hover, still visible, in the air would be the sneer. The only compensation for Lamont must have been that MPs were so eager to prove that he had made a mess of the past that they never got round to proving he was going to make a mess of the future.

When the Chancellor was not glaring at his notes, he was staring in a strangely fixated way at both his cuffs, which had emerged completely from the ends of his jacket arms. I briefly considered the possibility that the government's new economic policy may have been written on his cuffs, but dismissed it. One cuff would have been more than sufficient.

Good Ship Hezza Finds Safe Harbour

22.10.92

Michael Heseltine faced an angry Commons to defend himself following the withdrawal of the government's pit-closure proposals. . . .

What a magnificent sight! His rudder broken, his argument in shreds, his navigational charts scattered to the four winds, his hull torn apart by enemy fire, and shipping water by the bucketful, the fighting ship HMS *President of the Board of Trade* rode triumphantly into harbour yesterday, his torn sails billowing in the wind as Tories roared their support behind him.

The noise was fearful. Labour chanted. The Chair screamed. Strangers and onlookers simply gaped. And, their anger rising as every new affront broke across his bows, Michael Heseltine's own backbenchers blew up a gale of sympathy, indignation and encouragement.

Harried by the Opposition, Heseltine threw away his speech. He began to shout. Labour shouted louder. He raised his voice to breaking point. All the Tory rabble behind him yelled him on. As Opposition breakers smashed hopelessly against the rocks, reason, if reason ever entered this, blew away.

It started as a painfully complex argument about pit closures, with Heseltine on the losing side. Labour confidence rose. The Opposition became a rabble. The Chair all but lost control. Within fifteen minutes, and most unwisely, the Opposition had pushed what had begun as a trial into a lynching. It became apparent that Heseltine was struggling for his survival. With ancient visceral wisdom, his party sensed that this wasn't just an argument about mines: indeed, it wasn't an argument about mines at all. It was an argument about *their* government's authority. They sensed their man's despair, and closed ranks. The battle then turned.

Perhaps significantly, Neil Kinnock turned it. He told Heseltine that domestic coal had traded in a free market. Rubbish, roared

Heseltine, departing his wretched brief and treating Kinnock to a rant about the evils of a nationalized Britain in which you got what you were allocated and paid what you were ordered to. Labour, shouted Heseltine, had learnt nothing. This acted as a signal to his own side to quit the hopeless ground on which they had bogged down – the 'moratorium' – and go on the ideological attack.

Mr Heseltine launched into what was really a reprise of countless party conference triumphs. Labour backbenchers – who would have done better to sit back and giggle – began a serious attempt to barrack him.

This was when Michael Cartiss (C, Gt Yarmouth) sounded the bugle which began the rally which became the charge which, six hours later, was to pound into the division lobby, carrying the government to victory. Ironic that as Cartiss tried to rise, Richard Ryder, the chief whip, tugged furiously at his coat-tails to stop him.

But Cartiss would not be stopped. He had come to this debate, he told Heseltine, troubled about the pit closures. But '*these people*,' he shouted, the veins in his neck standing out with fury as he gestured at the Opposition, 'have ensured that *this man*' (he pointed at Heseltine) 'has my *total* support!'

Wisely, Michael Heseltine never returned to his text. The old warrior knows when to drop anchor. He brushed aside his speechnotes and, filling his sails with the wind of loyal Tory cheers, surfed past the sea-wall back into harbour. His first planned expedition had failed. His revised journey had had to be abandoned, and his whole strategy was now in ruins. But he was still afloat.

Westminster Wallies in Fool's Paradise

23.10.92

The duel between our political leaders is fast coming to resemble those early black and white movie comedies from the *Keystone Cops* era, in which combatants vie with each other for title of Biggest Fool. You remember the sort of thing: slapstick artist number one would advance on slapstick artist number two, raise his axe above his head, overbalance, and fall backwards; whereupon his intended victim would step forward to strike, step on the end of rake, and get whacked in the face.

With both prostrate, in comes joker number three to finish them off – and falls down an open manhole.

Yesterday at PM's Questions, John Smith fell down the manhole. Let me remind you of events leading up to this latest twist in our own saga of the *Westminster Wallies*.

Of Paddy Ashdown's exquisitely embarrassing whoopee-cushion, well before the election, let us not speak. Then came Mr Major's turn to get real egg on his face – after which Mr Kinnock devised his own high-tech custard pies at Sheffield and walked into them.

'Advantage,' we were about to say, 'John Smith.' Mr Smith unveiled his shadow budget and the bucket above the door dropped on his head.

Advantage Major – or so it seemed on 10 April. But the Danes let off a surprise stink bomb and President Mitterrand slipped on the soap. Bang went the ERM – an exploding cigar – leaving Mr Major with no eyebrows.

Advantage Smith. So now comes Mr Smith's big moment: his rallying speech at Blackpool. A total bummer. Then Ken Clarke fluffs his lines and Norman Lamont attempts to combine a double somersault with a tight fiscal stance, and splits his trousers. Heseltine laughs up his sleeve and arrives at Westminster, club and loin cloth at the ready. Through the trees he swings – 'Aah-ooh-aah-ooh-aah-ooh!' – and *wham* – misses his vine and whacks straight into a pit prop. Tories panic; advantage Labour . . .

And so to their leader's big moment at Prime Minister's Questions. Surveying the government front bench opposite him yesterday, John Smith must have come as close as any politician can to experiencing what a key striker in a football team must experience as he sizes up an open goal, or what a batsman must feel as a long hop bounces towards him. Total horror. The knowledge that *everyone* is expecting you to score. That's when you always miss the ball.

Someone must have told the Labour leader that, since Mr Major's style is wooden and his position awkward, a smirkingly smart-alecky little question from Smith would most discomfit him.

Well, maybe. But 'Given the daily changes in policy we all observed this week, what does he have in mind for his next U-turn?' just didn't pass muster.

To cries of 'bring back Kinnock', Smith tried to maintain a fixed grin, while the PM told him that his question fell 'a little below the level of events'.

Sadly, Mr Smith had a second unsuccessful joke up his sleeve. 'A policy a day keeps the backbenchers at bay,' quipped our droll Scottish advocate.

Laugh? We hadn't laughed so much since Bob Dunn (C, Dartford) unveiled, minutes earlier, the government's new weapon against 'travellers and ravers'.

'Unwashed benefit-grabbing socialist anarchists who deserve a good slap and a wash', he cried.

Quail, ravers! Faced with the prospect of being slapped and washed by Mr Dunn, which of us would not scamper home on the double to a mock-Tudor semi in Dartford?

Tories with Attitude

27.10.92

In America, militant groups like the self-styled NWAs and QWAs ('Niggers with Attitude' and 'Queers with Attitude') shake fists. Now, on British back benches, appears a variation – TWAs: 'Tories with Attitude'.

This breed, almost extinct, has revived. Fed by Euro-sceptical resentment and miners' anger but mostly by the slimness of the prime minister's majority, your Tory backbencher can smell fear as dogs can. He has seen the terror in the chief whip's eyes, noted the pits' reprieve, anticipated the Jubilee line rescue. He is emboldened.

Yesterday at transport questions, Tories with Attitude sprouted from every bench. Matthew Carrington (Fulham) wanted a new station on a new Tube line through Fulham. He did not actually *say*: 'You missa my constituency, I smasha your face,' but the implication was clear.

Taking note, a minister, Steven Norris, almost bowed. John Bowis (Battersea) wondered with menacing courtesy whether this line might extend under the Thames to Battersea. Before he could add 'or I'll send the boys round', Norris was on his feet to 'take your suggestion on board'.

By now other Tories were leaping up and down, no doubt with

new Tube lines and stations of their own to propose. Norris was fascinated by each suggestion.

As questions proceeded the prospect grew of a vast new Underground network in London, through which gleaming modern trains conveyed mollified electors to and from brand new Tube stations constructed in the constituencies of every London Tory with Attitude.

The handful of government backbenchers still willing to bowl soft balls at their ministers looked uneasy. Might they have sold at too low a price? Your sketchwriter remembers a time, under Mrs You-know-who, when a backbencher would return to his constituency at weekends to be asked what he had done to help the government. But today's TWAs are asked: 'What did you threaten to rebel on this week, Sir Bufton? Only the agriculture bill? And what have you brought back? Only a couple of hill-livestock premiums and a turnip subsidy? No new railway? No airport? No six-lane by-pass?'

Finally came Peter Brooke, the new heritage minister, with news of 'restoration of important national monuments', of which the return to office of Mr Brooke is a fine example. Asked about sites English Heritage might relinquish, he offered a hypothetical example in Wales, then, to heckles, quickly withdrew it.

'Does he know Wales isn't in England?' I asked a colleague, later. 'He does know,' replied my friend, 'much of the time. But short periods occur when he does not know.'

Stylish Dame of the Pantomime   *28.10.92*

In recent weeks, the presence behind Mr Major's shoulder at PM's Questions of Dame Jill Knight, redoubtable member for Edgbaston and cornerstone of the 1922 Committee, has lent an air of opera *bouffe* to proceedings. A retired actress and one-time star of the *Girls' Gang Show*, the dignity which in latter years has settled upon Dame Jill only adds to the diva quality so unmistakably hers. She is the Tory party's cuddly version of Kiri Te Kanawa, perhaps a shade larger and a little more mature.

And she dresses the part: never less than striking. Last week, in almost every TV picture of Mr Major in crisis, viewers saw a lady behind him robed in something which might have been designed for a Sabena air hostess in the futuristic fifties. It was Dame Jill.

PM's Questions yesterday were an important test for Mr Major. The Dame's outfit made that clear. To call it arresting would understate. It was inky black, setting off the violent colours of something more a mantle than a collar: a great plunging V described by two broad stripes, one within the other, the outer stripe turquoise, the inner one magenta. At the sharp end of the V hung a large medallion. The effect was of a cross between an Olympic swimmer and Dr Who.

On to the benches opposite strode Jimmy Hood MP (Lab, Clydesdale) dressed in a zoot-suit whose colour can only be compared with pinky-orange blancmange. Rather too old to be a gangster, Mr Hood looked too loud to be an MP. He and Dame Jill settled into their seats to watch.

It would have been hard for Mr Major and Mr Smith to live up to the backdrop or the moment. They didn't. Major must be judged the winner because he stayed cocky and upright when Smith ought to have been able to floor him.

We dare not advise Labour leaders what to ask, but we did rather think the question of the day was whether or not the PM deemed the coming Maastricht debate an issue of confidence. Major would not have answered, of course, but it might have been fun to *watch* him not answering.

Instead, we watched Mr Smith stage a minor volcanic eruption on the subject of the economy, to be answered by a minor tidal wave of facts and statistics from Mr Major. The commotion went on for some time, augmented by a small attempted earth-tremor from Paddy Ashdown. Eventually we were rescued by Roger Evans (C, Monmouth) who reminded MPs of the real threat to our nation: 'the curse of new age travellers'.

With infinite relief the Prime Minister turned to deal with this question, at some length. This gave Edwina Currie the time to get out her 'I [picture-of-heart] BASILDON' sticker, which (to Madam Speaker's distress) she held up for the cameras as Basildon's David Amess rose with a helpful enquiry about plummeting mortgage rates in Basildon. Then Labour's Kim Howells (Pontypridd) called Mark Thatcher a 'grease-palmer', a case of discourtesy mitigated by dyslexia.

. . . And normal pantomime service resumed. Dame Jill's medallion flashed in the television lights as Mr Hood inspected his pink suit for soup-stains. Madam Speaker gathered in her gown. Dr Spink (C, Castle Point) polished his big specs in preparation for his '10 minute rule bill' on pornography, and Mrs Mary Whitehouse (or was it Edna Everage?) watched, fascinated, from the special gallery.

Debate Murders English

3.11.92

Desperate times, they say, justify desperate measures: but MPs' use of language turns the old rule topsy-turvy. Famines, earthquakes and wars elicit from suave foreign office ministers the blandest of phrases: but bring the Commons back for social security questions on a drizzly Monday and all at once the language goes wild.

Mild men in glasses whose names nobody can remember wave their arms and speak of carnage, treachery and deeds of darkness down at the local benefit office. The more colourless the speaker, the more colourful his adjectives: the drabber the subject, the more violent the prose. At home, a delay in processing a welfare claim is an atrocity. Abroad, the slaughter of thousands is an unfortunate setback in the peace process.

'Too little, too late,' cried a little-known Opposition social security spokesman called Keith Bradley (Withington), to be upstaged within seconds by a Mr John McFall (Lab, Dumbarton) behind him. McFall painted for MPs a word picture in which 'loan sharks' cruised the tenements, removing from his despairing constituents a limb here, a three-piece suite there.

'When,' he intoned in a Gaelic cadence, rolling his rrrs dramatically as though declaiming Longfellow or Sir Walter Scott, 'will some shaft of sanity penetrate through all the years of foolish actions and botched thinking?' Mr McFall could with no discontinuity have rolled onward into:

> 'Come back! Come back!' he cried in grief,
> Across the stormy water,
> 'And I'll forgive your Highland chief,
> My daughter, oh my daughter!'

The subject under scrutiny was a review of the allocation of social fund money to local DSS offices.

Not to be outdone in the inter-regional hyperbole eisteddfod, Merseyside's Robert Wareing (Lab, Liverpool West Derby), chimed in with an impromptu passage about the Cabinet 'sacrificing the aged and the disabled on the altar of their own incompetence'.

As the minister stammered out his reply, Dennis Wheatley-like images of butchery and pagan sacrifice, severed limbs, broken walking-sticks, smashed zimmer frames, mangled wheelchairs and the pitiful bleatings of the elderly wheeled through the caverns of our minds, mingling with the cackles of Tory ministers swinging bloody axes in druidical robes.

The question was about the maintenance of the real value of social security benefits during the next upgrading.

And now rises Labour's Donald Dewar, who sneers at Peter Lilley for his anonymity and offers advice on how to stay as unknown as he is.

Lilley hits back. 'Talk about anonymity comes a bit rich from the hon gentleman, whose only claim to fame is that he is less well known than I am.' Dewar seethes. Madam Speaker consults her books of photographs, lest she forget . . .

And we, readers, must leave them. Outside it is drizzling. Within, the lights are bright, tempers hot and the prose blazing. As MPs move, firing on all metaphors, to a discussion on 'amending the income support regulations to extend entitlement to the severe disability premium to claimants living with non-dependants' (question 9), the parliamentary clerks sit snoozing, the English language lies bleeding, and we tiptoe quietly away.

4.11.92 # Major's Cattle Crush the Insects

A crucial EC vote looms. . . .

'Because,' remarked Edmund Burke, 'half a dozen grasshoppers under a fern make the field ring with their importunate chink, whilst thousands of great cattle, reposed beneath the shadow of the British oak, chew the cud and are silent, pray do not imagine that those who make the noise are the only inhabitants of the field or that, of course, they are many in number; or that, after all, they are other than the little, shrivelled, meagre, hopping, though loud and troublesome, *insects* of the hour.'

Yesterday in parliament, with tonight's moment of truth drawing closer and Euro-sceptical grasshoppers chinking ever louder in the press, the great cattle of the Tory backbenches judged it timely to moo.

James Hill (C, Southampton Test, approx 15 stone) has been chewing the cud down in Hampshire over the weekend. He is increasingly irritated by the grasshoppers. He hasn't, you understand, committed the whole Maastricht treaty thing to memory – suspects, indeed, that bits of it are pretty rum (hasn't the PM said as much himself, dammit?) – but he does know a bit about Europe, which is more than some of these young whippersnappers calling themselves the '92 group seem to. Hill is part of the '68 group. On the threshold of his second quarter century in parliament, he is described in Roth's *Parliamentary Profiles* as 'broad, thickset, genial, specs . . . rooted, pragmatic, commonsensical, local gut-rightwinger; well-heeled pigbreeder and ex-pilot'. A chap who crewed flying boats for BOAC ('47–'58, with three years in Aden Airways) knows a thing or two about loyalty to your mates in a tight spot.

James Hill attends assiduously but does not speak too often – not one of your twitterers about every damn thing. Yesterday, however, with the order paper showing his name attached to question number two to the PM, was a time for helping a chief in trouble.

If his broad, thickset, genial, local gut-rightwing, well-heeled, pigbreeding instincts had not told Mr Hill as much already, the whips would have, several times: and then reminded him again after lunch. And, if Mr Hill had not already seen in Monday's *Times* a letter from top industrialists stressing the importance of Maastricht to British industry (and pigbreeding?) then the whips would have drawn that, too, to his attention. 'You might,' they would have added (in the respectful way you do to a broad, thickset person) 'care to draw the House's attention to that letter, James.'

But Mr Hill doesn't need whips to tell him that. The importunate chink of the grasshoppers all around him does. At 3.18 pm he rose, slowly, testily but with immense dignity, as might any great beast of the field, disturbed by insects. His moment had arrived. The Prime Minister was agog.

Hill lumbered through the letters page of Monday's *Times*,

summarizing the gist, which was that Europe was good for industry, and that it is (he mooed) 'absolutely *essential* that we ratify M . . . Mm . . .'

Here occurred a tiny but electrifying moment's hesitation. Would Mr Hill get stuck on the Mm of Maastricht? Might 'Mmmm . . . you know what' have to suffice? No. Whips wiped their brows as Hill finished the word successfully.

From all around him came a lowing of supportive moos, as other great beasts raised their heads approvingly. The grasshoppers were momentarily silent.

The Words None Dare Utter

5.11.92

He called it a point of order. He rose, all 19 stone of him, from his customary seat on the government back benches. His great frame shuddered as he drew breath, shirt rucked violently along a belt-line which bore all the marks of a zone of intense struggle. His suit looked utterly defeated. His big, wide face was wet with perspiration. A handkerchief hung damply from his top pocket, a small white speck upon the whole picture, dwarfed by the perspective.

The great man was ready to speak. This was more than a member of Parliament: this was a phenomenon.

'Mr Geoffrey *Dickens*!' called Madam Speaker. 'Oh!' called 400 MPs.

'*Madam!*' bellowed the phenomenon. His shoulders heaved, rising and falling like a ship upon the swell of giggles, whispers and murmurs that greeted him from all corners of the chamber . . .

'Madam: I, like many members, am having difficulty knowing what today's debate is all about.'

Not for the first time, and not (we are confident) for the last, the member for Littleborough and Saddleworth, colossus of the Pennines, scourge of paedophiles, aficionado of the rope and hammer of the practitioners of witchcraft, articulated what none other dared say. Geoffrey K Dickens spoke for the nation.

The Best Class of Insult

6.11.92

The government had, the previous night, won a crucial motion on the Maastricht bill. . . .

John Major entered the Chamber yesterday during an exchange with agriculture ministers on the subject of illness among bees. Junior minister David Curry was lending his usual passion to a statement extending the *cordon sanitaire* around infected hives, but was probably surprised by the immense roar that greeted his determination to hold the varroa mite back at the banks of the Humber. The arriving PM, for his part, glanced with mild curiosity at Curry waving his arms and holding forth excitedly about sick bees.

The House forgot bees, and began raking over the coals of the previous night's dispute. Up jumped John Smith. 'In the midst of all our present miseries,' he began. Considering the defeat he had suffered, it was not the wisest start. He was engulfed by mocking Tory laughter before he could pin those miseries, as he had hoped, on the Prime Minister.

Smith tried again. 'In the midst of, er, this situation . . .' The laughter recommenced. There were some jovial shouts of 'resign' and assorted hand and finger gestures of the kind that pass as the small change of human pleasantry at Westminster. Where, in other places, one might call out 'good morning', 'nice weather we're having' or 'how's the wife?', in parliament you shout 'resign' or 'traitor' conversationally across the Chamber, or jerk your thumb down in a good-humoured motion. Should you seek a more substantial exchange of courtesies, you might (as, in recent memory, Labour's Tony Banks did to the Tories' Terry Dicks) compare your fellow parliamentarian with an inflated pig's bladder on a stick.

They love each other dearly, do MPs.

Teddy Boy Boris Shines

11.11.92

Have you ever organized a social morning at an old folk's home when a Special Visitor is to call (and perhaps show slides) and residents gather in the lounge? If so you will have recognized the mood in the Royal Gallery in the Lords yesterday. The Special Visitor was the Russian President, Boris Yeltsin, but he did not bring slides.

Peers were in excited mood. Theoretically, the occasion was for both the Lords and the Commons and equal seating had at first been set aside: but a few rows of seats were enough for the handful of MPs who turned up and the rest were filled by peers. Age brings an appetite for pomp and circumstance, and besides, they have time on their hands.

The Royal Gallery is Victoriana at its most absurd: neo-Gothic excess and fevered braggadocio: on opposite walls hang two vast oil paintings, one of victory at Trafalgar, the other Waterloo. Apparently, when President Pompidou visited, the French embassy insisted these be draped in muslin.

Headphones had been placed on each seat. Bewildered peers fiddled with these until a voice over the loudspeakers said: 'You will find a listening device on your seat. There is an On button which you switch on. It cannot be switched off. English is on channel 1, Russian on channel 2.'

It was nearly 11 am. We had been waiting since shortly after 10 am. 'Make way for Madam Speaker!' shouted a flunkey. Peers struggled to their feet, getting tangled in their listening devices, as guards in brass helmets stood to attention. Betty Boothroyd, knocking 'em cold in black and gold, tore down the aisle, pursued by footmen. 'Gosh, what a pace!' whispered a nearby peer, enviously, to his chum.

'Make way for the Lord Chancellor!' came the shout. Lord Mackay careered past in a cloud of brocade, moments later. Like buses, people in garters don't come for hours, then they all come at once. Then Dame Janet Fookes bustled down the aisle, in violent purple. Dame Janet doesn't need ceremonial dress for these occasions: her everyday clothes are sufficiently remarkable.

Now came a brass fanfare, followed by the unfortunately timed trumpeting of a peer upon his handkerchief. And in strode Boris Yeltsin, his white hair swept back in an impeccable quiff. He looked like a Teddy boy dad at parents' day. The President stood between Lord Mackay and Madam Speaker: the two in identical gold lace and black silk outfits: a glorified version of those matching his 'n hers carcoats you can order from Sunday magazines.

The President, Russia's answer to John Prescott, struck me as a powerful orator. His speech, which was in substance routine, was full of light and shade and gentle humour, and a bold oratorical use of silences.

True, something of a shudder ran down our backs at a passage which twice repeated the phrase 'there is no alternative!' – the *niets* ringing out with Thatcherian vigour. Was he – heaven forbid – turning into . . . ? '*Da!*' he cried – 'Yes! We have made mistakes . . .' The audience relaxed. No, he was not.

Irish Fog Befuddles Martian

12.11.92

If a Martian were to have wandered into the Strangers' Gallery for yesterday's statement on the postponement of talks in Northern Ireland, he would have been utterly baffled.

Fluency in English would have been no use. A detailed biography of every member speaking would have shed no light. Even a careful reading of Irish history would not have unlocked for him the meaning of the exchanges. The whole thing was completely Irish.

Sir Patrick Mayhew, the Northern Ireland secretary, read a long and painstaking statement. He spoke of 'Strands' – the word appearing first as 'strand', then as 'Strand'. He never explained what a strand was but, whatever it was, there were at least three of them, perhaps more.

Our Martian friend, having drawn a blank on the detail, might have said to himself: 'Well, regardless of exactly what it was Sir Patrick was aiming for, *is he succeeding*? Have the talks got anywhere?'

But again the Martian is confounded. 'We have not yet succeeded in the ambitious task of securing an overall settlement,' Mayhew said. Ah: failure. But perhaps they got part of the way? 'Nothing will be finally agreed in any strand until everything is agreed in the Talks as a whole . . . so the question of partial settlement did not arise.'

So no progress? 'Nonetheless, the Talks have seen substantive and detailed engagement on issues of the first importance.' Ah. Hopeful signs, then? 'Madam Speaker, the whole House, although doubtless disappointed . . .' Oh.

And then, finally: 'We have a duty not to lose patience with what is a deeply historic problem, not to give way to exasperation, not to recriminate.'

This was the signal for the recriminations to begin. As Labour's spokesman Kevin McNamara spoke of the Anglo-Irish agreement there were cries of 'Shame! Disgraceful!' from the Ulster Unionists. Our Martian began to get a sense of ill-feeling, or impasse . . .

Until up jumped Jim Molyneaux, leader of the Ulster Unionists. 'We have moved forward,' he said. 'Six months in the history of Ireland is but an evening gone,' Patrick Mayhew added, cheerily. Whereupon Ian Paisley rose.

Dr Paisley always sits beside Peter Robinson (Belfast E). Between them they made up two-thirds of his Democratic Unionist party. Paisley is a big, booming, beefy man, often apoplectic. Robinson is a thin, pale fellow in glasses, with an expressionless stare and a strangely limp look.

It has been rumoured that Paisley is a ventriloquist and Robinson his dummy, and it is easy to imagine that if Paisley moved away, Robinson might flop on to the bench into a heap of lifeless rubber. But my own theory is that this is an elaborate double blind, and that it is Robinson who is the ventriloquist. I could not see his right arm yesterday, but his thin lips seemed to be twitching as Paisley bellowed, and I fancied that one tweak from those hidden, bony fingers and Paisley's whole great body would jerk into action, railing and gesticulating against Popish plots.

Robinson and Paisley gave our Martian a strong impression that all was not well. 'Illegal, immoral, criminal' was Paisley's description of the Irish position; then Ken Maginnis (UUP) said it was not the time for recrimination and went on to accuse the Labour party of 'contradictory gobbledegook' and the Irish of a lack of goodwill. Heaven help us when the time for recrimination comes.

At this point, an Englishman blundered in. Barry Porter (C.

Wirral S), his eyes unaccustomed to the Celtic fog, wondered if 'failure' was the word for what had happened. This seemed to unite Irishmen of all persuasions. Heads shook pityingly. Poor fellow: how little he understood.

Sir Patrick gave a tolerant smile and declined to engage with such language. Parties to these talks call each other illegal, immoral and criminal. One participant might find another utterly devoid of goodwill. Indeed, the talks might have broken down. But never speak of failure! And never, never speak of success.

Onward they go as evening falls, waving their arms and their adjectives. One by one the English MPs had slid from the Chamber. So has our Martian. Mars is a long way from Ireland, but not as far as England.

Mr Brown's Bullets

13.11.92

Shadow Chancellor Gordon Brown replies to Norman Lamont's Autumn Statement. . . .

In vain did Gordon Brown spray the Chancellor's getaway car with a hail of bullets. These bullets you can see among the paragraphs which follow. In Fleet Street a 'bullet' is one of these: •. Many years ago Mr Brown abandoned ordinary English prose and began to speak entirely in lists prefaced by bullets. His speech yesterday was composed of fourteen lists, strung together with angry conjunctions.

He said that Mr Lamont had caused:
* unemployment to rise
* the deficit to worsen
* greater poverty
* cuts in the aid budget
* more bankruptcies.

Britain was, furthermore, bottom of the EC league in:
* growth
* investment
* output

- employment.
  Yet he had promised he would:
- stay in the ERM
- not devalue
- get unemployment down
- bring recovery.
  Now he planned to:
- break up training schemes
- tear up promises
- scapegoat home-helps.
  This would:
- add to unemployment
- prolong the recession
- damage productivity
- hit the poor and weak.

At one point Mr Brown fumbled in his pocket and we began to fear he would bring out a crumpled list and declaim:

- bread
- tea-bags
- 1lb tomatoes . . .

But no. He stuck to the economy. It was a tragedy, he said. Millions faced:

- cuts
- joblessness
- starvation.

. . . Pencil poised, I waited to continue:

- impetigo
- beri-beri
- rickets . . .

But he omitted these, predicting:

- tragedy
- disaster
- catastrophe
  . . . and sat down.

The Fearsome Road to Bettygate   *17.11.92*

If you want a reliable sign that a once-fashionable word or phrase
has been flogged to extinction and entered the *Dictionary of Cliché*,
then watch for the moment when MPs start using it. That is when
you know it has died. MPs are always the last to catch on to a chic
new quip, so by the time they do, you can be sure it isn't.

'Blood on the carpet', 'too little, too late', 'hearts and
minds' . . . the Commons is a sort of elephants' graveyard of ghastly
discarded phrases. They get their trendy metaphor, you see, from
TV commentators who (not known for valour) never venture a
smart new buzz-phrase until lots of other people have used it first.
The store where MPs shop for their prose sells only phrases already
clapped-out.

If books were cupboards and their contents the metaphors
crowding their pages, then *Hansard* would be a nursery wardrobe
piled high with broken children's toys. 'Massive cuts', 'beacons of
excellence', 'loony lefties', 'the dead hand of socialism' . . . what are
they but lifeless rag dolls and soiled, eyeless teddy bears beloved of
tired old politicians with nothing to say, tumbling from the pages of
every debate.

Yesterday they bowled out the latest weary retread. 'Gate'.
Watergate, Irangate, Dianagate, Fergiegate, Jennifer's-eargate
. . . already you yawn? You guess what's coming: Iraqgate. If we had
Iraqgate once yesterday, we had it a dozen times.

Various hecklers tried to introduce Iraqgate into Welsh questions
but without success, as Madam Speaker was in a fearsome mood.
Miss Boothroyd achieved what is (in my recollection) a parliamentary
record: she threw out three questions in a row, aborting each one
before the poor MP could finish. '*No!*' she shouted at Allan Rogers
(Lab, Rhondda) half way through his routine hi-jack of an answer
about railways in North Wales, which he bundled aboard his
question about railways in South Wales. Other Speakers would have
been grateful that we were still on the railways and still in Wales, but
not Betty: 'No! I know my Wales! Rephrase that!' Rogers couldn't,
and sat down, shocked.

'*No!*' she shouted at John Marek (Lab, Wrexham) who tried to
take us from the Welsh railways to the ministers who were

responsible for them, yet had received no election mandate from Wales, and ought to resign, and . . . 'Sit down, I'm on my feet. That was by *no* means a parliamentary question.' Faceless officials cut off Dr Marek's microphone and he retired, speechless, mouth open.

No! she shouted at front bench Labour spokesman (no less!) Rhodri Morgan, who tried to nudge the next question (about the Neath and Port Talbot Hospital – Neathgate) gently in the direction of corrupt Tory appointments, placement on health boards, Freemasonry, 'and, if I roll up one trouser leg Madam Speaker . . .'

'No! *Not* a question. This is about *hospitals*.' Morgan, the third Welsh casualty in as many minutes, keeled over, mute. Perhaps Miss Boothroyd had spent an exceptionally wet weekend in Wales and was taking her revenge.

Finally, provoked by a backbencher trying to tell her what she might have heard on the radio, she stood up. '*Sit* down. I've been *much* too occupied over the weekend to listen to the radio!'

Oh? And how, pray? Do we have . . . I can feel it coming on . . . Bettygate?

They Call It Education

18.11.92

'We're on the up and up and we're rolling!' declared junior education minister Eric Forth to the Commons, yesterday.

Not since *Three Men in a Boat* has there been as hilarious a trio as the government's education front-bench team. None of them would be allowed near a school sports day, let alone a classroom. On parade for Tuesday's questions, they made as unlikely an advertisement for Tory education policy as it would be possible to imagine.

In his personal political philosophy. Eric Forth belongs to the Libertarian-Thug tendency. He may well not believe in schools at all, preferring a Rousseau-esque state of nature in which mothers band together to tutor their offspring as baboons do their young. Yesterday Mr Forth arrived looking like a middle-aged swinger togged up for a country and western reunion. Single-breasted suit with waistcoat was set off by a royal blue shirt with white collar and a floral tie, and decorated by a blue silk handkerchief and a double-looped gold chain from which dangled a gold bauble as big as a conker.

Beside him sat the newest ministerial recruit, Nigel Forman, in a dark suit, jacket slightly too tight, white shirt and thin grey-green tie. With worried forehead and dark, receding hair, he looked like a typewriter mechanic.

'Choice and diversity,' cried John Patten to Labour questioners, himself an exotic choice for education secretary. With his Beau Brummel bearing and bouffant hair Mr Patten resembles the kind of men Princess Margaret used to go out with in the early sixties, but the Queen would never let her marry.

Rent-a-Rants

25.11.92

'There are people whose position in life is that of the interjection, without influence on the sentence.' – Kierkegaard.

As interjections go, Nicholas Winterton (C, Macclesfield) is an Oh!, a 'Go to hell!', or an 'Aaargh!' This Mr Angry of the Tory back benches is able, from a standing start, to go puce in the face, instantly, on any subject you care to mention. In a panel game in which contestants are required to lose their temper for 60 seconds (without hesitation, repetition or deviation) on quite random topics, Winterton's success could be guaranteed. Only one other Tory MP can do this.

To him we shall return. But first to Winterton: he sprang up during defence questions and stood like a human exclamation mark, daring Madam Speaker not to call him. She did.

His own regiment was to disappear in a merger! 'The Fourteenth Twentieth King's Hussars,' he declared, reddening already, 'are to be merged with the Royal Hussars, to become the King's Royal Hussars!' Fair enough, we thought . . . 'The *supreme* cavalry regiment!' he yelled. We were disinclined to quarrel.

'Are you prepared to give an *assurance*' (he was glaring at Malcolm Rifkind, the Secretary of State) 'that the new regiment will be able to have a *regimental band*?' He turned to include the whole

House in his glare. 'A regiment feels the loss of a band!' Losing a band, he roared, risked losing medical cover 'because, as many in this House know, bands double up as medics'.

Images of tuba players scattering their musical scores to the winds as they rushed to administer the kiss of life tumbled through our minds as Winterton bellowed.

Having reached the required shade of puce, he sat down suddenly. Mr Rifkind tried to calm him, remarking that he was fully conscious of all this.

The next question was about amphibious helicopter carriers and not nearly so interesting to MPs, as you knew where you were with a brass band.

You know where you are with David Evans (C, Welwyn, Hatfield). If, in the apoplexy stakes, Winterton holds the Tory backbench crown, Evans represents his main challenger. Their styles are different. A Winterton rant is a small but perfect dramatic performance: it builds to its climax and has an internal logic. An Evans outburst is a sudden, unprompted burst of sound, a sort of primeval scream. In no sense is it an argument but on sheer decibels it wins hands-down.

I *think* Mr Evans's subject at PM's Questions was immigration. At a volume and in accents which render Alf Garnett effete, and gesturing violently at the Opposition benches, Evans could be heard from as far away as Karachi shouting '. . . *We* know that lot! *They* couldn't care less. Seven hundred, seven thousand, *seventy* thousand! Let them all in – that's what *they* say!'

Answer that.

27.11.92 ## Taxing Questions About Monarchy

Maastricht? Forget it. Gatt? *Quel ennui.* Council tax? Spare us. Suddenly, even Norman Lamont was yesterday's news: demands for a Commons statement on his Access statement blew out almost before they began. From the tearoom to the Chamber itself, only one topic held MPs transfixed: the fire at Windsor – 'Who pays?' – and now proposals for Her Majesty to contribute to Treasury coffers.

Is the cynicism of the government's news managers bottomless? To take the heat off Norman, Douglas, Michael and John, they had turned the heat on Elizabeth. Who started that fire? Where were the whips?

Nothing gives Tories greater pleasure than calling Labour republicans. Nothing pleases Labour more than calling Tories palace poodles.

Picture, then, the Chamber yesterday, as John Smith rose for his bi-weekly challenge to John Major. What subject would he choose? The asylum bill, the council tax bills or the Access bill? Edinburgh, Peking or Paddington?

Mr Smith seemed unusually eager to bowl. Mr Major looked unusually confident as he strode to the crease. MPs pinned back their ears for the usual high-decibel mutual misunderstanding. But Smith sounded thoughtful.

'In view of the evident public concern, could the PM tell the House if he has had discussions with Her Majesty the Queen on the subject of taxation and the Civil List payments?'

Behind him, Labour MPs pricked up their ears. At last! Their John was getting stuck into the royal fat-cats. Tories groaned. Impertinent Leftie! *Their* John would soon sort him out.

But Mr Major only smiled. Odd, but he seemed to be expecting the question. Instead of a 'keep your thieving socialist hands off our lovely Queen' sort of reply, the PM pirouetted through a gracious little tribute to the royal family, and then read a detailed and helpful account of the very thing Mr Smith had requested.

At this point, clever Tories realized that the thing was rigged. Smith was on-side. His question had been planted. Their PM had just achieved the highest-altitude plant in hostile terrain that anyone could remember. Unclever Tories jeered at Smith, shouting things like 'Gotcha!' No doubt (they thought) he would now withdraw in confusion.

He did no such thing. 'The whole House,' he said, 'will welcome the fact that consideration of these questions has been initiated.' Then he asked about the timing, and likely content, of the proposals. Major turned to page two of his script.

The Labour benches had by now fallen quite silent, but I have to report that dimmer Tories had still not clicked. Shouts of 'Woo-err', 'Boring!' and 'We don't *know* yet, stoopid' greeted him. Someone giggled. Their John would now tell Smith to mind his own business.

Their John said nothing of the kind. He answered both questions, quite fully.

Both groupings of political groundlings were now quite winded. Labour were dumbfounded that their man had asked what they wanted him to, but hadn't thought he would, and the PM had come back with what they thought he wouldn't. The Tories were dumbfounded that the Labour chappie had demanded what they didn't think he ought to, and their man had given him what they hadn't thought he would.

Both sides were reassessing their position. In the silence which followed, the first fledgling cheep of the next stage of the argument was heard. It was Skinner. 'It's a fix!' he growled.

Molluscs Toast a Cockleshell Hero

4.12.92

Parliament yesterday proved a lucky dip of the exotic, the hilarious, the intriguing, and quite a lot of sawdust.

There is no time to tell you about the statement entitled 'Flooding: Wales' to which English MPs hurried, interested to find out how long it would take to flood Wales. Nor have we room to examine the proposals of the President of the Board of Trade for a 'one-stop shop'. With Heseltine at the check-out counter, MPs were examining their change.

And we must move fast through agriculture questions, starting with question 1, about fraudulent farmers. Why was a Portsmouth MP asking about this? The last time we noticed David Martin (C, Portsmouth South) was when he became upset about homosexuality in Her Majesty's forces. Having transferred his interest to agriculture, he was yesterday spared the Opposition cries of 'Give us a kiss' and 'Hello, sailor'.

Our perplexity deepened as the rich Welsh tones of Gareth Wardell (Lab, Gower) called us to question 2, about 'processing bivalve molluses'. An unilluminating ministerial reply had Wardell back on his feet crying in the accent, and with all the passion, of a chapel preacher that 'there is no way, Madam Speaker, that the

cockle-gatherers of Pengower' who had been 'cockle-gathering since
the Middle Ages' could cope with new rules. Added, now, to Jones-
the-milk and Di-the-post, Gareth-the-cockle will be the toast of
bivalve molluscs all along the Gower peninsula.

Brows still furrowed, we pinned back our ears for a lament from
Anthony Steen (C, South Hams). The question was about
agricultural set-aside (a scheme whereby farmers are paid not to
farm). Steen's complaint was that there were now so many golf
courses in his constituency that ramblers were in more danger from
flying golf balls than from bullets on the military training ground on
Dartmoor.

Laughter had barely subsided when the enormous Nicholas
Soames – gourmet, food minister and butter mountain – rose to
agree with a back-bench colleague that planners were often too
obstructive. 'The countryside cannot be preserved in aspic,' roared
Soames. 'If it could, you'd eat it,' shouted a Labour wag, to general
merriment.

Merriment increased when Blackpool's Nick Hawkins, a young
Tory who has taken his town's commercial instincts to heart,
confessed to 'my concern for the large mushroom growers of the
North West', and asked ministers 'to join me in congratulating Pixie
House Mushrooms' who had just won a business award . . . Hawkins
paused . . . 'sponsored by First Leisure plc'.

'After that short break,' began the Secretary of State, John
Gummer, in reply.

All good stuff. But did the question on fisheries have to follow one
from Peter Pike (Lab, Burnley)? And, only when the minister, David
Curry, had painted a mouth-watering North Sea picture of 'all those
haddock out there' and declared to the nation's fishermen that 'if we
find there is as much as one fish left, we will authorize them to catch
it,' did Madam Speaker have to call out, barely suppressing a giggle:
'Mr Salmon!' Alex Salmond (SNP, Banff and Buchan) rose, with all
hope of his question receiving serious notice already lost.

When Madam Speaker addressed Iain Sproat (C, Harwich) as 'Mr
Sprout', some of us felt that the comic possibilities of food, farming
and fisheries questions had been all but – well, milked.

Domestic Drama Upstairs

10.12.92

The Prince and Princess of Wales are to separate. . . .

Few of us with distressing family news to impart can expect such grand messengers as yesterday conveyed the royal news, indirectly, to the nation. Where other couples might pay for a small insert in the Personal classified section of the local paper, this couple had the PM nip down to the Commons with the news, and the Lord Chancellor drop into the House of Lords to let peers know.

Your sketchwriter watched from the Press Gallery in the Upper Chamber as their lordships crowded in and jostled round the throne to hear the penny drop. Bishops hovered anxiously. The air was rent with the sort of high-pitched electronic whistle that sends dogs mad, as a variety of hearing aids, turned to maximum volume, were pressed against a variety of noble ears. Lord Mackay of Clashfern rose to tell us what we had already guessed.

It cannot be said that peers liked it. There was a very faint gasp as the Lord Chancellor said that the separation did not affect the possibility that the royal couple might be king and queen. When he said that they were now entitled to a little privacy, there was a gentle moo of sympathy, for their lordships do not like the *Sun* at all. However, when he quoted the PM's expression of support and sympathy, there was absolute silence: not a hear-hear to be heard. Almost audible was the thought among them that *many* of one's friends don't get on – indeed Lord and Lady Thistledown have been barely on speaking terms and living in separate wings of Thistledown House at Thistledown Magna for as long as one can remember, but nobody has ever felt the need for a public statement.

This sort of thing is not good for the monarchy. And what is the monarchy but the foundation stone of the extensive and rambling structure we call the aristocracy and of which some of those assembled in the Chamber are crumbling outer battlements, isolated towers, lonely hunting lodges or amusing follies? Touch the monarch, peers thought, and the whole structure trembles. Hearing aids were pressed a little more anxiously to grizzled ears.

Nobody really wanted to say anything. For Labour, its new Leader in the Lords, Ivor Richard, mumbled about 'regret and sadness' and snarled something about 'the tabloids' ('hear, hear!') and sat down. For the Liberal Democrats, Lord Jenkins of Hillhead rose and said that he was not going to say anything, but said it in a very grave and noble way, and sat down.

From the absent Archbishop of Canterbury in Kuala Lumpur came a message delivered by the Archbishop of York. Dr Habgood rose and for three or four minutes gently buried himself and his presumed intellect in a blizzard of confused abstract nouns. 'Sharing . . . sorrow . . . unique and stressful . . . expectations . . . implications . . . compassion . . . pain . . . the lesser evil . . . comfort . . . strength . . . way forward . . .' – a soft, remorseless snowfall, burying sense.

A Tale of Two Presidents

21.1.93

On the day Bill Clinton is sworn in. . . .

The President sat yesterday, head bowed in silent prayer. His responsibilities were awesome, his mission immense. Before him lay an ocean of difficulty, for upon the high office he had inherited depended the lives and livelihoods of millions of his countrymen. And all around him sat enemies, rivals waiting for him to stumble, critics ready to seize upon the slightest slip.

The prayers passed so quickly. All too soon came the agony of decision. The ceremony over, his great task began . . .

'Is my Right Hon friend aware that my local council, the Kirklees metropolitan council, are extending a smokeless zone to rural areas of my constituency, thus further reducing the demand for domestic coal?'

Michael Heseltine's brow furrowed. The remit of the President of the Board of Trade is impossibly wide. How could he be expected to deliver a judgement on every footling regulation enacted by every footling town hall in the country? He muttered something politely vacuous to his questioner, a gawky youth of an MP, Graham Riddick (C, Colne Valley) took an irritable but half-hearted swipe at environmentalists in general, and sat down.

It was teatime in England, almost noon in Washington. Momentarily the President ceased to listen to parliamentary proceedings. Could he hear, ringing however faintly in his ears, the sound of a very different prayer ceremony, in a very different capital, for a very different President?

'. . . And will he make a statement concerning the work of the industrial competitiveness division?'

Bother. This one was for him. Some little squit of a Tory back-bencher wanted to know about some obscure branch of his ghastly concrete blockful of civil servants in Victoria Street. Wearily the President rose. 'I attach the greatest importance to the work of the industrial competitiveness division of my department.' Mr Heseltine sat down again.

He shut his eyes to the green leather benches around him. Could he see, however dimly, the balloons, the bright costumes of the massed choirs, the drum majorettes . . . ? *Major*-ettes! Aaargh! And were those the brass buckles of marching bands glinting in the New World winter sunshine – or just the mace glinting in the fluorescent Commons lighting? The mace! The mace he had so impetuously grabbed all those years ago, first in a small but fatal series of follies that had brought him to this.

He blinked and was back at that other ritual. There stood the President, and beside him a smiling blonde lady . . . *Blonde* lady? *Aargh!* With a start he was back on the front bench. Someone was asking him a question. '. . . And when he expects to announce the conclusions of his review of energy policy?'

Drat. Another Tory toad. Fumble through civil servants' briefing notes. Shouts of 'get on with it Hezza!' from socialist morons opposite. Stumble to feet . . .

'. . . And it is critically important that all aspects of the energy policy are taken into account in our review,' intoned the President. *Intoned.* Ah – 'I do solemnly swear that I will faithfully execute the Office of President of . . .' The Board of Trade. Wednesday 20 January 1993. London and Washington. A tale of two cities. A tale of two Presidents.

Kelvin MacKenzie Ate My Committee

22.1.93

You guys must be nuts! MPs blinked. This was a select committee, dammit! They were not used to being spoken to like this by a witness. Kelvin MacKenzie, editor of the *Sun*, was offering MPs his opinion of them amid the baroque splendour of their committee room 15.

MacKenzie had been summoned to assist the national heritage committee's enquiry into press intrusion. Possibly they expected a tabloid editor to be bowed, apologetic. They had been planning what MPs call a 'grilling'. There was a grilling: MacKenzie grilled the MPs. He treated them to a display of insouciance, impertinence, jokey camaraderie and contempt.

Striding in, flanked by two aides (one shaking visibly) the editor of the *Sun* turned to the doorkeeper: 'Can I say what a pleasure this is?' He grinned to the surprised policeman. It set the tone.

MPs picture tabloid editors in one of two forms: either tattooed and crew-cut with bovver boots, or sharp-suited and blow-dried with medallions. But before them, hunched and brooding, sat a big fellow who looked like a clever boxing manager, soberly dressed; by turns bored, thoughtful or belligerently frank.

'Go right ahead,' he barked at a surprised chairman, Gerald Kaufman, who had presumably intended to. 'We have no views on anything,' said Kaufman, assuring us of his open mind. 'I don't believe that,' said MacKenzie.

Winded, Kaufman wobbled into a question about Camilla Parker Bowles whom (it seems) MPs include among the 'ordinary people' they seek to protect. On these criteria, MPs too may be ordinary people.

'Of course you gentlemen could just troop down to the Strand and pick up a huge amount of tax-free wonga from the libel courts,' MacKenzie sneered.

Most were unsure how to react. Columnist Joe Ashton (Lab) had questioned *Sun* coverage of a man's confusing superglue with haemorrhoid cream. 'John's gone potty and glued up his botty,' cackled the editor, recalling his own headline. To Ashton he began: 'After many years of taking the tabloid shilling yourself, Joe . . .' Ashton smiled.

Others looked dazed. The committee failed to press its advantage, for MacKenzie was careless, murmuring in bored tones: 'We only write the truth, now.'

Nobody enquired when it was that his paper had adopted this pratice, or what had been his previous habit. It was a curious session. MPs grinned when their witness referred to 'Lindi St Clair, a woman known – or not known – to some of you'. She kept a list, he said, staring into space. 'There are some extraordinary names in there.' Just his little joke. 'Everybody's having a good time,' said Mr Kaufman. In a way they were.

At the end of *Animal Farm*, Orwell describes a scene in which the pigs and the humans, sworn enemies, begin to drink and play cards together. A similar impression grew on this sketchwriter. In committee room 15 sat two opposed estates: rival careers but with something in common.

In different ways both of them were in the business of playing to the gallery of the masses. And both were in the habit of aiming low. The tabloids do it better, that's all. That's why MPs are angry. They're jealous.

'If we knew as much about the editors of tabloids,' John Gorst asked Kelvin MacKenzie, 'as you do about us, would *we* have the same low opinion of *you*?'

'Probably,' said the editor.

Cheerful Chappie in Parliamentary Pantomine

26.1.93

It seemed somehow fitting that the first two Tory backbenchers to speak in support of the national lottery bill were Kenneth Baker and David Mellor. Something in the demeanour of both has long proclaimed 'Roll up! Roll up! Wonderful prizes!'

And some instinct in us has demanded we check that the tickets were not forgeries and the prizes were real.

Mr Baker's great delight, he told MPs yesterday – his whole aim in life, we gathered – 'the cause of cheering us all up'. Cheering us up!

He grinned. Mr Baker does not have (as peacocks have) a many-splendoured tail, nor does he have painted wings (as butterflies have) to spread in the sun.

But he has a way of pausing during a speech, holding himself still and beaming gently, which suggests that were he a peacock this would be the moment for the tail to quiver while we marvelled; and were he a butterfly this would be the time to pause upon some honeysuckle blossom and fold and unfold his wings in the sunshine while his little feelers waved. One looked back on Mr Baker's record as education secretary, home secretary, environment secretary, industry minister, campaign manager, Chancellor of the Duchy of Lancaster and Conservative party chairman, and remembered the troubled history of his areas of responsibility, the self-destruct tendency of so many of his intriguing initiatives. There were the prison riots, the national core curriculum and 'Baker days' at school. There was the poll tax, the infotech revolution, the CTCs, the Dangerous Dogs Act . . .

And suddenly one grasped the key to this puzzling charade of a life. *It was all a joke!* Mr Baker's whole career has been an elaborate trick designed to cheer us up: a sort of exploding cigar writ large. The self-sacrifice leaves you breathless.

Hard-core Politics

27.1.93

It was sex, sex, and more sex at the Commons yesterday.

The Chamber, of course, was not where the real action was. One or two MPs did look in – but, frankly, given the choice between a free private showing of the hard-core porn video *Red Hot Dutch* (X) in committee room 19, and a live performance on the floor of the House by Mr Tony Newton (PG) many MPs took the view that their responsibilities to their constituents demanded that, however painful the duty, they sit through the whole disgusting video, then stagger ashen-faced . . . (etc).

Your sketchwriter chose the mainstream cinema downstairs, *Red Hot Tony*, at the Commons ABC.

Charming though Mr Newton is, you would not at first expect to find him on screen in a Soho club. Were he involved at all he would be washing the glasses. Leader of the House and MP for Braintree, Essex, when Newton's name is mentioned the sex which comes to mind is the second syllable of his county. So, understudying for the absent PM, Newton found the cinema less than packed for his own show – unfair, for Mr Newton is not without satellite appeal. The signal is a little scrambled and you need a decoder, but there is a niche in the porn market for his performance, and yesterday afternoon your sketchwriter identified it . . .

There is (I once discovered when wandering by mistake into a pornographic bookshop, and lingering there by mistake) an erotic specialization known as 'bondage' whose followers like to chain each other up, or down, or reduce each other to total helplessness. Faced by a squad of MPs intent on tripping him up and tying him down, Newton adopts a wonderfully woebegone look and plaintive tone. Bondage freaks would be screaming in the aisles. There's a bright future for him in videos of this type.

The Banal Vision Thing

2.2.93

Is there nothing so banal that it is safe from becoming the centrepiece of a modern statesman's vision for the next millennium? At his conference last year the triumphant Mr Major, fresh from his election victory, promised lavatory stops on every motorway. This week, Labour is promising to double-glaze every home in Britain. Meanwhile, Liberal Democrats propose new efficiency standards for fridges and ideas for recycling yoghurt containers.

Now is the hour of the anti-heroic. Gone are the grand sweep, the broad sunlit uplands. In has come the elevation of the humdrum to the status of political art.

This week, a press handout from Chris Smith, Labour's tousle-headed environment protection spokesman, promises a Britain fit for double-glazing salesmen to live in:

'1. a basic package of water tank lagging, hot water pipe lagging, supply of low-energy light-bulbs, thermostats on heating systems and radiators, draught-proofing to doors and windows, and 6 in-thick loft insulation; 2. for those with cavity walls, the provision of cavity wall insulation; 3. the installation of double-glazing.'

Exhausted by so much vision, I looked into yesterday's debate. Maastricht rebels were trying to interest parliament in the question of its own sovereignty.

Feet on the table, ministers fidgeted. This was time-wasting. This would build no motorway loos.

Swift Retreat by General Rifkind   *4.2.93*

Terry Dicks, the maverick Tory MP, has arrived in Britain with a pump-action shotgun purchased in Calais and smuggled into Dover. Mr Dicks wants to prove that we still need frontiers. He may care to donate the shotgun to The King's Own Scottish Borderers who, we learnt yesterday, are not to be abolished.

There are limits to a Tory MP's appetite for spending cuts. Nothing better illustrates that than proposals for defence cuts. Try monkeying around with ancient regiments, for instance. Suddenly Conservative backbenchers are on their feet. Accountants scuttle as Tories fumble for language that Labour MPs reserve for threatened pits: 'Unquantifiable human costs, threatened communities, proud traditions . . .'

There are limits to a Labour MP's enthusiasm for reductions to our armed forces. Nothing better illustrates that than proposals to make soldiers in his own constituency redundant. Suddenly, a regiment ceases to be a war machine and becomes a valued employer. Up jump the Opposition benches, beating ploughshares into swords and fumbling for the vocabulary they have heard Tories deploy: 'policing the world order', 'Britain's international responsibilities'.

A government minister's enthusiasm for reorganizing his empire is not limitless. Nothing better illustrates that than when proposals turn out to anger colleagues on whose support his career depends.

Suddenly the most cerebral of strategists finds himself hastily scrambling the plans he had made. Out goes the paragraph on matching commitments to resources, in comes a footnote on matching resources to commitments. He fumbles for the phrases about 'leeway', 'flexibility' and 'sensible adjustment' he has been wont to despise in intellectual inferiors. Thus it was that Malcolm Rifkind, the stooped and donnish Defence Minister, found himself yesterday stiffening the sinews, imitating the action of a tiger, and bounding backwards in energetic retreat from army cuts he once called far-sighted, while socialists murmured approval of a reprieved imperial role, and Conservatives roared their support for a state rescue scheme.

It was Sir Geoffrey Johnson Smith (C, Wealden) who summed it up. 'Rapid reaction forces,' he told MPs, 'are the single most important component of our defence structure.'

We reflected that Malcolm Rifkind's reaction had been rapid indeed. There's nothing rapider than the reaction of a shrewd Tory minister to a brewing back-bench revolt.

Pillock in a Kilt

10.2.93

Do you know, reader, what Betty Boothroyd thinks the word 'pillock' means? Or what Bill Walker wears under his kilt? You shall learn.

Mr Walker (C, Tayside N) strutted up, to Labour wolf whistles, in a kilt. 'I stand before you, Madam Speaker, wearing the dress of Highland Scotland.' We were happy to take this on trust, but not Sir Nicholas Fairbairn (C, Perth and Kinross), who told the Chair on a point of order that this kilt was *not* Walker's national dress; and – worse! – 'I have reason to believe that under it he is wearing little red underpants.' Walker was wearing a little red face. Fairbairn did not say how he knew and Miss Boothroyd looked very unwilling to take his enquiry further. She told him so.

He desisted but the episode seemed to have aroused the sneak in his colleague, Barry Porter (C, Wirral S). Porter sits opposite Labour's Terry Lewis (Worsley), famous for his outrage over BT's 0898 porn-lines. Mr Lewis, Porter told the Chair, had 'used the word "pillock" not once, not twice, but *four* times'. It seems he provides a parliamentary pillock-line, and Porter wanted Miss Boothroyd to ban it. Did she know what this word meant, he asked?

To our surprise, Miss Boothroyd said she had not the least idea what pillock meant. Funny, that. She's in charge of 650 of them.

Forbidden Fruit in Garden of Eden   *11.2.93*

In the Beginning, there was Nicholas Soames; and the MP (C) for Crawley was without form, and void. And the Chief Whip recommended that he be made food minister; and Soames was given dominion over the fish of the sea, and over the fowl of the air and battery farms, and over the cattle, and over all the earth and large sections of the agriculture ministry, and over every creeping thing on the Tory backbenches that taketh an interest in food.

And it was all going pretty well. Unfortunately, however, Mr Soames had reckoned without Gavin Strang. Labour's principal agriculture spokesman is, as the Good Book says of the Serpent, 'more subtil than any beast of the field', but his role in yesterday's parliamentary drama differs sharply from Genesis, 3. Strang had come to the Commons not to commend the apple, but to denounce it.

Strang warned MPs about toxicity in apple juice. He took Soames to task for failing to alert the nation earlier. The problem was a substance called patulin, present in certain apples.

'Patulin,' cried Soames, 'is a naturally occurring toxicant which has been with us since the Creation. It is produced by moulds.'

'Good heavens!' said John Carlisle (C, Luton N).

Of course, Deadly Nightshade is also naturally occurring. As Strang put it, 'the fact that a substance occurs in nature does not mean it is not dangerous.'

'Like socialism,' shouted Tory wags.

'It is to top independent scientists that the government looks for toxicological advice,' Soames protested. Fruit was 'a natural product which has been with us since Adam ate the apple and thus made a career decision.'

MPs scratched their heads. Which career decision had Adam made by eating the apple? Soames seemed to be suggesting that upon leaving the Garden of Eden, Adam and Eve had gone straight into the cider industry, perhaps in partnership with the Serpent.

Speaking for the Serpent, a number of Tory backbenchers with constituency commercial interests to defend arose and said that they drank apple juice themselves, and behold it was very good. Glamorous Emma Nicholson (Devon W and Torridge) managed a prime-time plug, in husky contralto tones, for Inch's Cider. A few pints of this, she cooed to Soames, would produce 'a wonderful result'. The thought of Miss Nicholson in fig leaves was as pleasant as that of Mr Soames without them was alarming.

Jacques Arnold (C, Gravesham) advised Soames to 'ignore the chattering classes'.

Glenda Jackson (Lab, Hampstead), who represents them, rose. We remember her without fig leaves in *The Music Lovers*. She wasn't touching the apple. Pregnant women in Hampstead had drunk of its juice, she said, and behold they were sore afraid. Mr Soames said that they weren't to worry.

You would have to drink 140 litres of apple juice a day, said that doughty defender of the orchards of Kent, Andrew Rowe, to be in danger. Rowe (C, Kent Mid) had addressed the wrong man; the enormous and *bon-vivant* Soames is the one minister whom we can imagine achieving this level of consumption.

With shouts of 'What about bananas?' and 'Let's have a windfall tax!' ringing in my ears, I left the Gallery. Teresa Gorman (C, Billericay), in cerise with five medallions, was advertising herself as proof that drinking apple juice produced no harmful effects. MPs rushed from the Chamber to destroy every carton they possessed.

12.2.93 Mrs Gorman's Short, Sharp Chop

Its finger, as ever, on the pulse of world events, the House of Commons yesterday discussed the Gloucestershire County Council's budget, the tax status of the Royal Yacht, the temperature of deep freezers in Torquay hotels, and proposals for cutting the goolies off Billericay rapists.

We start with goolies: Mrs Gorman's word, not ours.

Or is it? A problem the biographers of Teresa Gorman (C, Billericay) will face is that it is difficult to know when the MP herself is speaking, and when the voice is that of the Billericay Conservative Association.

Teresa Gorman is a theoretical intellect, and a woman. In Billericay, where knuckles are hairy and Proust is hardly read, they have little time for philosophy and none for philosophical women. In Billericay, an ethics girl would be one who does not believe in extra-marital sex.

Yet Mrs G is proud of her constituents, and wants to please them while remaining true to herself. Most MPs do this by occupying a mid-point between their constituents' beliefs and their own. Mrs Gorman is different. On Mondays and Wednesdays she is Teresa, and on Tuesdays and Thursdays she is Billericay.

Of one whose tongue has been loosened by drink we may say it's the beer talking. Of Mrs Gorman we may sometimes say it's the Billericay talking.

The real Teresa is passionately anti-state. Her parliamentary notepaper is headed with a quote from Frédéric Bastiat beginning: 'The state is the great fiction . . .' When (some months ago) Mrs G found herself proposing a bill requiring immigrants to take an oath of allegiance, it was the Billericay talking.

When, on Wednesday, she told ministers that Britain should learn from Poland, whose government was falling apart, taxes went uncollected, laws were unenforceable, and the economy was booming . . . it was Teresa talking.

And when, yesterday, she told the home secretary that British judges were too soft on rapists and 'perhaps we should do something more drastic, like cutting their goolies off', it was the Billericay talking.

Poor Charles Wardle, the minister deputed to deal with Mrs Billericay, all but crossed his legs then sank beneath a sea of giggles as he agreed that 'stiffer sentences would be . . .' – the rest was lost.

Brer Garel-Jones and the Bramble Patch

16.2.93

If I were Tristan Garel-Jones I should stay indoors this week. For it emerges that this Machiavelli of a foreign office minister has been acting as decoy. He has lured the Tory Euro-rebels and the whole of the Opposition into a trap together. Yesterday the trap sprang shut.

Garel-Jones is piloting the Maastricht bill through parliament. Labour thought they had him and his bill surrounded. Over the weekend they had started to close in. And on Monday – hey presto! – up popped Douglas Hurd to declare that the bill was safe. Garel-Jones had escaped down a legal burrow with it.

Do you remember the tale in which Brer Rabbit is cornered? He begs his captors to inflict any humiliation they choose, but please *not* to drop him in the bramble patch. In the Commons tale the bramble patch is played by the social chapter, and Mr Garel-Jones plays the Welsh Rabbit.

Ten months ago, the Labour party framed an amendment to the Maastricht bill which aimed (indirectly) to force the social chapter on us. Ministers' apparent horror of this fuelled rumours that the amendment might scupper the treaty.

Even Tory Euro-sceptics, who hate the social chapter, began toying with the idea. Interest in the amendment grew. Enemies were closing in.

Last month, Brer Garel-Jones upped the tempo. Skipping out of his foreign office burrow, he called to his foes that Labour's amendment would be disastrous for his beloved Maastricht bill. It was the most fearsome of bramble patches, he said, giving them a quick flash of his little white bobtail: please, please don't drop him in the bramble patch. Their desire to do so grew.

And by this weekend it seemed that they had got him. Encircled by enemies, the Welsh Rabbit and his foreign office friends were being pushed backwards towards the hated bramble patch of the social chapter, protesting their horror all the way. Arithmetic suggested there was no escape.

Until yesterday. It fell to the Foreign Secretary to make the statement. Labour's Jack Cunningham looked ready for the kill.

From the peers' gallery Lord Tebbit leered down. Tristan Bobtail sat quietly on the bench, his very serious expression ruffled by the occasional little grin. Hurd looked embarrassed by the effrontery of what he was about to do.

And, in a moment, Douglas had kicked through the legal undergrowth to reveal a hidden tunnel. The government didn't *mind* about the bramble patch, he said.

They were content to be in it, if that's what their persecutors wanted.

All that stuff from Tristan Garel-Rabbit about the treaty being wrecked if they were thrown into this patch had been – well, a *mistake*. Even as he spoke, Tristan Bunny-Jones scampered down the legal burrow, to safety. It was the neatest of tricks.

All the same, it *was* a trick. A measure which until yesterday had been described by ministers as vital was suddenly reclassified as a piece of legal frippery, a modest thing, probably unnecessary, popped in by super-cautious draughtsmen, an act of obsessive tidy-mindedness, just in case.

Just in case, that is, Britain should be taken to the European court over its exemption from the social chapter? Alone among MPs, Geoff Hoon (Lab, Ashfield), put his finger on it. Wasn't the Foreign Secretary, asked Hoon, only pretending that Labour's amendment would not injure the bill?

Hurd floundered in his denials. People know when they are cheating. It was interesting that John Major stayed away.

Condemned to an Eternity of Interruptions

17.2.93

Your sketchwriter learns what names and faces he can, but gaps remain. One such, a new Tory backbencher, rose yesterday. 'Will the Prime Minister send the congratulations of the House to Sir Ranulph Fiennes . . . (blah) . . . fine example of voluntary effort . . . (blah)' and so on.

I whispered to an adjacent journalist: 'Who's that?'

'A berk,' he replied.

John Major did not think so. Endorsing the apprentice poodle's congratulations, the PM added: 'It does show that if you keep going you will get there in the end.' One reflected that it depends whether you know where you are going.

John Smith is in no doubt, but suffers from a different problem: he has forgotten who he is. Yesterday he launched a boomerang attack on 'sharp lawyers' and 'slippery manoeuvres'.

Any thought that Smith was experiencing a rare moment of self-criticism was dispelled when he made it clear he had Major in his sights. Major gently suggested that sharp lawyers in glass houses shouldn't throw stones.

Indeed. Yet MPs show a remarkable facility for applying criticism to everyone but themselves. They seem to lose consciousness of themselves as objects, and the air at Westminster is thick with flying boomerangs. Few professions blind people faster or more completely to what monkeys they appear.

Take Bob Cryer (Lab, Bradford S) for instance. A member of the Angry Left with a thin face, gingery hair, a voice that carries and a sour turn of speech, Cryer keeps both his intelligence and his humour *almost* secret. In tones half way between a Yorkshire bellow and a North Country whine, he has spent much of this century in a sedentary position, interrupting Tory MPs.

Yesterday, a Tory MP interrupted him: and you wouldn't *believe* the fuss he made! A convinced nuclear disarmer, Cryer was trying to call for a nuclear ban: but, before he got far, Phil Gallie (C, Ayr) started yelling 'Rosyth! Rosyth!' at him. Labour MPs have clamoured to keep this nuclear dockyard open.

Cryer stopped, amazed that anyone should do to him what he had been doing to others for 20 years. Winded, he struggled on to the end of his question, then sat down, seething.

But it was more than he could bear. He was back up in seconds, trying to raise with the Chair the shocking treatment he had received. 'Madam Speaker, I deserve the *right* . . .' he could be heard protesting, before jeers drowned the rest.

Should the Good Lord conclude that a few ages in hell would be appropriate for Gallie *and* Cryer, He could do worse than sentence each to make speeches to the other, interrupting each other for all eternity.

Call That Work?

'Work is of two kinds: first, altering the position of matter at or near the earth's surface relative to other such matter; second, telling other people to do so. The first is unpleasant and ill-paid; the second pleasant and highly paid.' – Bertrand Russell.

If so, then MPs have the perfect job. Their work, which is of the second kind, divides into two sub-categories. MPs spend half their time complaining that there are too many laws, and the other half making new ones. Often the same MP adopts both attitudes, but on different occasions. Some MPs even do so simultaneously.

Take questions to the President of the Board of Trade yesterday. In between quizzing him on the subject of orbital two-stroke technology (first question on the Order Paper) and seeking his comments on the use of the Queen's head on stamps (last question), MPs had trooped in hoping, variously, to attack the general idea of 'regional development areas', and to ask for Orders in parliament creating these in their own constituencies; to demand energy strategies, conservation strategies and export strategies, and to demand that government stop interfering with industry.

Bob Cryer (Lab, Bradford S) complained tellingly (and the Tories' Anthony Steen agreed) that this supposedly deregulating government made 3,499 statutory instruments in 1992, the largest number in history. As chairman of the select committee on statutory instruments, Cryer knows. But look, on the Order Paper, at the ambitions of his Labour colleagues!

Tony Banks wanted to ban *pâté de foie gras*. Jim Cunningham wanted further regulation of free-flight offers. Dr Tony Wright wanted laws against disreputable timeshare companies. Malcolm Chisholm wanted to ban standing charges for gas and electricity. And John Denham wanted a new regulatory framework for the travel industry. That was just Wednesday afternoon.

And that was just Labour. From the Tories came requests for assisted area status in three new places, and trade missions in every direction. The President himself started boasting about what sounded like 'my "one Sock Shop" initiative'. Was this the government's drive to reduce British industry and commerce to one Sock Shop? No. Apparently the phrase is 'one-stop shop', another mystery.

The unreal nature of the afternoon was heightened by the latest instalment, from Rupert Allason (C, Torbay), of the horrors besetting hoteliers in Torquay. Allason claimed that hoteliers there are obliged by new regulations to paint their kitchen ceilings twice a day. Last week he told us they have to check their fridge temperatures three times a day. A bizarre picture of catering life in Devon is emerging.

So it was a relief when the nightmare ended at 3.30 and a breathless young chap came to tell us about bicyling: Andrew Robathan, the Tory who has replaced Lord Lawson in Blaby.

It is not easy to imagine Lord Lawson on a bicycle, but Mr Robathan gave every appearance of having only just got off one. Fresh-faced and enthusiastic, eyes bright, shoulders square and a sky-blue handkerchief peeping from his breast pocket, the ex-soldier told jaded MPs that cycling was 'clean, non-polluting, cheap, quiet, relaxing, therapeutic and aerobic'. Sadly, though, 'my brother who bicycles in from Clapham has been knocked off his bike three times'. He was worried about cyclists' safety and . . .

Oh dear. There you go again. Mr Robathan wanted another law.

Been Here Before, Said Pooh

19.2.93

Dennis Skinner asked the Secretary of State for Employment 'if he will provide the latest unemployment figures, both nationally and regionally, and if he will make a statement . . .'

The Secretary of State for Employment (Mr Norman Tebbit): 'At 14 October, the number of unemployed people claiming benefit in the United Kingdom was 3,049,008. Lower inflation and interest rates provide a firmer base from which industry and commerce can regain lost customers at home and abroad, thereby generating more jobs . . .'

Or so the columns of the Official Report tell us. The year was 1982.

Readers whose memories go back even further will remember chapter 3 of *Winnie the Pooh*, 'In which Pooh and Piglet go Hunting and nearly catch a Woozle'. They will remember how the pair set off from a small spinney of larch trees. Later they reach a small spinney of larch trees, and find some mysterious tracks in the snow. So round this spinney went Pooh and Piglet . . . Round a spinney of another sort went government and Opposition MPs yesterday.

'Three million!' shouted Labour. 'Resign!' 'Lower interest rates . . .' shouted the Prime Minister, 'inflation down . . . We have put in place the conditions for economic growth . . .'

It was exceptionally boisterous. John Smith slipped into much the manner that Neil Kinnock and Michael Foot before him adopted, whenever unemployment reached a new high: he combined rage with bafflement; rage that so many people could be out of work, and bafflement that Tories could adopt what he considered a supine approach.

Mr Major, under pressure at the dispatch box, grows like his predecessor. Yesterday he came armed with lists: lists of what the government was doing and what was planned; lists of all the hopeful signs he could find in the economy; lists of everything wrong with Labour. To each shout of 'What are you doing?' he would throw another list at MPs, the whole performance approaching the classic Thatcherian rants of the 1980s.

Paddy Ashdown followed well-trodden Liberal tracks. He deplored slanging matches and called for positive thinking, offering none himself. I reached for my nursery story . . .

'Wait a moment,' said Winnie the Pooh, holding up his paw. He sat down and thought, in the most thoughtful way he could think. Then he fitted his paw into one of the tracks . . . and then he scratched his nose twice, and stood up.

'Yes,' said Winnie the Pooh. 'I see now,' said Winnie the Pooh. 'I have been Foolish and Deluded,' said he, 'and I am a Bear of no Brain at All.'

Government and Opposition MPs were busy, yesterday, furiously making new tracks in the snow, new columns in the Official Record for 1993. So busy and so furious that nobody tried fitting their paws into the tracks of the Official Record for 1982.

Perhaps in another 11 years the record for 2004 will take parliament past a spinney of larch trees, to be joined (should anyone look back 11 and 22 years) by *two* mysterious sets of tracks in the snow. And the hunt will go on – the hunt for what politicians call 'sustained economic growth'. The rest of us are scratching our noses and beginning to wonder whether it might be a Woozle.

23.2.93 **House with Mod Cons Inc Hot Air**

The redoubtable Stan Orme (Right Hon Stanley, Lab, Salford East, born 1923: this column's nomination for first president of Britain in 2003) yesterday raised with ministers the funding of libraries. With serious juvenile crime much in our minds, he said, surely public libraries should be spared?

Salford must be an unusual place. 'Oi, Darren' (we imagined). 'Library don't stock no Proust. Tory cuts.'

'Bleedin' 'eck. Let's nick an Escort XR3i then.'

Later, MPs came together in a rare display of real passion, detailed knowledge and all-party concern, to discuss their own facilities.

Ian Bruce (C, Dorset South): 'What financial provision is being made to extend the office facilities of hon members and their staff?'

Alan Beith, answering for the Commons commission, said new offices were on course for completion in 1998. He hoped that all members would have adequate facilities by the end of the century. 'Resign!' shouted some elderly MPs in quavering voices.

Mr Bruce began to describe the amenities that were an MP's due: rooms of their own, easy access . . . 'Baths!' shouted Tony Banks (Lab, Newham Northwest).

Mr Bruce misheard. 'With or without a bar,' he responded disapprovingly. But it was too late: Harry Greenway (C, Ealing North) was stirring. Mr Greenway is on record as having submitted a request that the sticky bits of Commons envelopes be peppermint-flavoured.

Up he jumped. What, indeed, about baths and showers, he enquired of the mild-mannered Mr Beith? Mr Beith assumed the air of a bed-and-breakfast proprietor under pressure from an awkward guest. But Mr Greenway had not finished: 'And while we're on the subject,' he said, 'what about provision, for members of the public visiting this House . . .'

'Of baths!' cried Mr Banks.

'You need one!' shouted a Tory determined to raise the level of debate.

'. . . of refreshment facilities?' concluded Mr Greenway, struggling to finish his question.

Mr Beith was unable to promise so much as a coffee bar, let alone a bar, or a bath, to visitors. He yielded to Anthony Steen (C, South Hams).

'Can you explain,' Mr Steen asked, 'why *hair dryers* are being put into lavatories in this House? Is this a proper use of public money?'

Elderly Tories sat bolt upright. So that was what those devices plugged into the walls of their loos were for. Hair dryers! Well I never! What was wrong with a good old rub with a towel? The things these young chappies seem to require these days. A few old boys silently thanked their lucky stars they hadn't tried to use them as ear-trumpets.

Mr Beith didn't know about hair dryers, but promised to enquire.

Mr Beith (Berwick-upon-Tweed) is a Liberal Democrat. His party can usefully be divided into two groups: those who know about hair dryers and those who do not. These groups are socially and philosophically quite distinct, and political scientists will find that membership of the hair dryer/not hair dryer categories is a reliable predictor of attitudes towards (for instance) abortion, public spending, homosexuality, marijuana and whether to form a pact with Labour.

Mr Beith, who is a Northern Methodist lay preacher, may never have seen a hair dryer and has certainly never touched one. Paddy Ashdown, on the other hand, knows all about hair dryers.

Business in the Bored Room

25.2.93

Recently I reported John Major's annoyance that John Smith is pursuing what our PM called 'sound bite' politics. Nobody could accuse Mr Major of that, but we identified a sound suck in one of his answers, and went on to spot sound gargles, sound chews and sound chokes from the back benches.

Yesterday brought the sound dribble. It came, I fear, from the new Liberal Democrat MP for Cheltenham, Nigel Jones.

How shall we describe him? Mild-faced and bearded, in early middle-age and doubtless a worthwhile and interesting chap to all who know his work, Mr Jones achieves, as an orator, a rare and surprising feat. He is so boring that he actually draws attention to himself as a parliamentary phenomenon. Nobody can believe that anyone can be so boring. They drop what they are doing and look up in wonder. As he drones on, all talk ceases in the Chamber. Heads shake disbelievingly. Senior MPs recall other hon members, now departed, famous for their boringness, and inwardly concede that this latest, from Cheltenham, takes the biscuit.

Mr Jones had something to say about local government spending by the Gloucestershire County Council, but nobody can remember what it was. Journalists' jaws and pencils dropped, stunned into inactivity. On Mr Jones went, and on, and on: his voice soft, his beard waggling gently, his argument strolling down every corridor in Gloucester County Hall.

It was supposed to be a question, so after what seemed an age, Miss Boothroyd, who had been fidgeting wildly, shot up like a scalded cat, and, in tones that hardly hid a sort of internal panic, asked MPs, *please*, to be 'crisp'. The realist in Jones told him he will never be crisp, but that he had better be brief. He sat down.

Firm Hand for Delinquent Tories

3.3.93

Juvenile offending was our MPs' theme yesterday. The Home Secretary spoke of 'secure training orders' and 'supervision in the community'. Even the Prime Minister denounced the erosion of discipline in modern Britain.

He should know. Smirking behind him sat delinquents, juvenile and otherwise, who have wreaked havoc in his party.

There is glue-sniffing Bill Cash, fixated Euro-bore, eyes glazed with Maastricht's small print; 'rat boy' Teddy Taylor, crouching in the ventilation shafts of amendment 443; and ram-raiding, treaty-smashing Tony Marlow.

And there are the joyriders: petty offenders such as young Liam Fox (C, Woodspring), working their way back to respectability. He and Alan Duncan (C, Rutland and Melton) were among new boys convicted of political joyriding after the Danish referendum last year.

They lept into an anti-Maastricht resolution where they had no right to be, hijacked it, and drove it across several newspapers. Eventually they crashed. Fox is 32 and Duncan is 31. Hormones are a problem with young men at this age.

They crashed into the Law – represented by chief whip Ryder and his menacing subordinates. Ryder (on orders, it is said, from the Prime Minister) placed secure training orders upon both of them, and some other new boys, too. They were to be incarcerated on the back benches.

Despite their brains, none was to be allowed near a job in government. They were offered a discreet cold shoulder whenever they tried to be helpful.

Both tried yesterday. Duncan asked a powerful question, reminding the PM that Labour spokesman Tony Blair had voted against reforms which toughened sentencing. Duncan was greeted by a huge cheer: hearts had softened towards the young offender.

But Major can be strangely unforgiving, and replied only 'my hon friend makes his own point in his own way'. Doubtless what the Americans call 'tough love'. Young Alan's supervision in the community continues.

Liam Fox may soon have paid his debt to society. If discipline is not instilled in the home, he said ruefully, the law steps in. Mr Major took pity and gave him a nice smile. A whip made a note: 'Parole soon', perhaps?

What, though, has been poor Ian Bruce's offence? During a question about students who drop out, the inoffensive ginger-haired youth (C, Dorset S) confessed to Education Secretary John Patten that 'I only lasted six months at university'.

Yes, snapped Patten to the MP, young people do drop out, 'often as a result of making a wrong career choice'. Bruce's pals sniggered. How *does* a chap please the front bench?

Black Days for Knights

The honours system is to be reformed. . . .

It cannot be out of order for a Labour MP to accuse a Tory, in the Chamber, of being 'obedient', and it is probably just about permitted for MPs to call each other 'hacks'. Whether there are circumstances in which the term 'lickspittle' is in order, we must doubt. And when fiery Paul Flynn (Lab, Newport W) told the Prime Minister that knighthoods for the 'obedient, lickspittle hacks' on the benches behind him were automatic, we *knew* he was out of order.

Madam Speaker confirmed it. 'Withdraw those words!' she cried, and, like the obedient – *ahem* – helpful fellow he is, Mr Flynn immediately did so.

But the Tory benches were in uproar. Tories who have already been knighted were indignant at the suggestion that they owed their knighthoods to having behaved like obedient, lickspittle hacks. Tories who have behaved like obedient, lickspittle hacks for decades, and *still* not been knighted, were indignant that their efforts were being overlooked by Flynn – and, indeed, by the PM.

There is no way you can stir a hornets' nest like the honours system, as Mr Major rather valiantly did yesterday, without yourself being stung by the necessary absurdity of any such system. The moment the Prime Minister rose to make his statement, you knew that the few short yards he dare venture would be shrugged off as an obvious step, while the rolling acres of snobbery and corruption upon which he dare not trespass would be pointed to by all with cries of anger.

With both the last two Labour prime ministers now in the Lords, John Smith still seemed unabashed in his denunciation of political honours. 'That is not the view,' said Mr Major, smiling with the confidence of a man carrying a dozen Labour applications in his pocket, 'held by a great many hon members in his own party, as the Right Hon gentleman privately knows.'

The Liberal Democrat leader asked why we couldn't have a single honour, with different gradations. MPs giggled. 'The Right Hon Paddy Ashdown, OY (I)' (Order of Yeovil, first class) sprang to mind. Or perhaps recipients could be decorated according to a system of proportional representation (single transferable vote)?

Tony Benn supplied the historical perspective. 'Ever since William the Conqueror took us into the Common Market . . .' he began.

Knights rose at their peril. Sir Peter Tapsell punctured the laughter by taking the bull by the horns: 'As an example, perhaps, of the somewhat haphazard way in which routine political honours are awarded . . .'

'My hon friend understates his own distinction,' the PM protested.

Ministers rose at their peril, too. Long-serving Anthony Steen (C, S Hams, Mr) had no time to speak, before several of his younger colleagues chorused 'arise, Sir Anthony!' Peter Mandelson (Lab, Hartlepool, Mr) who – if Neil Kinnock had won the last election – might have been Lord Hartlepool by now, asked why the Tories had brought back hereditary peerages. Interestingly, Major replied that he did not plan to create such peerages. Hard cheese, Lady T. Douglas Hurd, beside him, gritted his teeth as dreams of a viscountcy flew away. Absent from the Chamber, Michael, Duke of Henley, was not there as his dukedom crumbled.

Finally, the PM cited arch-rebel Sir Teddy Taylor as evidence that prime ministers do not try to bribe with honours. Some of us see Sir Teddy as evidence that they try without success.

After the Black Eye

10.3.93

The government had suffered a defeat during the passage of the Maastricht bill. . . .

John Major entered the Chamber of the House yesterday to the most enormous cheer.

There is something blood-curdling about the Conservative party cheering. It is more chilling than their enmity. Resonating within it is the folk-memory of a thousand treacheries. In recent months the cheering has been growing louder. Yesterday it approached the pitch accorded his predecessor in the weeks before her followers knifed her. If Tories carry on cheering Major like this, he would be wise to bring bodyguards.

The Prime Minister arrived in the final minute before he was to take the floor. As the digital clock flicked to 3.14, and still no Prime Minister, faces on the government front bench tightened. None who knows Mr Major ever *quite* discounts the possibility that he might just send a note saying he had gone back to mother.

He did turn up, and great was the cheering. What remained of defence questions was inaudible as late arrivals jostled to find a place. Jabbering filled the air.

It was like the atmosphere at sunset at an African water hole as the animals come down to drink. Jackals sniffed the wind, hyenas giggled among themselves, and smaller scavengers sneaked their way to ringside seats. On the front benches, big cats stretched or snarled in a desultory way, while monkeys chattered. Here and there a crocodile lifted an inquisitive eye about the surface of the pond. I cannot say the mood was grave: it was excited. Back-bench life is usually so dull.

Blair Evades Roadblock

11.3.93

As the Prevention of Terrorism Order passes the House. . . .

Security dominated yesterday's debate. Tory MPs joined MPs from Northern Ireland and crowded into the Chamber to hear the Home Secretary outline a strategy for dealing with the most insidious danger Her Majesty's government has faced in decades: now a daily threat which every member of the Cabinet, from the Prime Minister downwards, must live with.

Kenneth Clarke was to unveil the centrepiece of the government's defences. It is called the Prevention of Tony Blair (Exclusion of Sound Bites) Bill (1993).

With every month that passes Blair becomes more dangerous. Well-dressed, well-spoken, good-looking and immensely plausible, Labour's principal home affairs spokesman is just the sort of smoothie to lull the British public into forgetting that they are playing with fire. Confronted by the manicured moderation of a man like Blair smiling into the television cameras, it is all too easy for ordinary citizens watching from home to overlook the ruthless tendencies of the underground organization he fronts.

In recent weeks, at the dispatch box and at *Any Questions* sessions up and down the country, Blair has been posing as the policeman's friend, deploring crime and holding himself out as guardian and protector of every little old lady in the land. He has even smooth-talked his way into the *Daily Mail*. 'I'm Tony Blair,' he announces, seldom mentioning who has sent him. Elderly, naïve or confused electors have been inviting him into their living rooms, many quite unaware that he is not a Conservative. Charmers like this must be denied the oxygen of publicity.

Unfortunately, the government has not yet found a way of banning Blair from the Chamber itself. He kept getting up and sounding reasonable. His blue suit was beautifully cut, his shoes shiny and his posture good. His hair was perfect. He made the Tories look like the men of violence. 'It's no good standing up and looking steamy-eyed,' snapped Clarke, plainly exasperated.

But that was the problem. It *was* good. Blair is good. His case against parts of the act was perfectly arguable. To imply that this was unpatriotic was plumb stupid. Clarke was left manning a useless roadblock while, once again, the wily Blair had slipped through his net.

Steer Clear of Big John

12.3.93

Time is kept in the Chamber by a big digital clock above hon members' hon heads. PM's Questions end at 3.30 sharp. As this time approaches, eyes stray to the clock. Yesterday the Prime Minister began his last reply at 3.29. 'Productivity's up,' he cried, 'house sales are up; retail sales are up; car sales are up.'

'Time's up,' said Madam Speaker. It was 3.30.

The final whistle could not have come too soon for Mr Major. The PM has become increasingly irritable in recent weeks.

John Smith, for a start, got it in the neck. He only seems to have one question: 'Here's a fine mess and what's the government going to do about it?' Yesterday, as we might have predicted and Major had, job losses at Rolls-Royce were the subject.

Here's a fine mess and what's the government . . . etc., Smith asked. Major's eyes began to swivel rather as Margaret Thatcher's used to. He launched into an ill-tempered rant about how bailing industries out was tried in the sixties and . . . etc.

At this, Smith decided to get passionate, which in Mr Smith is signalled by the adenoids: he changes from sounding as though he has a bad cold, to sounding as though he has a very bad cold.

He had a little splutter about how it was a Tory PM who had rescued industries like Rolls-Royce. On the foremost bench below the gangway, Ted Heath, in his blue socks (always a dangerous sign), nodded. Perhaps Major saw this, for he became even crosser. 'There he goes again!' he barked at Smith, and began to rage about the 'nanny state'.

He was still fuming when Paddy Ashdown was unwise enough to intervene, the Liberal Democrat leader's public sanctimony undimmed by a week's private horsetrading, ultimately unsuccessful, with Tory whips over Maastricht. This was more than Major could bear.

He spat out something about 'principle' as opposed to 'practice'. It was unclear what he was trying to say, except that he meant to conclude with the phrase 'until he's *done* it'.

Unfortunately Mr Major hit the word 'done' slightly too hard, even for the emphasis he intended. His voice broke. The result was that, though the 'until he's' and the 'it' were delivered gruffly, 'done' came out in a sort of yodelled squeak. It rather undermined the majesty of the Prime Minister's rage. Two Cabinet ministers covered their mouths to suppress a giggle. One did not even try.

17.3.93 Doleful Norman Corners the Market

The Budget. . . .

In a performance of mind-boggling tediousness that reduced most of the House to stupefaction and rendered some MPs insensible, Norman Lamont yesterday wrote out a 20,000-word job advertisement for the post of Chancellor of the Exchequer (1993–6) designed to ensure that there could be only one applicant for the position: himself.

'WANTED: Tory taxgrabber: Senior minister to implement three years of shocking tax increases of a scope and intricacy calculated to drive MPs to despair.

'Applicants must combine a careful intelligence with an instinct for suicide. They must be prepared to defend and execute a harsh yet unexciting programme, already decided. The post offers little scope for glory, originality or personal initiative. Command of dry tax-detail essential. Massive paperwork required.

'Hours long, subject matter dull and no scope for originality. Willingness to disappoint a wide range of individuals and interest groups, break a variety of promises, and concoct plausible responses to shivering pensioners is essential.

'Rewards will include being booed during three successive Budgets and blamed for every setback. Successful progress, however, will be credited to the applicant's predecessor. Hopes of further advancement must be shelved.

'Applications should be addressed in triplicate to the Chief Whip, enclosing a draft publisher's contract for political memoirs, and endorsed with the words: "Honestly I'm not joking".'

As the shadows lengthened yesterday afternoon, so did the speech. So did the Chancellor's reach into the future. It was far longer than recent Budgets. By 4 pm we had reached 1994, by 4.30 we were framing the Budget for 1995 and by 5 pm we were finalizing plans for 1996. Then 5.30 loomed. MPs prayed that extra time be replaced by a penalty shoot-out, before Lamont turned his attention to tax bands for the next millennium.

'Lord, make me virtuous, but not yet,' St Augustine prayed. A similar thought has occurred to St Norman. He unveiled a fearsome catalogue of horrors to be implemented – one day – but it was so dull that he had lost the House long before he reached his destination. Perhaps he meant to.

Despairing of analysis, your sketchwriter fell to MP-watching. Opposite, in the 'overflow' gallery above, sat Hugh Dykes (C, Harrow E). As the Chancellor described the '94–95 wedge' Mr Dukes closed his eyes, the better to think.

As we reached the North Sea PRT regime, Dykes's head fell back against the oak panel, so intense was his concentration. The 20 per cent band for mortgage interest relief found Mr Dykes's mouth dropping open, no doubt with surprise. The special measures for VAT collection needed such careful study that Mr Dykes fell a little sideways, to think about it from that angle. And, as the detail of the Chancellor's reforms of advance corporation tax emerged, Dykes's head lolled forward in shock. Moments later he walked, trance-like, from the Chamber. I think he was dazed by the Chancellor's brilliance.

'My next measure,' droned the Chancellor, 'is a little less opaque.' It was too late. Dykes had left. If Lamont can do that to the remaining 648 of them, he may be in with a chance.

Weasel Tendency Prospers in Hamsters' Clothes

19.3.93

'What weasels our politicians are!' a colleague said as we left the Press Gallery after PM's Questions yesterday. It had been another wearisome session. John Smith tried to 'nail' John Major with his 'betrayal' of manifesto promises on VAT. Major tried to 'clobber' Smith for his habit of 'talking this country down'.

Spare us. Even lifting the pencil seemed pointless. Returning to my desk, I repeated the question: *are* they weasels?

The weasel is quick, sleek and beautiful, perfectly adapted to its role. MPs try to be sly but they are not very good at it and no joy to watch. Besides, a ghastly blandness infects our politics. Weasels in hamsters' clothing abound. For want of a better word, though, 'weasels' will do. But who made them weasels?

We did. The nation and its news media have created for politicians a habitat where only the weasel can survive. If weasels prosper at the expense of nobler beasts then should we sneer?

Take the two pseudo-issues which surfaced yesterday in the House. The VAT election pledge now seriously embarrasses the Tories. Major said there would be no increase. 'Surely,' we think, 'he realized it was foolish to give so firm an undertaking?'

Of course he did. But imagine if, placed on the spot, he had given the honest answer: 'We believe no VAT increase should be needed, but who can be sure?' Labour would have fallen on this with glee. Would political editors or columnists have brushed the reply aside, explaining that no party leader can ever say never? No. We would have splashed it: MAJOR FAILS TO RULE OUT . . . etc.

Or take Labour's 'talking Britain down' – a theme on which the Tories have been harping for months. Imagine Mr Smith made a speech supporting (as he does) some of the economic reforms the Tories have achieved. Or that he was to celebrate good economic news and say he hoped Britain was turning the corner. It would be dug up by Tory central office and rammed down his throat ever after. The press would speculate that he lacked the 'instinct for the jugular' an Opposition leader needs.

Or suppose a Tory minister were to enter the fray about energy prices by remarking what everyone knows: welfare beneficiaries will be compensated for VAT increases, but not to the full extent; that this is regretted, but that many pensioners are quite able to pay their share . . . just picture the fuss! The media, and much of its audience, would call this minister a hooligan.

We punish as 'indiscreet' any politician who ruffles the smooth surface of our bland political culture. We may *disagree* with his opinion, but it is the suggestion that the incompetence lies in *expressing* it, which so damages a frank politician. It becomes hard for serious MPs to touch any sensitive debate.

Smooth-talkers prosper, but the cleverest of all – rough-talkers who tell us only what we want to hear – prosper most with the English. Mrs Thatcher did that for her audience, as Dennis Skinner does for his.

Run through the names of famous politicians relegated for being insufficiently 'political' – Alec Douglas-Home, Keith Joseph, John Biffen, Peter Shore, Paul Tsongas – or less famous names – Richard Needham, Jeff Rooker, John Cartwright, George Robertson . . . and reflect. Doesn't the press, don't the electorate, persecute the non-weaseloid tendency? Have we any right, then, to scratch each other's backs and giggle at the survivors, the weasels?

Prescott's Tunnel Vision Goes Off Rail

23.3.93

It is easy to know when John MacGregor is in trouble. He goes red in the face and starts saying 'the fact of the matter is'. On difficult days or after railway accidents, the transport secretary's fact-of-the-matter-is count has been known to rise to 15 in half an hour, and his face to remain pink from lunch time to tea.

But yesterday, announcing plans for a high-speed channel link, MacGregor's f-o-t-m-i count sank to only two in an hour and his colour never rose once. We conclude that the government has got it right.

It is harder to know when John Prescott is in trouble. The problem with Labour's transport spokesman is that, whatever happens, he only has one response: he loses his temper. Mrs Prescott must possess huge reserves of internal calm, for, if her husband's dispatch box performances are anything to go by, every breakfast chez Prescott must be like a storm breaking anew.

'*Kippers!* I *hate* kippers. How dare you insult me with kippers? Kippers are the last thing I wanted. Kippers are an object of horror to me. Kippers are a symptom of everything that's wrong with this unspeakable Conservative government. Kippers disgust me. Kippers are a scandal, a disgrace, a Tory whitewash, a Cabinet plot, a conspiracy against truth itself, a catastrophe waiting to happen. Kippers are . . .'

'But John, dear, you *asked* for kippers, yesterday, when I gave you egg and bacon, which, you remember, you threw at the wall. You . . .'

'*Egg and bacon!* I *loathe* egg and bacon. Egg and bacon are anathema to me. Egg and bacon are a symptom of everything that's wrong with this obscene, child-murdering Tory government. Egg and bacon are a cover-up, a scam, a rip-off, a trap. Even kippers look good by comparison. That was my point yesterday. I was grotesquely misreported by the Tory press . . .'

Yesterday, reacting to MacGregor's rail link, Prescott lost his temper. But the difficulty for Prescott-watchers is that, reacting to Cecil Parkinson's rail link (when Parkinson was transport secretary) Prescott was seized with a rage whose violence few had seen the like of before. Later, reacting to Malcolm Rifkind's plans, Prescott fair bust a gut.

Since then he has blown fuses without number at the government's failure to put forward any plans at all. They have now done so. MacGregor's new proposals abandon many of the previous ones which Prescott had found so objectionable. Naturally, he went wild. 'A government of blunder and blight . . .'

Mr Prescott ransacked the thesaurus, missing blether, bladder-wrack and blockheads in his rage. 'A decade of misery and uncertainty . . .' but no mention of grief, panic or despair: is he mellowing? '. . . Lacking vision, commitment and common sense . . . ' not to say conviction, coherence, conscience, coriander, cloves, pepper, salt or tomato sauce.

Mr Prescott concluded by bewailing the '38 miles of tunnelling' envisaged in the first proposals, cut down to 27 miles in the next ones, cut down, now, to 'less than a third of that'. Why not more tunnels, he raged, far more? In an earlier incarnation Mr Prescott may have been an exceedingly belligerent mole, tunnelling furiously in a blind apoplexy of burrowing.

'Well,' replied Mr MacGregor, 'the fact of the matter is . . .' But this was his final f-o-t-m-i. Then all was calm, as one Kent Tory after another rose to tell him how reassuring they found his statement. Backbenchers loved the plans. They must be expensive.

Top Dog Speaks His Master's Mind   *24.3.93*

Offa, guide dog to David Blunkett, Labour's health spokesman, knows not only his master's name but his constituency, too. Yesterday, he growled at Dame Jill Knight (C, Birmingham Edgbaston) as the dame, referring to Blunkett by constituency alone, made a disparaging remark.

It is hard to guess, from Offa's growls, which are policy statements and which personal comment. It is hard to interpret the growls of the two-legged yappers at Westminster, too. Although unelected, Offa has much better manners than the elected mammals there, and rarely shows his feelings. He is the key, I think, to a riddle.

Beyond criticizing the Tories, Opposition thinking on health remains a mystery. Your sketchwriter's theory about Blunkett and his dog is that the dog is taking the lead on policy. Formulating Labour's health plans, Offa has decided to play it long, which is why the plans remain unarticulated. I have, however, noticed Offa's attitude to GP fund-holding mellowing.

Naïve members of the press try to discern Opposition policy from Mr Blunkett's speeches, but as much may be found in the raising of Offa's eyebrow as in a Blunkett press release.

In the absence of anything interesting from his master, Offa's snarl yesterday seemed to deserve study. But what did it mean? Dame Jill was strikingly dressed and the dog may have been expressing a fashion commentary rather than an ideological one. She wore her Sabena air-hostess outfit – navy skirt, tunic in three horizontal strata, violet on top, navy beneath, separated by a white band dipping to an aerodynamic V at the bosom. This could have upset Offa earlier, but, by the time that the dame rose, the dog was curled up behind the clerks' table.

'Could my Right Hon friend,' began Dame Jill to the health secretary . . .

The dog seemed to recognize this MP's voice; she often attacks Labour health policy in the person of Offa's master; Offa looked up. 'Could my Right Hon friend persuade, cajole or charm the hon member for Sheffield, Brightside . . .' She was being sarcastic.

At the word Brightside, Offa threw his head back and, hidden from Dame Jill by the oak table, curled his top lip back in a menacing snarl which he tossed with his head in the dame's direction. If he could only have seen it, his master would have been touched by this display of loyalty.

Knight went on to advertise the superiority of Tory health policies. Blunkett rose to respond that it was impossible to believe Tory pledges. Recognizing his master's voice, Offa wriggled his tail a little on the carpet in an understated gesture of affection. We, and Offa, awaited the health secretary's reply.

Virginia Bottomley launched into one of her hallelujah choruses for the internal market. These days she combines the joy of Julie Andrews with the punch of Arnold Schwarzenegger, a sort of Goldilocks on crack. NHS trust hospitals, she declared, were doing more and doing better, treating more patients, cutting waiting lists . . .

Head on carpet, Offa yawned. His eyes closed.

But he was not asleep. As John Smith arrived to question the PM ('why on airth doesn't he *do* something' etc) the dog looked up dismissively. Offa may be angling for that job, too.

Last Tango on the Back Benches?   *25.3.93*

For many years the whole House of Commons has been haunted by two abiding memories and one abiding horror. The memories are of the two occasions when Mr Geoffrey Dickens MP has danced. The horror is that he might one day dance again.

Dickens (C, Littleborough and Saddleworth) is a big-hearted, eager chap, tireless in the interests of his constituents. But his thoughts go beyond the north country. There can be no controversy in the nation, planet or universe, upon which he does not hold frank and fearless views, expressed daily and in violent language.

But he has few real enemies. He is without malice and personally kind, and there is a lovable naïvety about the man. All of at least 18 stone, with the bearing of a master butcher, the opinions of a taxi-driver and the voice of a foghorn, the sight of Mr Dickens's vast countenance rising from the bench like a pink, perspiring moon, mouth open and drawing breath in readiness for a new blast, brings a smile to all but the sourest faces. On the parliamentary sketchwriter's wall is a small box reserved for uneventful days: 'In case of emergency, break glass and reach for Geoffrey Dickens.' Yesterday was uneventful, except except for Mr Dickens and dancing.

Dickens danced first in 1981. At a press conference he called, journalists awaiting news of his campaign against paedophiles were astonished to be told instead that he was leaving his wife. Attending an afternoon *thé dansant* in Soho, he said, he had fallen in love with his dancing partner. By the way, he added, would reporters please not tell his wife until he had told her himself? Mrs Dickens, a wonderful woman, sorted all this out in no time. Soon Geoffrey was home, Soho out of bounds and dancing forbidden.

For a while. Mr Dickens next danced in the mid-80s, this time in circumstances none could censure, though some did deride. The all-girl pop group Bananarama made a video to advertise their music on TV. It featured Geoffrey Dickens.

For some time at Westminster the arrival in the Chamber of the burly MP was accompanied by requests from the floor. But shouts of 'give us a twirl, Geoffrey' met only a beaming smile. Perhaps Mrs Dickens had put her foot down again.

Or has she? MPs trembled yesterday as the northern member bellowed an apparent threat: 'the Lambeth Walk!' he announced.

This was a pun, referring both to the music hall dance and to alleged corruption in Labour Lambeth. Attention turned not to Dickens's argument, which was routine, but to the possibility that he might be about to dance, which was horrific. Did we imagine it or did he wiggle his hips teasingly as he spoke? Robin Squire, the studious, bespectacled minister to whom this was addressed, watched, frozen like a rabbit before a puff-adder, as Dickens roared.

Mercifully, he sat down without dancing. The whole House, Square said, was relieved that Mr Dickens had chosen not to dance. But Dickens hardly seemed to hear. Staring into space he looked transported. But where? To Soho? To Bananarama's studio? To the Yorkshire moors? We shall never know.

31.3.93 Baton-Charged by an Angry Dame

Rubbish! shouted Dame Elaine Kellett-Bowman at John Smith, her fearsome eyebrows beetling up and down.

She had already shouted 'rubbish' repeatedly at almost every Labour MP, so there was no special significance in her adding the Opposition leader to her hit-list. Let us not mince words: this dame was angry. Dame Elaine (C, Lancaster) was having one of her violent days. She had been in explosive mood since morning.

We first caught up with her before lunch, in the Jubilee Room. She was at a rally of her favourite trade union, the Police Federation. The mood had turned vicious. Let me explain . . .

The federation is lobbying MPs for the equipping of officers with the 'side-handled baton'. This is an enormous truncheon with a big, fist-sized joystick sticking out at right angles for extra grip.

Yesterday, hoping to appeal over the home secretary's head to back-bench MPs, the federation mounted an exhibition for members of both houses, issuing an explanatory leaflet describing the benefits not only of the side-handled baton, but also of 'Cap-Stun (registered trademark of ZARC International Inc)' made from 'Oleoresin Capsicum', an extract of cayenne pepper converted into an aerosol spray. Extract of cayenne pepper sounds like the kind of thing Dame Elaine would favour as a cologne, but sadly I missed any demonstration of this.

I arrived in time to watch a policeman ('Peter') and a policewoman ('Jacquie') perform, for MPs, a floor-show involving the side-handled baton. Muscle-bound Peter was in black leather arm-pads and reinforced leather breast-plate. Trim young Jacquie, hair in a chic close-crop, was in crisp white blouse and uniform. They took turns in twisting each other's arms, spinning one another to the floor, and choking each other.

MPs and peers, middle-aged and paunchy, sat gawping and grunting like ageing voyeurs, as the show progressed. And, in a ringside seat she had commandeered, sat the dame, wearing three badges. She looked absolutely transfixed. As Jacquie struck Peter in the throat she rocked with excitement. 'Want to see that again?' asked the ringmaster.

'Now,' he continued, 'let's see how she copes with the long, straight baton.' The dame sat bolt upright. Jacquie pinned Peter to the floor by his neck. Elaine licked her lips. Her eyebrows began to beetle uncontrollably.

They were still beetling when she arrived at education questions, shouting in sequence, 'no!', 'rubbish!', '*no!*', 'not your constituency!' 'complete rubbish!' and 'has it *heck*!' at Labour MPs and education spokesmen. When John Smith arrived with a crackpot question about the film industry, she began to writhe. Shouts of 'rubbish!' flew thick and fast.

She was plainly unsettled. Surely scenes of gratuitous violence should be kept from the elderly and suggestible? Dame Elaine is 68.

Welsh Flintstone Loves a Barney

30.3.93

Shrinking from the prospect of yet another set-piece battle between a wearisome Robin Cook and a stale Michael Heseltine, your sketchwriter looked in on questions to the Welsh secretary yesterday. Is there anything in Wales?

'There is a tidal wave in Wales,' declared Peter Hain (Lab, Neath), 'in favour of an elected Welsh assembly.'

'There is confidence in Wales,' cooed Welsh secretary David Hunt, 'there is great pride in Wales.' Labour denied it. Alan W. Williams (Carmarthen) said there was 'economic inactivity in Wales'. It seems there is little agreement about what there is in Wales.

But on two things we can agree. There is Walter Sweeney (C, Vale of Glamorgan) in Wales; and there is *not* John Marshall.

Mr Marshall was jeered as a non-Welshman when he spoke. He is the Tory MP for Hendon South, in London, but this does not prevent him having opinions about Wales, and almost everywhere else. Marshall is becoming a family favourite at Westminster, resembling TV's Mr Blobby. Readers who follow children's television will be familiar with this lovable chap, rotund of figure and orotund of speech, who is at the same time immensely voluble and completely unintelligible.

'The Right Hon gentleman,' he began, 'the immediate, former, past leader of the Opposition . . .' Mr Marshall was in unusually crisp form. Like Blobby, his mouth opens and closes and noises come out in the rhythm of human speech, but it never seems to mean anything. The conviction grows that, like Blobby, he is unlikely to say anything interesting: and yet with each year that passes we love him more and feel more certain we should be poorer without him. Thank you, Hendon.

More intelligible was Walter Sweeney, the Tory Euro-rebel. Coming to ministers' aid on the subject of new industry in Wales, he then intervened on a question put down by Win Griffiths (Lab, Bridgend). Griffiths was complaining at proposals to 'remove' various villages from Ogwr 'and place them in the Vale of Glamorgan' (it seems that Welsh secretary has assumed powers even Ceausescu would have envied). Sweeney welcomed the move.

Silver-tongued he was not: but he was solid. Tomorrow he will be in the Chamber rebelling on Europe: clumsy but steadfast. Listening, I regretted the cheap shots I took during Sweeney's first weeks as an MP last year.

It is not that he has changed, or that he is necessarily right, but that he has stuck to his guns so bravely. Mr Sweeney is a political primitive, a Fred Flintstone of the Tory back benches. But, like Fred, he has stone-age charm. We should not be surprised if he yelled 'yaba-daba-doo' as he stomped into the Chamber to club Euro-minister Tristan Garel-Jones on the head.

His style is wooden, his arguments basic, but he is utterly consistent. He has the smallest majority in the land (19) and machine politicians thought this new recruit from Wales would be a pushover. But whips' bullying and Tory central office arm-twisting in his constituency has not budged him. Night after night he is there, supporting his party in Welsh affairs and almost all else, but not Maastricht.

Not every backbencher is an orator and not every backbencher is always right, but some at least have spine. To a House full of blancmange the electors of the Vale of Glamorgan have sent flint. Thank you, Glamorgan. There is something, after all, in Wales.

Opposition Team All Dressed Up Like a Dog's Dinner   2.4.93

Those MPs who were not out celebrating victories at yesterday's 'MPs' dog show', sponsored by Woofit, looked in on questions to the Chancellor of the Exchequer. Suppressing the urge to see Norman Lamont as a plump Pekinese, and his shadow, Gordon Brown, as a slobbery Pyrenean mountain dog, I tried to concentrate on what MPs were saying.

In your sketchwriter's mind, another distraction was growing. I was unable to take in the economics.

With Easter in the air, fashion holds our attention. 'Grunge' is all the rage; and it strikes me that – almost a year, now, into the new parliament – Britain has a grunge Opposition.

I am not talking about their dress. Grunge, in clothes and lifestyle, can be defined as an anti-fashion youth cult, born out of the recessionary years of the early 1990s. It is a reaction to the glossy, shoulder-padded excesses of the 1980s. The grunge look consists of an unmatching collection of cheap and tatty garments, often bought from charity shops, inspired by the 1970s and earlier. There may be flares or platform-heels. There may be stove-pipes or turn-ups. There can even be parkas and earrings, afghans and midis, berets and waistcoats. The only unifying theme is that there is no unifying theme. The ensemble lacks coherence, borrowing from the cast-offs of different eras and styles.

Looking across this week at John Smith, Margaret Beckett, Gordon Brown, Michael Meacher, Harriet Harman, Jeremy Corbyn and Dennis Skinner, it seemed that we have, here, the concept of grunge elevated from the individual to the team, from the wardrobe to the ideological wardrobe.

How are the voters to match a Tony Benn with a Tony Blair? Blair alone makes a coherent fashion statement: 1980s Filofax. Benn has an integrity of his own: 1930s Socialist. However, Benn and Blair together are grunge.

Or take Clare Short and Margaret Beckett. Short is 60s Irish with a hint of Greenham Common. Beckett is 70s C & A with ideology and earrings to match the occasion – any occasion. Each alone presents a picture we can read. Together, we have grunge.

Put sober-suited Donald Dewar, social security spokesman and on the intellectual Calvinist right of his party, on a front bench with jovial, leftish, bearded Frank Dobson, shadow employment secretary, cheeks glowing from a mental mass trespass on Kinder Scout, and what do you have? Two coherent individuals, but, as a pair . . . grunge.

Here lies the reason John Smith triumphs as Opposition leader of a grunge party. Mr Smith is grunge, all by himself. As a political statement, Mr Smith achieves ideological grunge unaided. There is no need for extra colleagues to muddy the philosophical waters. A decade of boardroom dinners has supplied him with 1980s City cred. A Scottish presbyterian upbringing gives him 90s (1890s) non-conformist cred. His roots in the old Labour party give him

Keir Hardie Clause 4 cred. A lifetime's association with the trade union movement gives him TGWU dinosaur cred. Fighting Militant with Kinnock gives him New Labour cred. Any of these creds would do on its own. Together they present . . . grunge. Grunge not of the clothing, but of the mind.

Last week, Mr Smith was on about the cost of gas. This Tuesday, it was the Oscars. Yesterday, it was Bosnia. His glasses glint in the television lights, but the overall effect is . . . well, that's enough grunge for the Easter recess.

Paleskins and Fuzzy-wuzzies   *15.4.93*

The Conservative party squares up to the Balkan conflict. . . .

To the Tory backbencher, foreign troublemakers fall into two categories: paleskins and fuzzy-wuzzies. The paleskins are murderous fiends who will stop at nothing and are to be treated with the utmost caution. The fuzzy-wuzzies are troublesome hooligans who must be shown, if necessary with the butt of a British rifle, that aggression does not pay.

Depending on the category, entire armouries of moral and military reasoning must be switched. If the aggressor is Saddam Hussein (fuzzy-wuzzy – the slightest suntan counts, as do turbans, reading from right to left, Greeks, Italians and Argentines), then the vocabulary is of contempt: 'ludicrous', 'madman', 'bully', 'banana republic' etc.

The reasoning is clear. At whatever cost and for however slight an apparent prize, these louts must be taught a lesson: the rule of law must never be flouted with impunity. The military logic is that allies must be defended and important strategic goals (land routes/sea-lanes/exposed flanks, oil, etc) protected. The cost of recapturing Port Stanley or Kuwait can never be disproportionate. Victory over fuzzy-wuzzies is unconsciously assumed.

Dealing with a paleskin aggressor, a wholly different policy framework is wheeled out. Now arises what is called 'traditional British caution' or 'the prudence of a mature and adult European power'.

Thus it was yesterday, when Defence Secretary Malcolm Rifkind upheld HMG's Balkan policy of locking ourselves in the loo. Sage heads nodded along the Tory ranks behind him. Sir Nicholas Bonsor (C, Upminster, defender of the ancient rights of the fox-hunter), in tones as mellow and gruff as an Island malt, rumbled to his feet to 'welcome the caution' of his Right Hon friend. 'Our troops are sitting under Serbian gun-barrels,' he growled.

Was this the same Sir Nicholas who interrupted James Callaghan 11 years and eight days ago, to cry: 'It is imperative that the House now show its united resolution to see the sovereignty of the Falkland Islands returned to our people!'?

David Howell (C, Guildford) admired Rifkind's refusal to yield to 'the emotional heat of the moment'. Edwina Currie thanked him for not 'embroiling our troops in that dreadful conflict', and Shrewsbury's Derek Conway was relieved he had resisted the temptation to 'express emotions and anger' and chosen 'realistic judgement' instead.

With the exception of a small counter-Serbian expeditionary team – Major Patrick Cormack (C), Sergeant Campbell-Savours (Lab) and Corporal Tony Banks (Lab), commanded by Lt-Col Winston Churchill (C) (Lady Thatcher C in C) – nobody was calling for a fight.

Wisely, no doubt. But I cast my mind back to that war with Iraq. Our EC allies took a cooler attitude than Britain. MPs erupted in fury at this 'backsliding'. What in ourselves we call restraint, in the French we called cowardice. Shall we compromise and call it discretion? In the House yesterday it proved the better part of valour.

'The future is grim,' Mr Rifkind said. 'The noose is being drawn tighter. Other weapons are available.' For a moment I thought he meant Lady Thatcher.

There's No Danger of Success in the War against Crime

16.4.93

The Home Office (it was to have been renamed the ministry of the interior in Baroness Thatcher's fourth term, alas!) represents a sort of benign black hole in the political cosmos. For ministers it is just a great, roaring void in which all energy is wholly absorbed, nothing can be achieved, but no serious harm is ever sustained. For Opposition spokesmen like Tony Blair, it is a trampolining gravity force, as elastic, impervious and sterile as rubber, allowing a young athlete to show off, but without itself being dented by his efforts.

For backbenchers of all parties, the Home Office is a mysterious and life-giving source of outrage, quotes and local newspaper headlines. Like the restless ocean – ever-changing, ever-renewing, yet somehow constant – crime and the Home Office's efforts to combat it heave and swell, ebb and flow, rage, storm and crash on the political shingle – yet always within bounds. Dylan Thomas remarked that the sea sings in its chains. He might have added that a home secretary does, too.

Take yesterday's questions in the Commons. Backbenchers are outraged at the workings of the Criminal Justice Act, which obliges magistrates to vary fines according to the means of the accused. Anthony Steen (C, S Hams) wanted to tell us a story: once upon a time, a little old lady of 83 living all alone forgot to renew her TV licence. 'Oooh!' sighed sympathetic back-bench MPs. And, do you know, she was fined *eight hundred pounds* because she had put aside some savings.

Up leapt Labour's Gareth Wardell (Gower) with even more dreadful news: *he* knew a youth fined a *thousand* pounds for dropping a crisp packet. 'Oh!' shouted MPs in shock.

Appalling. But, you see, the wonderful thing about this opera is that the plot is circular. Soon the Home Secretary will change the rules, and everybody will cheer. Soon after that, a backbencher will rise to tell us a story. He knows of a millionaire duke who has been fined *thirty* pounds for speeding home from a casino in his Bentley, while a constituent with not a penny in the world has just lost his job and gone to jail because he could not pay the same fine they slapped on him when he rushed his wife, in labour, to hospital in his battered old Escort van. 'Oh!' 'Shame!'

It was A E Housman who spoke of 'the sure foundation of despair'. It is in despair that the magic of crime and punishment as an infinitely renewable political energy source lies. Everybody knows that crime is getting worse and punishments do not fit. As with 'falling educational standards', we are both dismayed and strangely comforted to conclude that things ain't what they used to be. A minister who claimed to be beating crime would be viewed with disbelief, but a minister who balefully promises to try is cheered to the rafters.

There is no danger of success, and no harm in failure, since it is expected. Whitelaw, Brittan, Hurd, Waddington and Baker changed their standing not one jot by going their allotted rounds in the Home Office boxing ring.

And nor will Ken Clarke. Yesterday, Warren Hawksley (C, Halesowen and Stourbridge) complained about rape, Sir John Wheeler (C, Westminster N) complained about car crime and Labour's Tony Blair complained about everything. Blows raining down, the Home Secretary gripped the dispatch box, his feet planted on the sure foundation of despair, and sang in his chains like the sea.

21.4.93

Major Was There

Joe Orton once remarked that the most any boy can expect of his father is that he should be present at the conception.

Somewhat to the astonishment of MPs, John Major yesterday told the House that his own son James had been luckier. James is the only boy in Britain who can honestly say that John Major is the first human being he ever saw.

It was Labour's Michael Connarty (Falkirk E) who elicited the news. During an afternoon otherwise dominated by Bosnia and the public sector borrowing requirement, Connarty asked the PM whether he had known 'the sheer joy of being present at the birth of his children'. Major leapt to the dispatch box to declare 'yes, twice'. It seems his daughter Elizabeth shared with James the surprise of arriving in this world to see the expression of considerable pleasure on Mr Major's smiling face.

Is Mr Major the first Prime Minister to witness the birth of his children? The answer must be no, as his predecessor was undeniably present when Carol and Mark arrived. If there were any way Mrs Thatcher could have pleaded a prior political engagement she would surely have made her excuses and left, so Major may well be the first PM to have been *voluntarily* present at the birth of his children.

The Unprintable Pursues the Unspeakable

27.4.93

Famed for his colourful language, Labour's anti-hunting Tony Banks was unborn when Oscar Wilde called fox-hunters 'the unspeakable in pursuit of the uneatable'. Now, Banks chases the chasers: the unprintable in pursuit of the unspeakable in pursuit of the uneatable.

Banks was back in the saddle yesterday, urging his Fox Hunting (Abolition) Bill upon MPs. He was nearly unhorsed before he started – by a point of order from young Alan Duncan, the Tory foxcub from Rutland and Melton, who complained about the long title of the measure: 'a bill to make the hunting of foxes with dogs illegal'. As every countryman knew, yapped Duncan, you hunt foxes with hounds, not dogs. Madam Speaker did not think that this ruled, Banks's bill out of order, and let him proceed.

As he rose, some wag on the Tory side with that gift for making funny noises with pursed lips which makes a boy a hero at infants' school but is rarely useful in Cabinet, achieved a sort of trumpeting sound, a simulated hunting horn. Nobody was sure who was doing it, but it caused widespread giggles. Banks was undeterred. The rules permitted him ten minutes to make his case, and he galloped off at a cracking pace.

The pace never slackened; indeed, what his argument lacked in rationality it made up for in vigour. Critics may complain that Mr Banks rather undermined his central contention by the manner in which he contended it.

The contention was that the pursuit of foxes brutalizes those who join it; but so aggressive was his argument and so violent his language that we gathered that the anti-hunting brigade brutalizes its adherents, too. Wild-eyed and angry, Banks's face seemed contorted with hatred for those of his countrymen whom he variously described as 'disgusting', 'sick' and 'perverts'. He would not choose such people for close friends, he said. They were 'on a continuum which ends up in the Bosnian massacres'.

The benign Nicholas Soames, Food Minister, picture of cordiality and keen huntsman, looked at Banks in mild surprise. Where Banks in a rage would make a half-way convincing Serb, it was very hard to imagine Mr Soames on a continuum to a Bosnian massacre, or any other kind of massacre, except perhaps of the sherry trifle.

Any continuum that Soames was on would have to be a reinforced one. Anyway, he is too much of a gentleman to use a word like continuum. Forced to guess its meaning, he would hazard that a continuum is what you get from eating oysters in a month with no 'r'.

Banks pressed on. Having slandered the hunter, he flattered the fox. It seems that these fluffy creatures have been maligned. Mostly they see their role as auxiliary refuse-collectors. They only take lambs, suggested Banks, when the lambs are dead, or at least terribly ill – a sort of ambulance service, specialists in ovine euthanasia.

Foxes eat beetles, mainly, added Banks. He did not mention rabbits, but we assume foxes spend their evenings frolicking with them, or bunnysitting while Mr and Mrs Rabbit go to the theatre.

The hard edge to the Labour MP's voice dissolved as he spoke of the real nature of foxes. He began to sound quite tender. Perhaps a socialist, having failed to fit his theories to human behaviour, turns to the animal world in pursuit of the gentleness that he has lost, and found lacking in his fellow men.

Bully Boy Tactics Fail to Unseat
Trouserless Hurd

6.5.93

Well, well, there we are, smiled the Liberals' Sir Russell Johnston laconically, as Douglas Hurd sat down. MPs were debating amendment 2, designed to queer the Maastricht pitch.

We did not, of course, know where we were. We had no more idea where we were than before the Foreign Secretary stood up. All we knew was that we had watched two distinctive parliamentary performers, one in brutish advance, the other in elegant flight.

There *is* something brutish about Jack Cunningham. Though he dresses with style and moves – a suave, handsome fellow – with a sort of lounge-suited self-assurance, he retains the air of a proprietor of a gambling club: ready to ingratiate himself with a duke, but quick to corner a troublesome debtor in the lavatories and smash in his teeth.

Labour's shadow foreign secretary spoke yesterday in the manner of a sententious bully: a deputy head boy, recently appointed, with seven half-way decent O levels and second place in the inter-schools 400-metre hurdles behind him. Never far from the surface was an undertone of menace, born of the knowledge that, this time, he had the troops.

Every syllable was stressed, and punctuated by an ugly glottal stop. European became Ee*yur*-ep *Ian* – as though he had a smaller boy by the ear, and was twisting it slowly round, one yank per syllable, as he spoke.

He was ramming home a clumsy argument with great self-confidence, knowing he could rely for its success in the division lobbies upon people who would vote that the moon was made of blue cheese, if that discomfited the government.

Once or twice he was interrupted. On these occasions Cunningham turns on backbenchers nastily, fast, and at the slightest provocation. He is quick to become personal. To Edwina Currie, who crossed swords with him over what was supposed to be the real debate – the social chapter – he sneered that he doubted she would succeed in her hopes of becoming a Euro-MP.

On and on he went, jeering at the Foreign Secretary; but Douglas Hurd refused to look up, airily leafing through a sheaf of papers as if engrossed in a superior French novel – Proust perhaps, or Stendhal.

He was in fact preparing his retreat. The retreat, when it came, was performed with great elegance, but nothing concealed the pain.

It will be called 'dignified' by the press but it was not really dignified. The amendment was tiresome, he said; it was undesirable; but it was irrelevant. It would have been 'preferable' to leave the clause intact, 'to avoid possible confusions'; but it was not necessary.

The Foreign Secretary stood there like a man deprived of his trousers but not his poise, arguing with style that it would have been preferable not to go out to dinner in his mauve polka-dotted boxer shorts – to avoid possible confusions.

For the sake of neatness it would have been desirable to wear trousers. But it was not necessary. He was not going to give his enemies the satisfaction of depriving him of his dinner, by cancelling on grounds of trouserlessness alone. To dinner he would go then, trouserless.

'I was in sackcloth and ashes last time, and I am not going to wear them again,' he told Cunningham. We reflected that the Foreign Secretary cannot feel as confident as he pretends: but, whenever Mr Hurd does appear in sackcloth and ashes, the sackcloth will be expensively cut and the ashes of the finest quality.

Battler Clarke Puts Bruised Blair out for the Count

14.5.93

An event occurred in the Chamber yesterday of the kind we may one day look back upon and say, 'Ah, *that* was the day we first got an inkling . . .'

It was the first time anyone had seen it happen. Kenneth Clarke annihilated Tony Blair.

Clarke has always been a prize puncher. A boxer, not a fencer, there is nothing of the weasel in him.

Plenty of aggression but no malice, his manner by turns jolly or belligerent, he is unguarded, intellectually confident and careless whether he knocks things over by mistake.

Who else could have got away with chortling that he hadn't read the Maastricht treaty, or describing the government as 'in a dreadful hole'?

If there remained any doubt that Clarke was a potential Tory leader, it was wiped out yesterday by a single punch.

As to Tony Blair, there never was any doubt that he is a potential successor to John Smith.

While Smith paws the air and frets 'Why on airth?' at the dispatch box, it has sometimes seemed that the Opposition has devised a system for picking each succeeding leader off the shelf just after his sell-by date has expired; and that Blair, still fresh and saleable, has been lodged on the shelf to stale little, while Smith loses the next election.

Talk of Blair's charms has been growing. He is persuasive and nice: a splendid debater.

Middle-class, middle-of-the-road and ideology-free, Blair does not sound as though he ever could have been a socialist, let alone be one now. His hair is perfect. Clarke is Home Secretary, Blair his shadow. Blair has been doing well, fulminating about rising crime, comforting old ladies and looking more like the policeman's friend than any Labour frontbencher has ever done before.

For the first time in their lives. Tories can see law-and-order as a potential vote-*loser*. Blair arrived yesterday as a rising stock.

The Home Secretary, by contrast, was in trouble. His Criminal Justice Act was not working, magistrates were in revolt and he had come to the House to climb down.

Clarke can do this sort of thing frankly and without apology, and his statement sounded confident, but nothing could disguise the retreat. Tony Blair rose – for the kill, we supposed.

He made a fatal mistake. Unable to resist the lure of a headline, or a slot on the six o'clock news, Blair began by ignoring the statement and demanding instead a statement on the 'royal bugging' story.

It was plainly offside. When he did turn to the Criminal Justice Act, his remarks lost force in a shaking of Tory heads, and disapproving clucks.

Clarke arose and gave him the most comprehensive verbal thumping anyone has seen Blair receive.

Pushing aside his notes, and with the Tories cheering behind him, the Home Secretary told him his priorities were utterly absurd: ridiculous allegations promoting a sleazy book. 'A tabloid politician,' he spat.

Would he care to 'turn away from royal scandals and the bugging of matrimonial rows, and turn his mind to something that actually matters to ordinary men and women?'

The Tories, who are feeling bruised, loved it. At last! A champ! . . . but – aye, there's the rub. What a contrast with the wooden exchanges at PM's Questions ten minutes earlier.

Labour, who had thought they were on to a winner, hated it. What? Our Tony, bested? . . . but – aye, there *was* that compensation: he'd been upstaging the boss too often of late. This should quell the muttering for a bit.

For Labour, then, a cloud with a silver lining. For the Tories an unexpected burst of sunshine: but with a rumble of distant thunder.

Sharpening of Claws at the Sound of Battle

8.6.93

It wasn't one of her better speeches, but who cared? It was herself. That's all people need to know these days.

She wore an old favourite for the occasion: the navy-blue two-piece suit with bold white piping round the big angular collar. The desired effect is perhaps of Britannia rising from the waves, but another impression was of Sailor Girl. She looked good. Show her a good scrap and the decades fall away.

The House of Lords was really only a backdrop. Is there any other British statesman who can brush away all that gilt and red leather, treating it as no more than an elaborate stage set? Even Roy Jenkins, an infinitely more accomplished speaker, adapts himself to the Lords' mode, appearing as a creature of the Chamber, albeit a noble one. She just shrugs it all aside: a big cat detained briefly in a poodle parlour, sharpening her claws on the velvet.

Lord Wakeham, leader of the Lords and former Commons chief whip, spoke first, for the government. A guinea-pig could have made a more inspiring speech on our European destiny. Next up, Lord Richard, for Labour, suggested kindly that Lord Wakeham's trumpet had been muted; to be frank, we never heard a trumpet, even muted: a tinkle on the triangle, perhaps, but no more than that. If this was Lord Wakeham's song for Europe, *nul points* was our response.

Lord Richard, promising that he, by contrast, would give us a positive Labour Party point of view, proudly quoted his own party conference resolution declaring that the Maastricht accord 'while not perfect, is the best that can be achieved'. Euro-breasts heaved with pride and the hair tingled on the backs of our necks.

Then came Lord Jenkins. To say 'Euro-realist' when you can't pronounce your rs is immensely brave. When Lord Jenkins suddenly told us that he was a Euwo-wealist, many of their lordships sat up in surprise, supposing that this was some kind of a German sausage.

Baroness Thatcher removed her spectacles and looked sharply across. Geoffrey Howe, behind her and only a dagger's lunge away, grabbed and held the knot of his tie alarmingly, as though choking.

Then she stood up, the anti-sausage, clutching a sheaf of notes, many of them hastily scrawled in the preceding minutes. It was a shambles of a speech, by degrees rambling, nit-picking or derisory.

Although it had little form, it achieved its apparent purpose, which was, firstly, to apprise us of a list of things we ought to know but might foolishly have overlooked concerning Europe; and secondly to deliver to the media three deliberate sound-bites of a robust nature, to be used on news bulletins last night and in this morning's press. These will duly appear.

Only the perforation, three lines, had been typed: the rest was jottings in blue felt-tip, interpreted rather as one might a shopping list as one steered the supermarket trolley randomly and somewhat headlong between the shelves . . . Who was that, next to the bolognaise sauce? Ah, Roy Jenkins. She had a piece of her mind for him – she'd written it down somewhere; now, where was the page?

'May I have a word about the European Court?' And could someone tell her where the gravy granules were? Casually she insulted all the members of the European Court. 'Finally, the referendum . . .' Really? What about the oregano? But her list was at an end and she sat down.

In the gallery her Commons disciples took notes, or gazed, dumbstruck in wonderment. Who cared *how* she said it? The point was that *she* had said it. It was herself who had spoken. They had seen her. They had been there.

10.6.93

The Sting in the Tail

An unmistakable sense of malice hung in the Chamber. Eyebrows arched, and pale – very pale, an almost ghostly pallor – Norman Lamont sat between a self-satisfied looking Kenneth Baker and a skull-faced MP in thin-rimmed spectacles. It was as though Anger had come to sit between Pride and Avarice. Genesis does not record whether Lucifer, after his fall, made a personal statement ('humiliating climbdown . . . devastating blow . . . shocked angels gasped as Mr Lucifer hit out . . .') but if so, it was only a curtain-raiser for yesterday.

The chamber was packed. Tristan Garel-Jones, newly retired to the back benches, fanned himself with a brown envelope. On the front bench, Kenneth Clarke and Michael Howard, assassins-in-waiting, muttered to each other. Michael Portillo, apprentice assassin, arrived late for the spectacle, squeezing himself between their reluctant knees. The chief whip managed a thin smile. Opposite, Margaret Beckett, deputy Labour leader, and Gordon Brown, heir-apparent, flanked their leader like prison warders, while joint-heir-apparent Tony Blair skulked behind the Chair. The sense of conspiracy in the wind rivalled accounts of the medieval Vatican. It would have made a magnificent oil-painting.

Mr Lamont will perhaps remember that at 3.26 the House discussed in vitro fertilization, moving at 3.29 to prospects for a bridge to the Isle of Skye. His hands shook through both exchanges. He rose on cue at 3.30. Nobody had the least idea what he planned to say.

We still didn't by the half-way point. His voice a little unsteady, and through gritted teeth, he had managed a cordial nod in the direction of loyalty to the PM, then ploughed through a half-way convincing but none-too-graceful apologia for the supposed policy errors of his chancellorship. None, it seemed, had anything to do with him.

Tory backbenchers, some of them sitting within feet of me, in the overflow gallery, began to fidget. Is this all we had rushed to hear? Yet another 'not my fault, guv' speech? 'Poor old thing,' you could sense them thinking, 'wants to put the record straight – who doesn't – but wouldn't it have been more dignified to wait for his memoirs?'

Then he moved to policy. No tax increases, he urged; an independent Bank of England; no immediate return to the ERM: spending cuts. Backbenchers pricked up their ears: another leadership bid? Already? He seemed to be putting down a marker with the centre-right. Michael Howard's eyes narrowed.

Even thus far into the speech it was clear that John Major did not know what was coming. At times he would smile nervily, or nod when his ex-Chancellor said something with which he could agree. Beside him, the new Chancellor, Kenneth Clarke, grinned and nodded too. They seemed to think the worst was over.

And indeed the speech was nearly over. There had been the occasional glint of steel, but we had seen no knife. Then came the flash of an unsheathed blade. In effect Lamont told Major he had no direction and no guts. Poor John Major looked like a schoolboy unexpectedly singled out for a verbal lashing in assembly. The muscles around his mouth tugged awkwardly. Kenneth Clarke, whose face does not set easily to granite, achieved the appearance of a frozen pudding.

The backbencher beside me sat up. 'Oh dear,' he said.

Redwood Shows His Human Nature   *15.6.93*

Years ago, this column was first to spot the entry into the Commons, under deep cover, of the only Vulcan ever elected to parliament. John Redwood had arrived on the Tory back benches.

Vulcans come from the planet of the same name. Their most famous expatriate (half-Vulcan) is *Star Trek*'s Mr Spock. They are super-intelligent and utterly logical, resembling humans in every respect except that they have no emotions, and many have pointed ears. The new breed, like Mr Redwood, have their ears straightened in private clinics, so it is very hard to know when you are dealing with a Vulcan, but a giveaway sign is a steady, emotionless voice and chilling stare. They also exhibit gaps in knowledge about the folksier side of life on planet Earth, and will occasionally react to human displays of passion or humour with complete bafflement.

When Mr Redwood became a minister, I recorded this first example of Vulcan penetration into the junior ranks of government. I also recorded doubts as to whether Messrs Lilley, Howard and Portillo were pure-bred humans. It now falls to this sketch, which we may rename *Vulcan Watch*, to announce that a full-blooded Vulcan has for the first time entered the British Cabinet. John Redwood, the Welsh secretary, came to the Commons yesterday to report on flooding in the principality (or 'testing zone' as they speak of Wales on Vulcan).

He was accompanied by his PPS, David Evans (C, Welwyn, Hatfield, human, very), recruited in an attempt to 'humanize' his master, teach him jokes, explain about love, merriment, sin, etc. Mr Evans has been having some limited success. At the weekend, Redwood's address to the Welsh Tory conference had featured the pseudo-humanoid singing 'God Save the Queen' in Welsh – it is a simple matter, you see, to programme a Vulcan with an extra language, even Welsh. So far so good. Yesterday's statement, his first as a secretary of state, was an important new test.

Alas, attaining power has caused Redwood to revert. Striding in, attempting, mechanically, to swing the arms as humans do, he sat down, then rose in one smooth movement, staring icily into space.

'The – damage – has – been – very – extensive,' he softly droned, in that BT directory enquiries machine voice, 'eighty – five – per-cent – of – eligible – expenditure – over – the – threshold . . .' Had he gone on to say 'the – number – you – require – is – Llandudno – 0 – 4 – 9 – 2 . . .' few would have been surprised.

Alan Williams (Lab, Carmarthen) decided to test him. The 'Bellwin rule', said Williams (a formula for allowing relief payments) 'is a fig leaf'. Vulcans are weak at imagery; Redwood activated his WordSearch program and established that 'Bellwin rule' does not mean 'fig leaf'. 'No – it – is – not – a – FIG LEAF,' he droned, aware of a need to hit the Indignation Key, but hitting it on the wrong word.

But the performance was not altogether discouraging. Various backbenchers tried to short-circuit his logic system by putting the muddle-headed proposal that uninsured householders should be compensated by the government. At this, I saw Mr Redwood's eyes swivel involuntarily. Through my sound-amplifier I just managed to eavesdrop the interference from his internal circuitry: (*very faint*): 'Il – log – ic – al!' (*crackle-crackle*) 'Il – log – ic – al!' But something (a tap on the shoulder from Evans?) stopped him. He rose. '. . . appreciate – problem. There – is – mayor's – fund . . .' he whirred. Our Vulcan is learning.

Naval Guide to a Commons Outing   *22.6.93*

Late last night the Commons approved the Army, Air Force and Naval Discipline Acts (Continuation) Order, 1993. Renewable every year, this gives statutory backing to forces' discipline. It includes provisions for dealing with a group not unknown at Westminster: male homosexuals. The Royal Navy's detailed guidance for officers or ratings who may suspect a colleague, and advice on how to gather evidence and cross-question suspects, has just come into your sketchwriter's hands.

It's an absolute hoot. I ask myself how many of my old MP colleagues would pass these tests – or indeed, submit to them. They ought to, for the preamble to the guidance explains most persuasively why a group of men and women working closely together in the national interest must weed out these dangerous elements from their ranks.

Before imposing the regulations on servicemen last night, the House might have looked at their guidelines (RN IC 2/87) with a view to their immediate implementation aboard HMS *Westminster*: for we are dealing, as the notes point out, with men and women who 'are required to serve in a wide variety of situations . . . at home or overseas, away from familiar surroundings, relations and friends . . . [and] subjected to unusual stress, when it is all the more important to retain absolute trust and confidence between [them]'. Members of the Cabinet will say 'hear, hear' to that.

There, and on the government back benches too, 'the potentially divisive influence of homosexual practices or other sexual deviations must be excluded. [Such activities] may also give rise to . . . doubt about an individual's fitness to have access to classified information'. Golly, imagine giving a minister whose sexuality is in doubt access to classified information. Heaven forbid.

The 'haunts' of these people, says the guidance 'are generally well known'. Ho, hum; we must keep a look out for Tory MPs there. What are the signs? '12. Note the general appearance. Look for feminine gestures, nature of clothing and use of cosmetics, etc.' I am bound to observe that as an investigative strategy, this does leave a slight chance that a few may slip through the net. There is also a danger that we may find ourselves hauling in the Serjeant at Arms, bedecked in his tights, plus a crop of MPs fresh back from the *Newsnight* studios, traces of TV make-up unremoved. The advice to look for homosexuals particularly among 'those who are known to have unstable backgrounds' eliminates few MPs, I fear.

Anyway, leaving doubts aside, let us assume that we have rounded up our MP suspects.

How shall we examine them? '10. The patient should undress while standing on a white paper sheet.' Say he refuses? '16. . . . A direct order should be given and, if still refused, an appropriate charge should be made.' Oh, and our MP 'must not be allowed access to toilet or washing facilities, other than under constant supervision'.

There follow descriptions of examinations that are impossible to repeat in a polite newspaper; examinations that would, I can assure the Admiralty and the Prime Minister, fail to identify about three-quarters of the servicemen, and MPs, we are looking for. Ah well, take heart at least from this: '5. A homosexual act of itself is not life-threatening.'

You bet. If it were, Mr Major would have lost his 18-strong majority twice over by now. Happily, they were there in force last night, to vote this measure through.

Calming Influence of the Voice-over for Every Crisis

29.6.93

Yesterday the Foreign Secretary urged an agitated Commons to support the US attack on Baghdad.

The really terrifying thing about our diplomat turned head of Mr Heath's political office turned Thatcher's Home Secretary turned Major's Foreign Secretary, Douglas Hurd, is the very thing that makes him *at first* so reassuring. Mr Hurd is so completely professional that you have absolutely no idea what he thinks himself. You have a suspicion that he does think himself, but no inkling what.

Whatever the government has done, Mr Hurd pops up (if so dignified a creature can be said to pop up) and explains in the calmest voice that there was simply no alternative. Have appeals been made to reconsider the convictions of the Guildford Four? Mr Hurd is sorry but the most exhaustive review has already been undertaken. The finest intellects have looked afresh. Mr Hurd regrets . . .

Are Vietnamese refugees in Hong Kong being dragged into lorries and carted off to the airport? Ah, how Mr Hurd shares your distress, how carefully he has considered every other suggestion, how plain it is that none would be workable. Is some appalling new tangle of Euro-bindweed called the Maastricht treaty threatening our sovereignty? Oh, but you have been deceived! Mr Hurd has read the treaty; please understand that its purpose is to *enhance* our sovereignty. Are Muslims being slaughtered in Bosnia? The pain is written across Mr Hurd's own face. If only he could help, you know he would. It is *almost* vulgar to suggest otherwise. You sit down to hear Mr Hurd, convinced there can be no way of talking our way out of this one. You end up embarrassed that you even thought there was a problem. Such is his relaxed, civilized self-confidence, his evident humanity, that every horror becomes a tragic necessity (or why would he tolerate it?), every accident a part of the plan.

He could be Foreign Secretary, he could be chaplain general to the armed forces, he could be UN secretary-general, he could be Master of Balliol, or he could be the expert voice explaining the cleansing effects of Harpic in your lavatory. He could be the instructions on the wireless after a nuclear bomb, advising us that all was well but would we please whitewash our windows, wait under the table, and not drink the water for the moment – just in case? Mr Hurd's is the ultimate voice-over to video pictures supplied by somebody else.

This weekend the video pictures were supplied by the United States. Yesterday came Mr Hurd's voice-over. We must stand by our US allies; repel state terrorism. We must not be tricked by Iraqi propaganda . . .

One had entered the Gallery with hackles raised by this attack, doubtful of its wisdom. But as that calm, decent voice washed, in polite waves, like his hair, over hearers, one's doubts began to seem so adolescent. Maybe we just needed a good night's sleep? Of course the Americans had been right. Of *course* the Iraqis would dissemble. Of *course* the Arab moderates would make a show of displeasure, at first . . . You don't need to listen to his words: the very cadence of Mr Hurd's voice says 'of course'. We had been making a fuss about nothing, of course.

Still, Labour's George Robertson made a good fuss. Passionate but coherent, he rallied the Opposition in a way they were beginning to forget. For once he had the entire Labour party singing the same tune. It was an old tune: 'Yankee Go Home'. But at least they knew the words.

A Punch in the Noise from Patten

2.7.93

Having been badly beaten up by the National Union of Teachers, the Education Secretary, John Patten, has decided to pick on someone smaller than himself: the National Union of Students. He came to the Commons yesterday to kick sand in their faces, while some of the weedier boys on the Tory back benches egged him on.

At last: someone he could push around. All the pent-up anger and humiliation of his recent bruising battle over schools testing found an outlet – a point not lost on the SNP's Alex Salmond. Patten strutted to his seat in one of his new suits – beautifully pressed – his hair representing to coiffeurs the triumph that a prize-winning *vol-au-vent* represents to a pastry chef. Patten never *quite* calls cock-a-doodle-doo from the dispatch box, but he comes close.

And not only was his foe puny, but his argument was easy. Patten made a persuasive fist of his case – that students should choose to join a union rather than be conscripted, and that public money should not be spent by unions on political causes – and punched his way through the argument with stylish aggression.

He carried all before him. The only convincing objection came from another Tory, Robert Jackson, an ex-education minister who asked why universities should not decide these things for themselves. Jackson's question was significant, but quiet. Jeff Rooker, a Labour spokesman, was not quiet, but unfortunately he was not significant. He was quite the noisiest thing that had been heard in the Chamber for months. MPs marvelled not only at the scale of Mr Rooker's fury, but at its duration. He stood there, quite literally yelling at the top of his voice, for what seemed like 20 minutes. Nobody is sure what he meant but shouts of ''igher education', 'stoodent unions' and 'disgrace' ricocheting round the Chamber suggested that Mr Rooker didn't agree. A secretly thoughtful man, Mr Rooker was guarding his secret closely.

Angrier and angrier he grew – ''ow this guvvermint 'as the bare-faced *cheek* . . .' – until we started to fear for his health. A slim, slight fellow, with a receding hairline and an advancing Brummie accent, he sounded, with every yell, less like a higher education spokesman and more like a bus conductor who had been provoked beyond endurance and finally cracked. One had the impression he had been building up for years towards this outburst. The whole thing was a bleedin' scandal and a flippin' disgrace. His hearers soon ceased evaluating his argument and started to wonder whether we ought to rush over and help him: a wet towel, perhaps, or a glass of water. Mr Patten looked delighted with the effect he had created.

Towards the end, Rooker's apoplexy reached such a pitch that he grew unable to understand his own speech notes, and started to read (instead of the text of the speech itself) the instructions he had written for himself. Thus, and without warning, Mr Rooker suddenly looked up at the cameras and shouted: 'Give two examples and ask the minister to explain why they would be inappropriate!' MPs scratched their heads.

But one of Rooker's objections we did understand. The three months the minister had given students to respond happened to coincide with the summer vacation. Spluttered James Pawsey (C, Rugby and Kenilworth): 'Twelve weeks is perfectly reasonable.'

So let the House Leader propose, just as the House rises at the end of July, that MPs' allowances are to be cut – and give parliament until October to respond.

Britain's Own Worst Enemies Left Sitting on Defence

6.7.93

Yesterday, government and Opposition unveiled rival plans. Each outlined its own proposals for a war machine to defend Britain into the next millennium.

The two outlines were very different in concept. Labour plans to approach future world conflicts armed with a comprehensive range of reviews. Yesterday their spokesman, Dr David Clark, described just a few of the sophisticated and deadly reviews his party hopes to deploy.

The Tories are arming themselves with 'abouts'. Yesterday, Defence Secretary Malcolm Rifkind hinted at some of the abouts with which Britain's arsenal will be buttressed. Almost every consignment of new weaponry comes equipped with an about or two. These are designed to confuse the enemy.

Unfortunately they also confused Sir Nicholas Fairbairn (C, Perth and Kinross), who has returned after an illness, and was cheered loudly. What, he asked, was the purpose of these abouts? Mr Rifkind, said Fairbairn, had promised that Britain's surface fleet will be setting sail 'with a force of about 35 destroyers and frigates'. Sir Nicholas understood the purpose of the frigates and destroyers, but what was the function of the about? Did it (as he believed) have a capability for varying the size of the fleet by as many as 15 ships – between 30 and 45? How in practice did the Ministry of Defence intend to use this about?

But of course Mr Rifkind was not saying. Half the value of such weaponry lies in the element of surprise. As Mr Rifkind explained, the enemy was no longer the reliable monolith of communism: 'That certainty has vanished, to be replaced by a broad spectrum of risk and uncertainty.' One immediately saw his point. If Russians were the enemy then of course weapons like bombs and tanks would be what Britain needed. But now that the enemy was a broad spectrum of risk and uncertainty, a whole thesaurus full of abouts, maybes and quite possiblys will have to be aimed in every direction at once. Yesterday Mr Rifkind made a start, 'to provide,' he said, 'what such a fluid setting demands'.

This was not Labour's way. They placed their trust in an old but trusty weapon, manufactured right here in Britain, relatively inexpensive, and available in unlimited quanities: the review.

Reviews come in all shapes and sizes, and Dr Clark was calling for a whole range. At the top, he wanted 'a full review'. This we took to be a conventional review, but it emerged that Labour also wants a nuclear review – two, in fact: both strategic and battlefield. The British helicopter commitment needed a review, and submarines deployment was also 'desperately short' of a review.

At the bottom of the range, a comprehensive review was urgently needed to take care of defence workers whose jobs might be targeted by some of Labour's other reviews. Dr Clark urged Mr Rifkind to order one immediately.

As the Defence Secretary and his Labour shadow did battle across the floor, Mr Rifkind letting fly from his large stock of abouts and Dr Clark replying with a few well-aimed reviews, the impression grew that each of Britain's main political parties has developed a highly appropriate range of weaponry for dealing with the other. Just how fearsome this arsenal looks to foreigners, however, is doubtful. Let us hope our attacker proves to be not the hun, the dago or Johnny Frenchman, but a broad spectrum of risk and uncertainty. For this we are well equipped.

Flying Visit Gives Beckett a Buzz   *13.7.93*

As Margaret Beckett harangued media representatives assembled in Christchurch to hear her kick off Labour's by-election campaign, a fly became caught in her hair.

Picture the scene. A crowded room, chairs, hot television lights, foam-covered microphones and a table graced by a plastic rose, the candidate and Mrs Beckett. She was in an arresting outfit of shamrock green and blinding white, with earrings. Nigel Lickley, her candidate, was dressed like a Young Conservative from the early 1980s, smartly suited for the slaughter.

For us, just another press conference in another town. For the luckless Mr Lickley, a bid to save another Labour deposit. For the fly, a whole new situation.

The fly became confused. Initially it had been attracted by the sugared coffee and oatmeal biscuits. Now, disoriented by the television lights and the ringing of portable phones, its compass failed. Spotting the fine, bouffant, blonde soufflé of Mrs Beckett's hair, it thought it had found a place of safety: somewhere soft and fluffy where it could take refuge and snuggle. It flew straight in.

In an instant it was trapped. Contrary to the soft appearance, each brittle, lacquered strand represented, to the fly, a girder: but twisted and crimped into a wrought-iron maze. This was a Margaret Fly Trap. Caged and fenced and struggling to find a way through, the insect clambered and fell further into the interior. Now perilously near the scalp, you could see that it was close to panic.

Then somebody asked Mrs Beckett about the Tories' pension plans. She flew into an agitated state. Eyes flashing, she lashed out: 'Every day brings fresh rumours,' she said, omitting to mention that she was starting them. In a display of contempt for Tory heartlessness, she shook her head fiercely. The fly tumbled straight through to her roots and lay on its back waving its legs. Maybe it was stupefied by the fumes of Spray-'n-Go.

Not far away, Mrs Beckett's striking white earrings waved alarmingly from her lobes. She began a quieter, reasoned assessment of prospects for the welfare state. Righting itself and seizing the chance offered by this temporary lull, the fly began to crawl back from the roots, seeking a passage to the surface. It made headway.

'*Tories* want to *cheat* pensioners,' Mrs Beckett raged, jerking her head with each emphasis. The insect was trampolined to left and right, bouncing between strands, spiralling back down. It lost ground and, almost, hope.

Mrs Beckett moved to NHS dentures, the hottest topic in Christchurch after VAT on pensioners' gas bills. She built slowly to her peroration. A window of opportunity for the fly! It made a final dash for freedom, scrambling through three coiffeured layers in the course of one paragraph of her argument about dentistry. 'When the going was good,' she said, 'they gave money to the richest taxpayers. Now the going is tough, they take from the *poor*!'

On the word 'poor', Labour's deputy leader climaxed, with a sudden wild sweep of the head. The centrifugal force spun the fly helplessly to the surface of her hairdo. 'They *don't CARE*!' she spat, with another neck-breaking jolt.

We had lift-off. Ejected violently into the air, the fly found its wings at last and accelerated to safety, resolving never, ever, to attend a political press conference again. Labour's deputy leader reached her closing remarks, and was still.

For Margaret Beckett, one more by-election. For your sketch-writer, a welcome distraction. For the fly, a nightmare.

Pity the English, Cornered by Celts   *20.7.93*

Allan Rogers (Lab, Rhondda) started it. During Welsh questions he called the Tories' Ian Bruce (Dorset S) a stool pigeon.

A word of explanation. There are three varieties of Celt in British politics, one coming from Ulster, one from Scotland and the third from Wales. They all have this in common: they are aggrieved. Politics, for them, is the pursuit of grievance. Grievance is their meat and drink, grievance their waking cry and daily song; and before they go to sleep at night they kneel in silent prayer: 'Lord, why are the English so horrible to us?'

But here the similarity ceases. Your Ulster grievance is a wild, paranoid fantasy in which the Englishman walks hand in hand with the Pope and the IRA, smiling sweetly and plotting murder. Your Ulsterman must shout this treachery urgently from the rooftops and back benches: drama its medium, betrayal its theme.

Your Scots grievance, on the other hand, is a demand with menaces. Your Scotsman lunges from the shadows of Hungerford Bridge, or the Labour division lobby, cursing and growling, fingering a penknife and rattling a tin.

But your Welsh grievance is different from both. It is a sort of continuous, censorious whine, a tugging at the sleeve. Never threatening, it carries always a hint of moral reproof. In pious sing-song the Englishman is informed that his injustice is an affront not so much to Wales, as to Heaven. Unlike your Scot, your Welshman is not trying to pick a fight, just letting you know what God thinks of your behaviour.

On the temple steps, then, the Englishman encounters the madman, the footpad, and the itinerant preacher soliciting alms: England's three neighbours. Yesterday, questions to the Welsh secretary, was the preacher's turn to importune.

27.7.93   Bastards Flock to Join Stool Pigeons

A feeling of injustice is troubling Labour MPs. Last week, Madam Speaker told MPs that, in addition to being forbidden from calling each other 'young pups' or 'hypocrites', and being banned from suggesting that other MPs have not told the truth, they are not allowed to use the term 'stool pigeon' of each other.

On hearing Miss Boothroyd's ruling, MPs bit their lips but bowed to her authority. Now they turn on their radios and hear that the Prime Minister is calling his Cabinet colleagues 'bastards'. There seems to be one law for Downing Street, and another for the rest of Westminster.

So dare a sketchwriter, these days, call that barrack-room lawyer of the Labour back benches, David Winnick 'mischievous'? Winnick (Walsall) rose to ask Miss Boothroyd 'whether *we* can say "bastards"?' Miss Boothroyd said No. 'I am not responsible for what hon members say *outside* this Chamber,' she added sternly, rather like a primary school headmistress regretting what some children's parents let them get away with at home, but determined that decorum will prevail inside the school gates. Winnick was left in no doubt. Hon members would employ 'moderate language' while she was Speaker.

Dennis Skinner, never slow to spot an opportunity for using a rude word about Tories, made it clear that he was only quoting the

Prime Minister, and asked Miss Boothroyd to help him find out which three of the many Tory bastards on offer Mr Major had in mind. Miss Boothroyd was not playing. She called Nigel Spearing: a sure sign that the Chair is in no mood for fun.

Mr Spearing (Lab, Newham S) is a formidable Euro-bore and proud recipient of a postgraduate degree in advanced pedantry. His very voice wears cycle clips. He even rises to his feet pedantically, checking each cuff and pausing slightly too long to make it clear he has the right to. 'Madam Speaker,' he said, in the voice of one whose wisdom this world has not entirely recognized, but will. 'I have three brief points of order to put to you . . .'

I exited, bought and drank a cup of tea, made two telephone calls, dictated a letter and returned to the Press Gallery.

'. . . And secondly, Madam Speaker,' Spearing was saying. Miss Boothroyd wore the expression of a woman who only by an immense effort of the human will was restraining herself from chewing the arm of her chair. It strikes me that she is only in her early 60s. She faces the prospect of another eight years of this. She cannot leave. I can. I fled.

Brown Plumbs the Depths

28.9.93

The Labour Party Conference. . . .

Here at Brighton everyone is talking about Omov. It sounds like a brand of Russian soap powder, but apparently it is more controversial than ordinary detergent.

Some think it is too strong. Others say that it is too expensive, and speak of semi-Omov, Omov-plus, or Omov-minus. By Wednesday they will probably have compromised on Radion.

But yesterday was only Monday. We had hardly begun. Delegates drifted in after breakfast to inspect the hall.

There seemed to be an order of precedence, David Blunkett's dog took the lead, followed by Mr Smith followed by Margaret Beckett. The dog lay down dreaming of Odov. His master's voice was expected in a debate on health; and, later that afternoon, Gordon Brown was to speak.

I am having a problem with Gordon Brown. It is becoming hard to take him seriously. Increasingly, style stifles substance. It is an odd style and getting odder. On the basis of yesterday's dreadful speech, four elements dominate the performance.

First (as we have noted before), he speaks in bullets, like this: •. Popular newspapers use them to lend zap-snap emphasis to their hard-hitting lists.

Second, he has now started smashing his fist on to the lectern wherever a sub-editor would insert a bullet. Amplified by his microphone, the bangs ricochet around the hall as though they were being submitted to heavy shelling from the platform, gun-boat or submarine. The effect is startling.

Third, Mr Brown has started *dropping* his voice half an octave for the last word in each sentence. It makes him sound like a teenager hopeful of buying cigarettes or someone doing the voice of Daddy Bear in a bedtime story.

Fourth, his speechwriting proceeds by repetitious couplets, trip-lets and quads, each component clause starting with the same words as the last, then moving the idea forward just one notch. Where you or I would say: 'I had bacon and eggs for breakfast today,' Gordon Brown would say: 'I had bacon. And I had egg. And I had them for breakfast. Today.'

Then he would bang the lectern. The intellectual content of his speeches, which is flimsy, will not bear so leaden a structure and the whole thing sinks.

Add to this the fist smashing down on the lectern and the sudden voice plunges and the effect is bizarre. Not far into his speech, Brown wanted to tell us he was in Brighton to preach the gospel of discontent about the evils of unemployment, pov-erty and the abolition of wages councils.

Let me, from memory, transcribe for you what he said, using (*bang*) to indicate a terrific bang on the lectern, and ▼ to indicate voice plunge.

'So I am here in ▼ Brighton – to preach the ▼ gospel – of (*bang*) discontent – about the (*bang*) evils of unem▼ployment.

'The gospel of discontent about (*bang*) ▼ poverty.

'The gospel of discontent about the (*bang*) abol▼ition, of wages
▼ councils . . .'

And so on. There were eight pages of it.

A whole cartload of tiny soundbites, stuck together into a
speech all negative, all ending in a dying fall, all going nowhere.
It was like a thousand caterpillar pelts stitched together into a
grotesque parody of a fur coat.

It was purely dire.

Verbal Bulldozer Clears Smith's Path

30.9.93

'I am a typical creature of the movement,' he roared. Terror
gripped the faint-hearted. Yesterday in Brighton, John Prescott
went 12 rounds with the English language and left it slumped
and bleeding over the ropes. Among the collateral damage were
thousands of Mr Smith's critics, many trade union dinosaurs,
several big composite motions and Margaret Beckett's political
career. And all this in quarter of an hour! Such gratuitous violence should be kept off our television screens for fear of frightening old ladies.

Other politicians pre-release transcripts of their speeches. The
very thought of a Prescott transcript is laughable. Before his
speeches are delivered, Mr Prescott is unaware of what he is
going to say; after they are over, nobody has the least idea what
he has said. Any transcript would be gibberish – nouns, adjectives
and unattached parts of speech lying among the verbal wreckage
like a rose garden after a bulldozer. Yet, somehow, everybody
guesses what he meant. I dare not offer a summary, any more
than I could provide the précis of a multiple pile-up, of which
Prescott's speeches are the literary equivalent. His off-the-cuff
rendering of the Lord's Prayer would read like this:

'Our Heaven which Thou art hallowed in Be Thy name Father
to give us ongoing daily delivery of this trespassing to Kingdom
come and will Thy be done on earth for Heaven's sake as it is!

And forgive us this day, our evil bread likewise also deliver us not into any leading temptations like we do if they do it unto us because Thy power is in the Kingdom of the Glory and ... [stops to pant] Amen! Comrades for ever! (wild cheers and standing ovation).

Prescott's relationship with his mother tongue ranks with *Moby Dick* as one of the great adversarial contests of all time: a life spent pursuing our language with a vengeful fervour. Yesterday he cornered and flattened it. The destruction, simultaneously, of political enemies was incidental.

Diva Delights in Cries of 'Encore'

20.10.93

Lady Thatcher answers questions and signs books....

The questioner whose chance came almost at the end summoned it up. Offered the microphone, and after a short pause, she said: 'Lady Thatcher, I miss you dreadfully.'

You could feel the groundswell of support for that. It welled up from most of the audience. Those who had come to mock, to take detailed notes, or to make enquiries of a practical sort, sensed the inappropriateness of our presence – like turning up at a revivalist rally in the hope of nailing down the preacher on his claimed healing powers.

This baroness – attired yesterday in imperial purple, diamonds and pearls, and draping herself over the lectern like an operatic diva there mainly to be adored and only incidentally to sing – has long passed the stage of needing to prove anything, or indeed do anything. She needs only to exist, to appear in the flesh, to *be* just what we always knew she was; to recite one or two of those famous sentiments, once more with feeling.

Would she consider setting herself up as an international one-woman political Red Adair? Ah, she replied, Red Adair only put the flames *out*. Did the Conservative party need a period in opposition, to recharge its batteries? '*Never* give up office! Hold on! You might not get back.'

Her voice is an octave deeper than it was: a semi-tone down for each of the 16-odd years since she first led her party. She has gained terrific stage presence, a powerful use of the controlled pause, and a sense of the spectacle she herself is creating which leads almost – but not quite – to self-parody. It teeters on the edge of pantomime. Good fairy? Wicked witch? Cinderella, stepmother or Widow Twanky? She played them all, rolled into one.

Lady Thatcher simply, obviously, unconcealably adores being told that nobody can replace her and she never should have gone. When the first questioner asked if she would consider resigning her peerage and returning to Number Ten, her 'no sir' came somewhere between a purr and a growl. We never heard a lady more capable of saying 'no' when she meant 'yes'.

It is when she speaks of battles that her eyes burn and her voice takes wing. Battles with Galtieri, battles with Scargill, battles with the Wets. All these chapters in her story are well known, but she went over each again, to the delight of her audience. Lady Thatcher has reached that lucky state when it really doesn't matter what she says. She symbolizes things. Her presence, to be seen, touched and to sign books is taken as evidence of the political verities, as might the appearance of some minor saint be evidence of religious truths.

At party conferences they have taken to magnifying the platform speaker on to enormous video screens to each side. But she stood at the Barbican last night, a tiny figure on a vast stage before a huge audience, and all attention was on her. There was no need at all for magnification.

Billericay Rocket Colours Future of Russian Politics

27.10.93

It is reported that Boris Yeltsin is to reconstitute the Russian parliament along new lines. It is to be called the Duma. Yesterday at Westminster the Russian Foreign Minister, Mr Kozyrev, was seen entering the ambassador's gallery and settling down to watch questions.

Is he here to pick up tips for the new Duma? That this might indeed be our distinguished visitor's intention struck me, in all its horror, as a well known backbencher leapt up to question health ministers. Mrs Teresa Gorman (C, Billericay) was about to show Mr Kozyrev how it's done.

She was sensational. And that's before she even spoke. Where other women paint their lips alone in that violent pink colour advertised as 'fuchsia' or 'crushed raspberry', Mrs Gorman was dressed in it from head to toe, with gold buttons. She looked like a killer fruit-drop, or hyper-active cherry.

What, asked Billericay's bouncing bonbon, was the minister going to do to promote hormone replacement therapy? 'It gives *amazing* benefits,' she said, 'of which I myself am an amazing example.'

The whole House cheered. The spring-heeled Mrs Gorman just stood there, quivering with suppressed energy. It was as though, even as she spoke, scientists in some nearby control tower were executing the final countdown . . .

'Ten, nine, eight . . . Mission Teresa, having failed to find intelligent life on Earth, is ready to depart . . . seven, six, five . . . lift-off is imminent . . . four, three, two . . . bye-bye Billericay . . . one . . .'

And off she goes, blasting into outer space, faxing her gospels to the passing planets and Tannoying the stars, seeking life-forms better able than ours to match her energies, shaming the sun himself, astonishing lesser meteors. She certainly astonished MPs.

Even the famously cocky Tony Banks (Lab, Newham NW) looked limp by comparison. Praising Mrs Gorman as 'radiant proof' of the efficacy of her own hormone treatment (she joined the cheers at this), he asked the prime minister, somewhat plaintively, whether it was not the case that men, too, could benefit from the replacement of their hormones?

Certainly it is true that Mr Banks's hair appears lately to have lost some of its previously spreading grey. Our guesses as to the cause of this may have been unfair. Is he on HRT?

Dennis Has Royal Beano   *19.11.93*

Briefly, yesterday, the Bash Street Kids took over. It lasted seven minutes. In what will become known as the Short Parliament, the Commons Chamber was occupied by a gang of desperadoes. While the Queen was opening parliament in the Lords, Dennis Skinner and his chums in the Commons passed an act abolishing her. It was like that episode in *Animal Farm*: the ruling pigs were at a party, and the other animals took over the farmyard.

They chose their moment well. The Tories and the respectable part of the Labour party had followed Madam Speaker to the Lords for the Queen's speech, and the coast was clear.

The Skinner gang struck. They occupied the Speaker's chair and proposed two new laws, abolishing not only the monarchy but the aristocracy too. They were on the point of disestablishing the Church of England when they were interrupted by the return of the grown-ups.

Last year, Mr Skinner challenged Black Rod to a game of snooker. This year he watched with an expression of amused scorn while the royal emissary declared: 'Madam Speaker, the Queen commands this honourable House to attend to Her Majesty in the House of peers.' Everybody upped and trooped out.

A moment's silence, then: 'Let's abolish the House of Lords!' Mr Skinner rose and climbed up to the empty chair. His mates giggled. He sat in it. 'Order! Order!' Bearded Jeremy Corbyn (Lab, Islington N) sauntered in, tieless. 'Are you dressed properly?' drawled Mr Skinner. 'The motion is that this House do agree that we abolish the House of Lords. All those in favour, say "Aye".' A ragged but enthusiastic shout of assent greeted him.

'All those against, say "No".' Silence. 'The ayes have it, the ayes have it,' declared Mr Skinner. At last the revolution! He must have thought he was dreaming. Up jumped Mr Corbyn: 'Mr Speaker, the second motion relates to the monarchy.'

'Are you suitably dressed and on your knees? Have you the appropriate kneepads?' demanded Mr Skinner. 'Yes, sir.' 'All those in favour of abolishing the monarchy?' 'Aye!' 'All those against?' Mr Allen shouted 'No!' but could find no seconder.

'I declare the motion carried,' announced Mr Skinner, refusing to take points of order, and swept out.

A motion to disestablish the Church of England was circulated, but before the revolutionary agenda could be proceeded with further, the enemy was at the door. Madam Speaker arrived back and climbed into her seat.

Did she notice it was warm? Would she, like Mummy Bear, ask: 'Who's been sitting in my chair?' It seemed not.

Mr Skinner had just provided us with the first break in constitutional authority since the Civil War. As in those ancient mockeries in which the Lords of Misrule temporarily take over, we had been reminded how thin is the line between order and chaos. Let us hope Betty never finds out.

(*She did.*)

Old Trouper Opens New Season

25.11.93

Rejoice, fans of the parliamentary pantomime: Michael Heseltine is back! Yesterday's performance had been eagerly awaited. It was his first Commons speech since the heart attack five months ago. Heseltine has been seen often on parade, but always silent. Might the fire have gone out? Might the master have lost his touch?

Those who know him suspected the news would be good. To Heseltine-watchers the maestro's appearance, mute, at Blackpool was anything but a sign of illness. It was final proof of a total cardiac comeback. For the first time in his life, the great man remained speechless on the podium. A deputy, Tim Sainsbury, made a quiet, unsensational speech.

Nothing, absolutely nothing, could put a more intolerable strain on the Heseltine heart than that. Deprived of an opportunity to speak! Forced to keep his mouth shut while an inferior addressed the multitude! This was the ultimate test. Top surgeons assembled in a nearby laboratory studied the Heseltine cardiograph print-out as Sainsbury spoke; noted the huge strain on his entire nervous system; cheered as his heart kept pumping; and pronounced his cardiac system healthy.

Perhaps the critical moment at Blackpool was when Sainsbury sat down, right beside Heseltine, and a thousand delegates applauded *him*, Sainsbury. Heseltine's lips tightened, his jaw worked, his eyes narrowed in suffering to slits – but his blood pressure remained within acceptable bounds.

Friends, then, suspected, before the President of the Board of Trade even rose yesterday, that all would be well. We were not disappointed.

Heseltine would have been forgiven for a low-key speech: for not making this the big test. Yet, careless of whether there were many to hear, he launched into a shameless blockbuster of a speech, tearing into the Labour party, pouring scorn on Cook and Smith, lauding the magnificent achievements of British industry under his own visionary leadership, thumping the dispatch box and waving his arms . . . and rousing the scattering of Tories behind him to attention, then interest, then excitement, and finally a great wave of cheering.

'Six thousand fingers,' he cried, 'clawed at the throats of the government front bench,' when the Opposition claimed that the insolvency of Leyland-Daf would bring 6,000 job losses. The job losses had never occurred. Instead, there had been new jobs. And where were those fingers now? 'Stuck, all 6,000 of them, in the dikes of Labour's crumbling allegations!'

When the president sat down, order papers fluttered in the air behind him, and Labour were left, slumped and sulking, across the benches opposite. His speech had been almost entirely devoid of content, but who cared? It had worked.

Wind of Change Ruffles Knickers

10.12.93

'You're just trying to get my knickers in a twist again,' cried the Baroness Trumpington to the Earl Russell, in her Dick Emery 'Ooh, you are awful, but I like you' voice. Is nothing sacred?

It seems not. On Wednesday Baroness Thatcher was forced to appear before a bench of inquisitors, an eagle pecked by ravens. On Thursday the House of Lords proposed to bring spies under the gaze of MPs. Nature is awry. No wonder the night had seen wild winds toppling walls.

Even the Lord Chancellor accepted that what peers were doing was breathtaking. 'I myself felt, during the debate five years ago, that the time was not right for such a step,' he said. 'What has changed?'

Lord Mackay did not say. It struck us that the Prime Minister has changed. We peered down into the ranks of peers – ghosts discussing spooks – and wondered what had drawn them to this debate. How many were ex-spies themselves – spooks of spooks? I spotted one eye-patch and a number of people with wires leading into their ears. 'Theirs,' said Lord Mackay, 'is not the high-profile, glamorous life . . .' The Lord Chancellor's own black silk stockings and little black slippers with silver buttons, combined with a silk cloak and full-bottomed wig, were hardly designed for snooping unnoticed in bus queues. Perhaps the whole thing is double-bluff, and Mackay is, if not M himself, then the big Mac.

He was followed by R, Lord Richard, Labour Leader in the Lords.

After R came . . . well, what shall we dub Roy Jenkins? 'W', I think. 'We welcome the thwust of this bill,' the ex-Glasgow MP told their Lordships. To have a woman in charge of MI5, he continued, was reassuring, 'even if not wholly *wationally* weassuwing'. And he conceded that the intelligence services seemed to have settled down recently: 'there's been an efflux of time,' he explained, without mishap. An *efflux* of time? Is this term common on the streets of Glasgow? We imagined Lord and Lady Jenkins at breakfast. 'I wonder why the toast hasn't popped up,' worries the great man. 'Hasn't there been rather an efflux of time, my dear, since you put it in the toaster?'

Later, Lord Jenkins spoke of a lacuna. A lacuna appears to be a vacant efflux. Lord Jenkins's speech took an efflux but was in no sense a lacuna. His lordship also spoke of a monoculture.

Lord Callaghan, following him, noted that he, Callaghan, had wanted a more accountable security service 14 years ago, whereas Jenkins had only wished for it seven years ago. Lest this be taken as a reproach, he added he would like to express pleasure at Jenkins's recently awarded OM.

We share Lord Callaghan's joy. But still we scratch our heads. Lord Jenkins was Home Secretary not once, but twice. Lord Callaghan was Prime Minister, and Home Secretary as well, not to say Foreign Secretary. There have been, if we may put it like this, considerable effluxes (*effluces? effluxen? effluxim?*) of time during which these men were not without influence. But we search the history books for references to their own versions of yesterday's bill, and what do we find? A lacuna. A monoculture. No wonder Lady Trumpington has her knickers in a twist. After the efflux of an hour, I left.

Arafat Stumbles into Occupied Territory

15.12.93

They arrived in order of importance, the lesser celebrities taking their seats first: the PM, the Leader of the Opposition, Jeffrey Archer ... and, finally, the big one. All eyes turned upward to the Distinguished Strangers' Gallery as the most famous tea-towel in history was borne to its appointed place, atop the head of a diminutive and smiling Yasser Arafat in desert khaki.

Prime Minister's Questions was in full swing. Mr Arafat sat down. Below him, MPs began screaming and hooting at each other without apparent cause. Madam Speaker, wearing the closest thing in the Chamber to full purdah, shrieked for order.

Fists were waved, fingers stabbed into the air. Strange orderlies in medieval black uniforms moved in and out.

What was this all about? Mr Arafat's smile was now tinged with anxiety. Even at its most unruly, the *intifada* had an agreed aim and unwritten rules of engagement. Here in this strangely decorated temple the walls rang to the sound of curses and the atmosphere bristled with suppressed violence; yet neither reason nor rules were clear. Where was the Red Cross? Who was in command of the Opposition forces?

The shouting continued. Mr Major – that courteous grey-haired English gentleman they had identified to him as the 'Prime Minister' – seemed to be yelling at his own compatriots. And they were yelling back. Everyone was too angry to make any sense. Was this not a curious kind of leadership? Had some international drama whipped up the rabble? Russian fascism? Gatt, on a knife-edge? The Arab-Israeli impasse? Feelings were plainly running high. The Prime Minister was incensed. Maybe the House was devoting its 15 minutes with its Leader to hammering out the settlement of some great historic conflict? No. MPs were discussing the cost of decorating Number 10. They had just finished discussing last year's drinks allowance for Downing Street.

Yasser Arafat leaned towards the balcony, peering over in disbelief, smiling politely, utterly baffled.

Adopting a desert metaphor in honour of his guest, Major accused the Labour party of throwing sand in people's faces. Then, under cover of a volley of economic statistics lobbed across the Mace at the heads of Opposition MPs, the PM departed.

... And still that frozen smile on Mr Arafat's face. So this was democracy. This was self-government. This was what he had taken his people through all those decades of slaughter to achieve. Casting his mind back to the days of grenades, mortars and Kalashnikovs, the world of blood and sand, Mr Arafat struggled with a strange emotion. Was it nostalgia?

A Shining Gateway to Portillo's Spanish Roots

26.1.94

In mid-grey suit, shining white cuffs and a restrained silk tie, Michael Portillo yesterday addressed the Commons not as one of the lads mucking in with the mob, but as a young flight lieutenant who has distinguished himself early in battle, and come back to talk to senior boys in his old school.

In civvies for the afternoon, he had laid aside his flying kit for a morale-boosting visit at a difficult time in the war. His complexion was fresh, his eyes bright, his brown hair – a mid-parted, squashed wave – looked as though he had just doffed his airman's leather helmet after four hours in a Spitfire over Germany. He looked earnest and brave.

Seated next to him – crumpled, jaded, trapped in a desk job with seniority but little leeway – sat housemaster, Kenneth Clarke. Easy enough, thought Mr Clarke, for these young daredevils to impress . . .

He did impress. Michael Denzil Xavier Portillo. Even the name adds a trace of exoticism. Which of us can boast an X among our initials? Careful though he was, speaking of the problems of the Prime Minister of Spain, to mispronounce Gonzales in the English way – his ancestors turning in their graves – you could not forget that Portillo was virtually, but not *quite*, English.

Portillo belongs in the Peruvian Andes, captaining the *Sendero Luminoso* ('Shining Path') rebels. Their methods are murderous but their message sounds clean.

Watching him speak yesterday, I observed a number of characteristic dispatch box poses, subliminally shrewdly selected. He rarely hunches or buries his face. His hand movements are open: clearly and boldly stated. *Portillo Luminoso.* The Shining Gateway. To those in search of simplicities, it has an appeal.

Good-news Doll Pops in

16.2.94

Only last week we described the arrival in the Chamber of Mrs Cheryl Gillan (C, Chesham and Amersham), all dressed in yellow, spreading joy among gloomy backbenchers in grey suits at PM's Questions. She shared with John Major her picnic-basket full of good news and helpful economic statistics. We compared her to a little primrose (well, a medium-sized primrose) peeping through the tarmac.

Yesterday, Cheryl was a poppy. All dressed in the red they would call 'fiesta' in paint charts. Mrs Gillan popped up on Question One to the Employment Secretary, David Hunt, to ask how much British industry spends on training. Mr Hunt told her it was quite a lot. Mrs Gillan was in rhapsodies. Did this not prove that we were ahead of the rest of Europe? This kind of thing was so very important for employers. Hooray!

Shortly afterwards, Mrs Gillan left. In the interlude before she returned we were left to ponder the possibility that she means to make a habit of this, tripping into the Chamber gaily attired, imparting any good news that has recently come to her attention, and then tripping out again, presumably in search of more.

Soon, Mrs Gillan will be automatically linked to happy tidings. The very sight of her on television will cause an optimistic blip on the Stock Exchange. Like the smiling figurine in those 'rain-or-shine?' toys, swivelling out from her wooden shelter to indicate sunny weather, she will no longer need to speak at all.

A Wee Cow'ring Tim'rous Beastie

23.2.94

Is beast-baiting a cruel sport? The question which divides anti-hunt campaigners gained a new urgency yesterday as the most famous beast of all, the Beast of Bolsover, was finally taunted beyond endurance. Dennis Skinner came out to fight.

Heaven knows the weekend past had been pretty bloody for him. Much of the *News of the World* had been devoted to a breathless account of his friendship with a lady who was not a miner's daughter and lived not in Clay Cross, but in Chelsea. The paper suggested that, disguised in a muffler, he had avoided recognition by lurking in bushes.

Your sketchwriter knows the lady in question: a gentle, modest person, by no means the wealthy Sloane Ranger the press has implied. But some stories are too good to check, and Skinner's own delight in throwing mud at his Tory opponents has made his come-uppance all the more delicious for government back-benchers.

Besides, has he not invited it by posing as an apostle of proletarian puritanism? Tories returned to the Commons this week aching to goad him into a playground fight.

Wisely, Dennis wasn't playing. Speaking not a word on Monday, he sat, arms folded, in his usual place. This was a wee, sleekit, cow'ring tim'rous beastie.

A silent Skinner is almost uncanny. How long could it last? As with a starling that refuses to squabble or an alligator unwilling to snap, one feels tempted to poke at the creature with a stick, to see whether it is still alive.

The Tories' David Evans (Welwyn Hatfield) wielded the stick. The question was about Lambeth Community Care Centre. Couldn't the care centre help, he asked, with 'hats and mufflers to keep Labour warm when they are hiding in these bushes?'

This was too much. Bolsover sprang from his lair. 'Chelsea!' cheered the Tories, and: 'Where's your muffler?'

On a rising wave of cheers – from Labour genuine, from the Tories mocking – a puce-faced Skinner stabbed his finger at the Tories. Let the Cabinet submit their own private lives to examination at the dispatch box, he roared, then he'd willingly submit his own. Let them call an election if they dared! Let the people judge! 'Then I'll be sat over there and some of them will be wanting a fresh job!'

Hm. Fighting talk, but not quite the beast's former song. The old refrain was 'I'm better than you.' The new one is: 'You're no better than me.' Behind a furious smokescreen, a significant retreat.

'This kid's not going to run away!' rumbled Skinner, as the storm abated. Indeed not. This kid's got pluck. But for some time to come, I suspect, this kid's not going to be giving chase, either.

At Last He Admits It

10.3.94

Mr Waldegrave had told the Scott enquiry that ministers sometimes lie. . . .

It is a mad world into which William Waldegrave has stumbled.

If you want to know why the British public and its news media get liars for their politicians, just look at what we do to those who try to tell the truth. Here we go again, sniffing around our political leaders, picking up the scent of any intellect bolder than the others, and hounding him down. Political commentary seems to consist in ambushing anyone so incautious as to tell us truths we do not wish to hear, shrieking 'gaffe! gaffe!' like parrots, and baiting him into oblivion. We take pot-shots at every head that appears above the parapet, then notice that we are left only with pygmies for politicians. Then we write columns bemoaning our leaders' lack of stature.

We mob, ridicule and finally destroy those who try to refresh our politics, and then complain that our politics is stale. Every time a politician stands up, we break his legs. We end up with those whose only posture is to crouch. And then we rail against timidity! Truly, we are a most hypocritical people.

In the mad world which Mr Waldegrave has described, the man who says he never lies is accounted more honest than the man who admits he might.

A Pocketful of Social Deference

16.3.94

We witnessed yesterday one of the last surviving examples of social deference at the Commons. A Tory barked at a Labour MP that he should get his hands out of his pockets. Despite himself, the socialist almost complied.

A century ago the first Labour MPs struggled under a handicap: in class terms the Tories were their 'betters'. Habit of respect for toffs died hard, even in men who had rejected the class structure intellectually. It is said that, before the war, working-class MPs often found it difficult to question Tory ministers with the insolence that Opposition requires. Deference lingered in the second natures, if not the conscious beliefs, of MPs born in Victoria's reign. That has gone.

Or has it? Male readers will know that, though nothing comes more naturally than to put your hands into your pockets, it is almost impossible to *keep* them there after a voice with any hint of social command has told you to take them out. So spare a thought for Labour's Alan Simpson (Nottingham S), a quietly spoken, polytechnic-educated 45-year-old. He had a question for the Prime Minister. Unfortunately none of us can remember what it was, for the occasion was swamped by hilarity.

Mr Simpson rose. More out of nervousness than disrespect he thrust his hands into his pockets. Addressing the PM, he began: 'Would the Right Hon gentleman . . .'

'*Get* your hands out of your pockets!' came an officer-rank bark from somewhere on the Tory side. Simpson reacted without thinking. One hand was out of his pocket, the other well on its way, before he remembered the class struggle. Too late to put back the hand! Aborting the withdrawal of the other hand, he thrust it defiantly in. One in, one out. MPs guffawed. The impact of his enquiry was lost. PM's Questions, commanding the premium they do, it may be years before he gets another chance.

Heseltine's Black Day Swings From
Bad to Verse

14.4.94

Something seems to have upset Michael Heseltine. Nobody and nothing pleased him yesterday. Labour questioners received terse, irritated replies, while even friendly Tory poodles were sent away with cursory lists of statistics, sniffily delivered.

Perhaps he was a touch disappointed about something? A little miffed, possibly, still to be there? Like waking up from a dream in which one has become a rock star, a football hero . . . a prime minister, even . . . one blinks, focuses on the heap of dirty linen on the floor that is yesterday's clothes, and realizes that these, after all, are the circumstances of one's life; and likely to remain so. Mr Heseltine's short fuse and depressed countenance put us in mind of that Tom Jones hit, 'The green, green grass of home':

> I wake up and look around me –
> At four grey walls which surround me.
> And I realize – oh, yes, I realize –
> I was only dreaming.

With no more than a slight effort of the imagination it was possible to imagine Heseltine doing a classic karaoke rendering, from the front bench, of Tom Jones's great hit.

With his frilly lace shirt unbuttoned half-way to reveal a tanned, hairy and medallioned chest, leather trousers far too tight, a toilet roll stuffed discreetly down them to enhance his leadership prospects, the Industry Secretary grips the mike and, belting it out with great intensity, sings:

> Yes, they'll all come to meet me.
> Arms reaching, smiling sweetly.
> It's good to touch the green,
> Green grass of . . .

. . . well, Chequers.

Then, laying down his mike for a moment, he looks around.

The Chamber is nearly empty. The television monitor screens say *Industry Questions.*

The tattered file of civil servants' notes on the table before him reads 'Trade & Industry: 13 April 94: supplementary briefing.' To his left sit a junior whip and a junior minister.

Sadly, the prisoner picks up his mike again, and croons soulfully:

> And there's a guard, and
> There's a sad old padre;
> On and on we'll walk at
>   daybreak,
> Again to touch the green,
> Green grass of . . .

. . . well, the DoI, 123 Victoria Street, SW1.

Janice and John Take Centre Stage

15.4.94

The stuffier element in the Parliamentary Conservative Party will this morning be deploring yesterday's performance at Prime Minister's Questions by David Evans (C, Welwyn Hatfield). Your sketchwriter is not among them.

This sketch takes the view that if you want people to perform with wet sponges, funny noses and custard pies, you might as well recruit a proper clown to do it.

Mr Evans, at least, is a professional. Yesterday he had us in stitches.

Mr Evans asked the Prime Minister to explain something to his wife. 'Janice wants to know,' he began, as Tories giggled, 'whether it was the Conservative Party that won the last four elections, with a record 14 million votes in the last?'

MPs pinned back their ears, for Evans had started quietly and he never ends quietly. There was more, much more, to come.

Labour groaned. This was not the first time Janice Evans had starred in parliamentary exchanges. Her husband celebrated her recent return from hospital by treating John Major to a range of her views, which bear a remarkable resemblance to Mr Evans's own opinions.

So carried away did he become that Mr Evans strayed from the subject of his wife, to be advised sharply by Madam Speaker to 'stay with Janice'.

Alas, Miss Boothroyd's advice does not seem to have sunk in. Yesterday Mr Evans stayed with Janice only moments longer. He had one more question on which (he told the Prime Minister) his wife needed Number 10's advice: 'Will he also tell Janice whether it was a *Conservative* Government which, in 1978, imposed a new, high rate of tax?'

MPs scratched their heads. As the Conservatives did not win power until 1979, David could surely have told Janice, on his own authority, that they were unlikely to have been setting tax rates in 1978. Had there been a breakdown of trust in the Evans household? Did Janice now treat even the simplest statements from her husband with suspicion?

Requiring the Prime Minister, in the presence of the whole House of Commons, to back him up, seemed to be over-egging the pudding.

Shrewder onlookers realized that this could not be all. Evans was only on the preliminaries. He had not yet reached a deafening bellow, he was only shouting. His face was only moderately puce. He was still on the runway.

Then came lift-off. Janice was left behind as Mr Evans established the level of Labour's top rate of tax. 'Was it *60* pence in the pound?' he yelled to Mr Major, across a sea of tittering Tories. 'No!' they yelled back.

'Was it *70* pence?

'No!'

'Was it *90* pence?'

'NO!'

'Was it *98* pence?'

'YES!' Grinning, the Prime Minister told Evans he could safely remind Janice of that.

The Epitaph Was Silence

13.5.94

For MPs, whose job is so often to express shock or grief when little is felt, real shock and real grief are almost strangers at their gate. They have ransacked the vocabulary of distress for slighter occasions than this. Now, like children in the face of something they cannot understand, they are all at sea. How can they show they mean it? How can they mark the difference they feel?

They tried very hard. Margaret Beckett spoke with real dignity. Struggling to control her voice, she recalled the previous evening and the last time she had heard John Smith speak. She touched a chord among Members on all sides when she said that he was a man 'who knew what he could do'.

He was more completely at ease with himself, she said, than any politician we know.

John Major was kindly and utterly unpompous in his remarks. Departing often from his notes he raised a smile when he remembered how friendly – and lengthy – had been his regular meetings with the Opposition Leader. 'Sometimes we drank tea,' he said, 'sometimes not tea.'

Was there a rueful smile behind the Prime Minister's remark that Mr Smith had been 'an opponent, not an enemy'?

When Paddy Ashdown, in his own tribute, remarked that this was a period 'when the public are not much given to trust politicians' one reflected on the irony that, over the short time when Mr Smith was Leader of the Opposition with Mr Major as Prime Minister, Britain has experienced the coincidence of two more decent political leaders than our political system has thrown together for decades.

But as the tributes continued, the words began to pall. Perhaps because they speak too much and too easily, MPs are curiously incapable of articulating the extraordinary. Even at times of genuine emotion, auto-tribute is an ever-present danger in the Chamber.

The most touching epitaph for John Smith at Westminster yesterday lay not in the tributes which began to roll from MPs at 3.30. It lay in their silence just after Prayers, at 2.30.

The Chamber was packed. For just a couple of minutes, as

Madam Speaker suspended the sitting for Members to collect their thoughts, a sort of emotional confusion reigned beneath the watching Press Gallery.

There was no buzz of conversation. Margaret Beckett was very close to tears. People tried to pat her on the back, or put an arm awkwardly on her shoulder. John Major looked simply staggered. Most of the Cabinet were there, Douglas Hurd and Kenneth Clarke at the Prime Minister's side. Between Sir Patrick Mayhew and Michael Portillo sat Nicholas Scott – suddenly yesterday's news.

The Labour front bench was too full to accommodate the Shadow Cabinet. Gordon Brown stood, by the Speaker's Chair. Every face was knotted with tension. Hands twisted and untwisted. David Blunkett's guide dog, stretched indolently on the carpet, occupied a tiny plot of unconcern in a field of tension.

Nobody really knew what to do. It was a moment, suspended in a sudden silence, between an event and the consequences of an event. These would flow soon enough. The speeches would flow sooner.

But, just for an instant, as it faced the unexpected intervention of mortality, the whole House of Commons added up to a strange, awful, uncomprehending pause.

27 Things You Didn't Know About Blair

17.5.94

Tony Blair becomes front-runner for the leadership of his party. . . .

Supporters of Tony Blair (wrote the political editor of *The Times* yesterday) are worried that his leadership bandwagon is racing out of control. There are fears that Tory enthusiasm and media 'hype' for Mr Blair might antagonize traditionalists in the Labour Party.

This is disturbing. Those of us who wish Tony well must act fast. As both an ex-Tory MP *and* a columnist, this sketchwriter must be as close as you can get to an Identikit picture of the sort of supporter Blair can do without.

In fact to improve his street-cred with the appalling types with unwashed hair, CND badges and training shoes who characterize his party's activists, I can best assist him by attacking him. Here, then, is a thoroughly nasty column about Tony Blair: Twenty-seven bad things you didn't know about the next Leader of the Labour Party (*oops! Sorry*).

☐ He has terrible teeth

☐ He looks like a vampire

☐ It is not true that Tony Blair is attractive to women. He's too pretty. He's a *man's* idea of a man who attracts women. Seven out of nine women in the Westminster Press Gallery do not fancy Tony Blair. Gordon Brown scores four

☐ He went to public school

☐ He went to Oxford

☐ His dad became a Tory

☐ He smiles too much

☐ He cannot possibly be as nice as he seems. All politicians must rise through a nasty political process, work with nasty people in nasty parties, and prosper. He has. He must be pretending to be nice.

☐ He cannot lack a simple ambition for office, as he claims. He must be lying

☐ He has never held down any job in Government

☐ He spends too much time on his hair

☐ He looks like a prototype for something, but nobody is sure what

☐ Nobody had heard of him before 1992

☐ He may be a Vulcan. This man is too good to be true. I believe that military strategists on the planet Vulcan, having infiltrated into Westminster an early attempt at an Earthling politician, John Redwood, have now learnt from the mistakes in this design. They have sent an improved version, with added charm. He has pointed ears

☐ He probably approves of Cliff Richard

☐ He may *be* Cliff Richard

☐ The Tories will say he's a boy sent to do a man's job

☐ Richard Littlejohn supports him

☐ He used to wear flares

☐ He was almost certainly a fan of Peter, Paul and Mary; the New Seekers; the Carpenters; Bucks Fizz; Abba . . .

☐ He probably listens to Classic FM now

☐ His father was a lawyer

☐ Tony Blair is the next leader of the Labour Party (*oops!*) but he could just as well have been the leader of the Conservative Party or the Social Democratic Party or the Liberal Party or the Green Party, or Archbishop of Canterbury, or a progressive missionary, or in charge of Bob Geldof's PR, or director of a major charity, or chairman of English Heritage, or general sec-retary of a small, service-sector trade union, or a management consultant, or King Herod, or the leader of the Dutch Social Democrats, or manager of a small plastics factory in Enfield where he is also sidesman in the local church and takes his daughters to pony classes in a newish Volvo

☐ He wears pastel suits

☐ He reminds us of Bill Clinton

☐ If he had ever smoked marijuana he would *not* have inhaled

☐ He doesn't fool me

Hope this helps, Tony . . .

Lucy Gives Tories Paws for Thought

15.6.94

Britain's dogs are fed up with party political bitching – and that's official. If David Blunkett's new dog Lucy is any guide then John Major's plea for amity in the Commons meets a warm response in the canine world.

Yesterday was Lucy's first day at the Commons. Her task was to lead her master, Labour's health spokesman, into the Chamber, guiding him to his seat on the front bench to the left of the Chair. For Lucy it was the canine equivalent of making the maiden speech. From a kennel in the Home Counties, Lucy's mother was probably watching the occasion on TV.

The previous dog, Offa, was a chunky labrador: slow but sure. Like the late John Smith (Offa's Leader) he always seemed calm. The old dog was playing a long game, but knew exactly where he was going. He never put a paw wrong.

Lucy is a contrast. Slighter and sleeker, her black coat shows traces of a discreet perm around the rump: 'retriever with a hint of poodle' perhaps. Lucy looks younger, leaner: eager for the fray. Like her new would-be Leader, young Tony Blair, this dog strains like a greyhound in the slips. Like Blair the eyes are bright, the hair bouffant. If Blair had a tail to wag he would have been wagging it. Lucy wagged hers for him.

She and Dave stepped forward: Lucy to the fore, on her harness. Disaster! Unhesitatingly and fast she drew her master straight towards a place on the Government front bench. Sensing something wrong, Labour's health spokesman put out an arm in time to encounter the corner of the table where the PM's dispatch box sits.

The dog looked round, triumphantly. Alone, she had done what the entire electorate failed to do in 1992.

It was a story her pups and grandpups will tell at family reunions years hence: 'The day Grandma led Mr Blunkett to the Government side.' Arms reached out, and the pair were led back to the Opposition fold.

Was it canine caprice? Shouts and guffaws of 'Tory dog!' filled the air and the Government whips looked ready to sign up Lucy on the spot.

Other interpretations of Lucy's astonishing initiative include the thought that this bitch knows an inviting political stench when she sniffs one; the suggestion that she saw John Patten's hair and thought it *was* Tony Blair; the idea that Lucy was making an ideological point about how right wing Labour has become in its quest for power; and that Lucy's canine intuition has already anticipated victory at the next election. Not dumb at all, she is simply three years ahead of the rest of us.

The Corfu Beach Bully

28.6.94

Major returns from blocking an EU appointment in Corfu

I have seldom seen this Prime Minister cooler, more convinced or more confident. If, as his critics claim, John Major talks as a hostage with one arm twisted behind his back by Tory Eurosceptics, he certainly gave no sign of it in the Commons yesterday.

He was helped by a string of damnfool questions from Left and Right which he hit for an easy innings of twos, fours, and – in Margaret Beckett's case – six.

Poor Margaret Beckett. To place Mrs Beckett in the position of urging upon the Government a more positive attitude towards co-operation with our European partners was rather like asking St Francis to deliver a lesson in baby seal clubbing. Labour's acting leader stood up, an inky sheaf of heavily amended notes in hand, no doubt recalling her own history of heartfelt horror of the EC and all its works, knowing this was on record, and suspecting the PM would have the record to hand.

He did. Major prefaced his answer with a brutal side-swipe. Effortlessly, he said, she had slipped from slavish opposition to blind assent. He quoted her own words from another era. Insisting on her opposition to Europe, she had declared: 'How can we be expected to put our consciences and principles aside?'

Paddy Ashdown did better. His gibe that the Prime Minister was presenting 'the Punch and Judy farce at Corfu as though he were Henry V at Agincourt' might have hit home in a more doubtful House than yesterday's gathering; but the mood was all against him. Every Tory but Ted Heath (who adopted a worried rather than hostile line and received a politely firm reply) backed the PM's stand.

John Major has returned from foreign holidays galore with his happy snaps to show the House, and found his audience unimpressed. Yesterday, admiring MPs were crowding round for a closer look. 'And here's one of me, kicking sand in a fat boy's face.' He gave every impression of enjoying it immensely.

Stuck Answers Are Safest

8.7.94

Liberal Democrat spokesman Robert Maclennan yesterday asked the Home Secretary to create a criminal offence of 're-chipping mobile telephones'. Michael Howard gulped. *Re-chipping* phones? His eyes dived toward his briefing notes.

Nobody can claim to see into a mind as Byzantine as Mr Howard's. We cannot with any finality assert that the Home Secretary had not the least idea what re-chipping a mobile phone would be. To suggest that he is hazy about how you would chip, let alone re-chip, a phone, is unfair. Perhaps the sudden look of panic on Howard's face was caused by indigestion, or the recollection that Thursday was his turn to pick up his daughter from her *cordon bleu* cookery classes.

It is therefore no more than your sketchwriter's hunch, unproven and unprovable, that the Secretary of State hadn't the foggiest what Maclennan meant. He paused to assemble his reply.

'It's something we're looking at,' he said.

The ring of 'doughnutting' Tories framing Howard for the cameras nodded wisely. Civil servants glanced at each other. If the re-chipping of mobile phones was not something we were looking at yesterday, you may be sure we are looking at it now.

It took your sketchwriter back to the days when he was a Conservative MP for a rural Derbyshire constituency. Shortly after being elected I found myself at a Tory fund-raising buffet in Ashbourne, saying a few words, and taking questions, standing on the stair in someone's gracious living room. Many of those present seemed to be farmers. A small, ruddy-faced man in a tweed jacket asked a question.

'What is Mr Parris's attitude to roll-over stock relief?'

I panicked. I had never heard of roll-over stock relief. As a new young MP aged only 29 I felt very much on my dignity. I was sensitive to the charge of being still wet behind the ears; of knowing little of the rough-and-tumble of rural life. The natural reply – 'What *is* roll-over stock relief, please?' – therefore struck me as unbefitting. I hesitated.

Were there any pointers in that question, if not to its precise meaning, then at least to the general policy area we might be discussing? The fellow looked like a farmer; 'stock' was a word (like 'beasts' and 'barren heifers') that rural types use when they mean cows of some sort; and 'relief' must refer to a variety of monetary compensation. Farmers are always wanting money from the Government for one thing or another.

But what? To my (by then) hysterical mind, it occurred that when cows die, they roll over. I was seized by the conviction that roll-over stock relief must be a form of state compensation paid to farmers whose cattle had become ill, and rolled over.

Even in my panic, however, I remained circumspect. Best to keep the reply unspecific . . .

'That's a tough question,' I said, 'on what is, as you know, a complex subject. You would not want me to plough unbriefed into a detailed off-the-cuff response. Let's be frank: I'm no expert . . .' I should have stopped there. '. . . But I shall be talking to the Minister of Agriculture next week. Let us see how *he* responds to your question.'

There was a murmur of approval from the other guests, who had no more idea than did I what we were talking about. I sensed that I had handled this one well. I did notice an expression of polite surprise on my questioner's face – he was, as I later learnt, a partner in a firm of accountants – but I put that down to his evident admiration for my aplomb.

I left the buffet with self-confidence undented.

The Tony Blair ABC

11.7.94

Last week, Tony Blair called for an initiative. Money spent on new police authorities should be diverted, he told the Home Secretary, to a 'drugs initiative'. He did not elaborate. I hugged myself with delight, for 'initiative' begins with the letter I. It filled the final gap in the Tony Blair ABC I have been compiling from the recent speeches and interviews of the soon-to-be Leader of the Opposition.

Here follows a guide not just to the preferred vocabulary of the incoming Blair regime, but to its mood and themes. Labour

MPs hoping for a job under the new leader would be wise to draw their speeches and their tone from this lexicon. Get ahead of the pack: get in tune with Tony now!

A is for Achievement. Achievements are one of the main things a Blair government will achieve. A is also for Abstract. Abstract nouns are another Blair achievement. A is for Absolutely, too. 'Absolutely' means 'yes' in Islington.

B is for Beliefs. Politics is about beliefs. B is also for Basic. Basic beliefs. B is for Broader society. And B is for the Battle of Ideas. 'Only by re-establishing its core identity, can the Labour Party regain the intellectual self-confidence to take on and win the Battle of Ideas' (Fabian/*Guardian* Conference, 18 June).

C is for Core identity; also Core beliefs; also Community, Citizenship, Cohesion, Compassion, Confidence, Coalition and Change.

D is for Duty: 'individuals owe a Duty to one another and to a broader society' (ibid). D is also for Direction, new Direction, and Drive in a new direction.

E is for Energy: 'the power and Energy of ideas and vision' (ibid). E is for Equality, too: 'social justice, cohesion, Equality of opportunity and community' (ibid); and for Ethical Socialism, as distinguished from unethical socialism.

F is for Fairness, for Freedom, and for Full employability.

G is for Global: 'First, the economy is Global' (ibid). Labour's foreign and defence policy are also likely to be Global.

H is for Historic mission. Also for Historic opportunity: 'a Historic opportunity now to give leadership' (ibid).

I is for initiative. No minister will be without one. As well as Initiatives, a Blair administration will have Ideas. 'The future will be decided ... through the power and energy of Ideas and vision' (ibid).

J is for Justice and social Justice (see Ethical Socialism).

K is for Key values and also for Key beliefs (see also Core values and Core beliefs). 'Socialism as defined by certain Key values and beliefs is not merely alive, it has a historic opportunity now to give Leadership' (ibid).

L is for Leadership (see Historic opportunity/Key values).

M is for Modern: 'a future that is both radical and Modern' (ibid). M is for Movement, too: 'a popular Movement in this country for change and national renewal' (ibid).

N is for National renewal.

O is for Opportunity. '. . . the chance to capture the entire ground and language of Opportunity' (ibid. See also Equality).

P is for Partnership. P is also for Purpose, Power, Potential and Pluralism: 'a greater Pluralism of ideas and thought' (ibid. See also Ideas and Thought).

Q is for Quality work. 'Central to my belief about this country is that we've got to give people the chance not just to work, but actually to have Quality work' (interview with Frost 12 June).

R is for Rediscovery, Responsibilities, Realization and Respect: 'We do need to Rediscover a strong sense of civic and community values, the belief that we must combine opportunities and Responsibilities, and the Realization that true self-respect can come only through respect for others' (speech to the CBI 14 June).

S is for Society; and plural Society, and shared Society, and broader Society, and changed Society, and Social . . . and 'Social-*ism* – if you will' (Fabian/*Guardian* speech).

T is for Tough: 'Tough on crime, Tough on the causes of crime'. T is also for Thinking, Thought, Trust and True self-respect.

U is for Urgency. 'Radical reform . . . should be pursued by a Labour government with Urgency' (ibid). U is also for United: 'a strong, United society which gives each citizen the chance to develop their potential to the full' (ibid. See also Society and Potential).

V is for Values. For Vigour and Victory too; and, more than all else, V is for Vision: 'a central Vision based around principle but liberated from particular policy prescriptions . . .' (ibid). You can say that again!

W is for Worth: 'the equal Worth of each citizen' (ibid). W is also for Welfare and Well-being.

X is for Factor 'X'. John Major doesn't have it, according to a survey conducted for Mazda cars. Tony Blair has Factor X.

Y is for Youth. Blair has that, too.

Z is for Zero-sum game. A Zero-sum game is a calculation in which if you add to one thing, you must take away from another. Blair's economics, as he has said, is *not* a Zero-sum game. This means that you can have your cake and eat it.

Moles in the Media Searchlight   14.7.94

Two MPs are trapped by newspapers into putting down Questions when promised payment. . . .

'I think, father,' said Tom Sheridan to the playwright Richard Brinsley Sheridan in the eighteenth century, 'that many men who are called great patriots in the House of Commons are really great humbugs. For my part, when I get into Parliament, I will pledge myself to no party, but to write upon my forehead in legible characters, "To Be Let".'

'And under it, Tom,' replied his father, 'write, "Unfurnished".'

Yesterday, as the House committed press allegations against two MPs to the House's Committee of Privileges, students of Parliament would have been intrigued.

The atmosphere was weird. The exchanges were not raucous, full-hearted or confident. Members' opinions did not divide upon wholly partisan lines. The dominant mood was angry, confused and troubled.

The Conservative Party is angry with itself, angry with its delinquent MPs, bitterly angry with the *Sunday Times* and in a state of near-paranoia about the media in general. It is troubled about the future for MPs' outside interests. Casting around for someone to blame, Tories' instinct is to blame the press, yet some of them do have a flickering recognition of what fools they are making of themselves by doing so.

The Labour Party is richly confused. Hating, as it does, media intrusion, the underhand methods of journalists, the Tory press in general and what MPs yesterday called 'the Murdoch empire' in particular, they now find themselves backing a Tory-leaning News International paper in an intrusion by underhand methods into the lives of two British citizens. It's just that they happen to be two Tory MPs, and the ammunition too good to ignore.

Labour's Nick Brown, Shadow Leader of the House, led the debate yesterday with a reasonable show of impartiality and a measure of good humour.

Most of his backbenchers opted to ignore (or even, in the case of Clare Short and David Winnick) to commend the *Sunday Times* and concentrate on the allegations. But admiring the paper came easily to none.

Of those I heard, Sir John Gorst's speech produced the most curious effect. It was a passionate attack on press methods, of which he cited first-hand evidence. It was patently sincere. It will read well in *Hansard*. It was impossible to argue with much of it: 'corrupt means, to expose corruption, are a corruption in themselves' is a fair statement of a fine principle. Yet in the circumstances it looked and sounded simply awful – and Sir John seemed to have no conception at all of this. However justified their argument, a group of politicians who have lost all sense of how they appear to the world outside is a worrying sight: like watching a mole creeping blindly across the lawn.

As for Labour, their arguments confirmed the Tories' worst fears. Tony Benn made so powerful a speech that, finally carried away by the force of his own rhetoric, he declared: 'When MPs take the oath they should swear to tell the truth, the whole truth, and nothing but the truth.'

Steady on, Tony!

Of Barges, Baronets and Bonsors   *15.7.94*

Yesterday, and after a little humming and haing, Sir Nicholas Cosmo Bonsor Bt (Upminster) swung ponderously but decisively Malcolm Rifkind's way. The Defence Secretary, we conclude, has won his case for a shake-up of our forces.

A view over the Thames from your sketchwriter's flat includes a large, broad-bottomed barge, moored to a buoy in midstream. This barge is a reliable indicator of the current. Breezes do not deflect it, but when the current flows one way the barge floats to that side of the buoy. When it flows the other, the barge floats round to the other side. When there is no decisive current the barge swings in between, rocking up and down.

The link between barge and current is fixed, but only a fool would suppose that it is the barge which causes the current. Nor – though the barge is always right – can we assume that it necessarily *knows*, itself, what the current is doing. Its position is determined, without need for reflection, by the natural forces on whose flow it rides, heaving gently in the swell.

Sir Nicholas, formerly of the Royal Bucks Yeomanry, a boxing blue at Oxford, a descendant of Nelson and Chairman of the Commons Select Committee on Defence, resembles this barge in more respects than one. A large, heavy, broad-bottomed MP, he is no slave to the fickle parliamentary breeze. But when the current of defence expertise within his party flows firmly in one direction, Sir Nicholas floats, in a dignified way, to that side of the buoy. When opinion moves the other way, Sir Nicholas will reliably be found, heaving gently in the swell, to the other side.

Much as we admire him, we would be hasty to conclude that the position of Sir Nicholas on any key question in defence actually *causes* a movement of military wisdom. Nor, though he boasts as free-thinking an intellect as any shooting man, member of White's, Pratt's, the Royal Yacht Squadron and (formerly) the Council of Lloyd's could claim, can we always be sure that the baronet himself knows, at any given moment, exactly what his own opinion might be?

But we can be sure that his position indicates it. Sir Nicholas is one of those Conservative MPs who absorb opinion and information not so much via the ears, eyes and brain, as through the skin. It is done by a sort of Smoking Room osmosis. Such MPs do not always know what they think, as it has not occurred to them to ask themselves. To find out, they need to stand up and make a speech. Once they hear what they have said, they know what they think.

It fell to Sir Nicholas to make the keynote intervention from the Tory side, after the Defence Secretary had delivered his statement 'Front Line First'. Mr Rifkind had sweetened cuts in personnel with a list of new tanks and 'Tomahawk land attack missiles' such as would gladden the heart of any boy soldier on the Tory benches.

But his *coup de grâce* was a reprieve for the Territorial Army. This plays a key role in defence policy. It exists to be reprieved after rumours that it is to be cut. During MPs' cheers, the minister rushes out the real cuts in the rest of the armed forces.

Sir Nicholas rose. Heaving in the swell, he seemed at first to float neither the way of approval nor of protest. Then, with little sighs of regret, he swung gently but decisively the Cabinet's way. Rifkind looked relieved. The party will wear it. When Nicholas reads his own intervention this morning, he will be able to reach the same conclusion.

Comet Tony Hits Earth

22.7.94

Mr Blair takes the crown. . . .

As fragments of Shoemaker Levy–9 thudded into the surface of Jupiter, Tony Blair stood up in Bloomsbury and released a barrage of abstract nouns of unprecedented duration and ferocity.

It was awesome. Grown men – hardened journalists – rocked against the walls in disbelief; camera crews – unable to cope with exposure to such sustained levels of intellectualism – staggered from the hall; Tories ran for cover. Even Liberal Democrats winced. Across the nation, TV viewers, watching the event live, shielded themselves as honour, pride, humility, community, excitement, conviction, trepidation, passion, aspiration, gratitude, courage and determination – and that's only the first page and a half – rocketed out of the television sets and across their living rooms, thudding into a million sofas.

Devices tracking Earth from Jupiter will have blown their fuses at the sheer philosophical energy unleashed. Never, even in Islington, have so many generalities been uttered with such passion by a single politician within one lunchtime.

For those inclined to doodle it was interesting to take keynote phrases ('the power of all for the good of each', 'ours is a passion allied to reason') and try swapping their constituent elements, to see whether it made any difference: 'the power of each for the good of all', 'ours is a reason allied to passion', or even 'the power and passion of each, allied to reason, for the good of all'.

The show was well executed: stagey without being vulgar, media-friendly, cunningly lit, pre-scripted, press-released, sound-enhanced, Autocue-supported, video-assisted, and cheap. Seating in the hall was divided into the three sections eligible to choose the Labour Leader: one third BBC, one third print journalists, and one third Labour Party. The trades unions had disappeared: something called 'affiliated organizations' figured on the video-graphics. There were no comrades either. Those present were addressed by loudspeakers as 'colleagues'. Next year we will be ladies and gentlemen. Blue was the predominant colour.

And another Tory feature is creeping into Labour occasions: incessant, fatuous applause. Tony Blair's speech was prefaced by some 15 seconds of applause, interrupted by 27 separate bursts of mostly polite clapping, each lasting about 10 seconds, and concluded with some two minutes' clapping.

Blair delighted most journalists. His skills would serve in those amusement-arcade 'Grand-prix' screen games. His own screen the Autocue screen, and his gaze rigid with concentration, Mr Blair drove at gathering velocity round a track littered with the death-traps of policy-commitments, swerving to avoid every one, fuelled by a tankful of abstract nouns. Meanwhile, in an event which cannot be unrelated to the discovery of Tony Blair, a team of scientists in a remote mountain range in New Guinea have discovered a species of whistling tree-kangaroo: the bondegezou. These kangaroos, held in huge affection by local tribesmen, are soft, furry, and completely unthreatening. They sit amiably on their branches, and when they see a human being walking below, they whistle a friendly greeting.

It remains to teach the bondegezou to intersperse its song with words like 'honour, pride, conviction' and 'passion', and to teach Mr Blair to climb trees. Then, British political life may become interchangeable with that of the New Guinea cloud forests.